Steamboat Legacy

The Life & Times of a Steamboat Family

BY

DOROTHY HECKMANN SHRADER

Introduction by

JOHN HARTFORD

Published by

THE WEIN PRESS

HERMANN, MISSOURI

FIRST EDITION, 1993

Published by
THE WEIN PRESS
514 Wein Street
Hermann, Missouri 65041

Telephone 314-486-5522

Manufactured in the United States of America

Library of Congress Catalog Card Number: 93-061111

ISBN 0-9638589-0-4
ISBN 00-9638589-1-2 pbk.

ACKNOWLEDGMENTS

*T*he historical authenticity of this book is in large part due to the help of a prodigious number of people and organizations. I owe a huge debt of gratitude to all who provided that help for me. "Steamboat Legacy" could not have been written without them.

MY APPRECIATION ... To my grandmother, Mary Miller Heckmann, for her faithful chronology of the life of a steamboat wife; to her sons, Edward and Norman, who thought enough of her diaries to preserve them after her death and then to bequeath them to me; to her son, William "Steamboat Bill" Heckmann, who chronicled steamboat events as only one who had lived them could; to her sons, Edward, George and Norman, who had their own inimitable style of recording their observations; to the "Hermanner Volksblatt" and the Hermann "Advertiser-Courier," the newspapers responsible for reporting the events as they happened, in a style long since lost. I am especially indebted to the Graf family, longtime owners of Graf Publishing, and to the current owner for permission to use the old files. The St. Louis and Jefferson City newspapers and many of the little papers—the Linn "Unterrified Democrat" and others—assisted in rounding out the stories. Special appreciation must be extended to E. B. "Doc" Trail, an early steamboat enthusiast who searched for and found pictures and some stories of the early steamboats.

MY APPRECIATION ... To my father and mother, who never realized that my nine years spent on the Str. John Heckmann would provide the background for "Steamboat Legacy." It was my good fortune that my mother was an ardent photographer. She provided many of the more recent pictures. My father, a friend of "Doc" Trail, saw to it that all the pictures in the Trail collection were available for the Historic Hermann River Room and the State Historical Society, as well as our personal collection.

MY APPRECIATION ... To the "Waterways Journal," the steamboatman's publication, for river news from day's past. The "Waterways Journal" also was responsible for the publication and preservation of the copious writings of "Steamboat Bill." Thanks to H. Nelson Spencer, publisher, for permission to quote from the "Waterways Journal."

MY APPRECIATION ... To steamboat friends and River Buffs who gave assistance and encouragement, especially to Jim Swift of the "Waterways Journal"; to Hermann

Radloff, who researched and found the financial records of the little steamers and presented them to me; to Ralph Dupae, unsurpassed photo collector of old steamboat pictures; and to John Hartford, for his introduction to "Steamboat Legacy."

MY APPRECIATION ... To Sandy Barks, editor and publisher of The Wein Press, for her faith in this project, her encouragement and her excellent editing. To Willie Boenker-Thomas and Linda Heck for their artistic contributions. To Lucinda Huskey for proofreading and clerical assistance.

MY APPRECIATION ... To the U.S. Army Corps of Engineers who provided maps and a picture of the U.S. Army Corps of Engineers Boatyards at Gasconade. Also, to "Corky" Heck, who gave my husband and me a wonderful firsthand look at the beautiful Gasconade River, the crooked little stream that once was the home of the steamboats that provided the melody in the Ozarks.

MY APPRECIATION ... To my husband Bill, the farm boy turned university professor, who had to learn to love steamboats, for his patience, endurance, and unfailing support while this book project was in progress—and it was a long time a'borning.

Credit for the pictures used belongs in large part to the Herman T. Pott Inland River's Library, Mercantile Library, St. Louis, Mo., the final resting place for the Shrader collection. Many of the pictures were taken by Alice Bock Heckmann; one is from the U.S. Army Corp of Engineers. Almost all the pictures also are on file at the Murphy Library, LaCrosse, Wisconsin. Copies are available through Ralph Dupae.

Research was carried out at many libraries and museums. Many of them had microfilm facilities and copy machines; all personnel were gracious and helpful in my research. My thanks to the Ames, Iowa, Public Library and the Iowa State University Library in Ames; the Western Collections Library af the State Historical Society of Missouri in Columbia, Missouri; the Historic Hermann River Room Museum in Hermann, Missouri, of which Capt. Kermit Baecker is curator; the James Memorial Library in St. James, Missouri; the Scenic Regional Library in Hermann, Missouri; and the Columbia, Missouri, Public Library.

To Bill, the pilot of my ship.

TABLE OF CONTENTS

INTRODUCTION

The View from the Pilothouse

by

John Hartford

I grew up reading and re-reading Steamboat Bill's columns in the "Waterways Journal." Then I devoured his book, "Steamboating Sixty Five Years on Missouri's Rivers." Steamboat Bill and Fred Way, who wrote "Piloting Comes Natural" and the "Log of the Betsy Ann," were my river authorities. But Steamboat Bill was "home," right up on the Missouri River in an area where I grew up and where I played a lot of music. He talked about catching the train in Kirkwood where all my cousins lived. And he even mentioned the Langenberg family. I went to school with the Langenbergs, and the Langenberg Hat Company in New Haven, Missouri, still makes the derbies I wear on stage.

Steamboat Bill stories went good on cold, wet nights by the fire with the smell of wood smoke and bacon. I could see "Old Rough Head" and his son hunting from the pilothouse as they nosed up the dark Gasconade River. And I could imagine the old captain coming down the river seated on a keg of nails—his raft floating just under the surface so it looked like the keg was coming downriver all by itself. I think about that story every time I see a barge loaded so heavy there is virtually no freeboard. It looks as though a floating sand pile is under tow.

The colorful Heckmann clan was a literary bunch. Steamboat Bill's brothers, Capt. Ed Heckmann and Capt. George Heckmann, were writers, too. With the publication of "Steamboat Legacy," Dorothy Heckmann Shrader, Capt. Ed's daughter and Old Rough Head's granddaughter, raises the voice of yet another generation of Heckmann writers.

The source of all this writing talent may well have been Dorothy's grandmother, Mary Miller Heckmann, whose diaries are the heart of "Steamboat Legacy." A shy Mennonite girl from Pennsylvania, Mary was an unlikely candidate for marriage to a flamboyant Missouri River steamboat captain. But she and Capt. Will Sr. produced 14 children and a veritable steamboat dynasty. Of eight sons, all but one followed their father to the river.

Mary's diaries paint a wonderfully candid picture of steamboating on the beautiful, convoluted little Gasconade River and on the powerful Missouri River, probably the hardest river to navigate in the whole Mississippi system. (Or the Missouri system if you, as many of us do, subscribe to the notion that the Missouri is the river that flows past the Jackson St. wharf in New Orleans and on into the Gulf and that the Mississippi flows into the Missouri.)

Steamboating was brutally hard work. Maintaining and operating a wooden boat in all kinds of weather was a huge chore, and steamboating was a strain on family life—even when a boat was tied up and cooled down someone had to keep a watchful eye on it. Lonesome to have her husband at home, Mary confided in her diaries her secret prayers for the boats to fail and her terrible fears that her prayers would be answered.

"Steamboat Legacy" tells of the glad times and the sad times of a large family. Mary's story of the devastating loss of a child is a genuine tear jerker—*When everything was in full bloom, all our trees were laden with blossoms. Everyone seemed very kind.* Laid to rest with lines we've sung many times—*Little Joe, in Heaven no larger will I grow, but any kind angel will know when you call for your own little Joe at the gate.*

The year 1894 was a hard one for Mary. *It is very unkind to write words of rebuke after anyone is dead, but never the less, the truth must be told: The old year of 1894 was one of the hardest ever passed through this country in times of peace.* In the 1880s and '90s Mary writes of summer droughts and no water in the cistern, putting out the washing down at the boat, rowing back and forth across the Missouri because there was no bridge at Hermann. At times the river was so low it was like *Pushing the boat over dry land, with a small boy walking ahead with a sprinkling can.* All this was part and parcel of daily living for a steamboat family.

Dorothy Heckmann Shrader has done a wonderful thing here. She has made a weave, like a braid of a woman's hair, with her grandmother's diaries, reports from the "Waterways Journal," the writings of Steamboat Bill, Capt. Ed, Capt. George and Norman and the reporting of the Graf family in the Hermann "Advertiser-Courier," all held together with her own commentaries. Dorothy Heckmann is a genuine river person in her own right, having grown up on the Steamer John Heckmann, her father's excursion boat.

My feeling for this book runs very deep. It is a book you can read straight through, or you can come in at any given point and inhabit. For river buffs, historians, folklorists, and readers in general—"Steamboat Legacy" is a keeper.

John Hartford

PREFACE

I Knew Her Not ...

*M*ary Louise Miller Heckmann was the grandmother I never knew, and yet I know her well through her diaries. Her records reveal the full strength of this woman; the very dailiness of her entries reveals much of her life, its trials and tribulations, along with the joys. Certainly, nothing in her preparation for marriage gave her any clue how to deal with the handsome, flamboyant, charismatic, freewheeling William L. Heckmann, whom she married in 1868. No man could have been further removed from the sedate Mennonite husband she had expected, and nothing in her upbringing had prepared her to be a steamboat captain's wife and the mother of 14 children. This is her story—the story of a steamboat wife.

The Miller family was living on a small fruit farm, aptly called Calmdale, near Avon Station, Pennsylvania, when the diaries began. The early diaries are tiny books. The writing is small and cramped, the entries brief. In time Mary expanded her writing to larger notebooks and more detailed entries. She called the diaries her "journals" and valued them enough to ask that they be kept safe after her death. It was also her wish that someone continue to chronicle family events after her death, but no one was interested.

It was my good fortune to have a father who treasured these family records, as did his youngest brother Norman. They were the sons who preserved the diaries when their mother died and later designated me as the custodian—a gift of rare value. I like to think that she would be pleased that 84 years after her death some of her records are being shared.

The diaries continued until Mary's death in 1909, thus concluding 43 years, 15,695 days, of faithful recording of the life and times of a steamboat family. She is, perhaps, the only woman to tell the woman's side of steamboating, not glamorous or pretty, but true and unembellished by romantic ideas. Mary could range from cleaning the kitchen on a steamboat to the latest idea for a new craft project or an order for new plants in one day's story. Nothing was too trivial to record. She captured the infatuation of man and the river, along with her own capitulation to the man, if not the river.

The diaries, as a whole, provide a picture of the life and times of a family from 1866 to 1909. Political views, book reviews, accounts of her various literary contributions, life and death were all a part of the panoramic view. The early diaries are a rather somber record of the domestic chores, interspersed with very simple announcements—another baby in the Miller household, for example. *Mother not well ... We got a baby boy last night.* This was the ninth Miller baby, so the birthing process was not a new one to Mary, the oldest child. The following week she comments, *Mother downstairs today.*

The life of a young Mennonite girl in Pennsylvania was simple, but arduous. The domestic duties were ongoing—washing, baking, cleaning, sewing and, in the case of Mary Miller, gardening, since her father was a horticulturist. Her diaries begin in 1866 when she was 18 and already being prepared for the duties of a good Mennonite wife. Mennonite "meetings" were usually conducted in the homes of members with a big dinner and often overnight guests. For Mary this meant extended visits to relatives. Even when at home she often took the railroad "cars" to go to neighboring meetings—this was fertile ground for finding the proper Mennonite mate.

The family move to Missouri may have cost her some tears, but did not dampen her interest in the trip. This she recorded in the daily journal. The move by rail and steamboat was carefully noted—again with little or no personal feeling. She had no way to guess that she was also rushing headlong into the love of her life. The daughter of a horticulturist had little knowledge of steamboating and this was her first exposure—but certainly not the last.

For 28 years after her marriage, she gave birth to a child every even numbered year, and her life was centered in domesticity. Eight of her 14 children were boys, and as the children grew she viewed with concern the desire of her sons to follow in their father's footsteps. Her efforts to steer her sons away from the wicked river that so captivated her husband and into teaching or preaching were futile. One daughter, to her great joy, did marry a minister. The sons, to a man, went to the river, although one eventually defected to the railroad.

This is Mary's story—a love story, a family story, a steamboat story— embellished by the writings of her sons, "Steamboat Bill" Heckmann, my father Edward Heckmann and my uncle George Heckmann, along with stories published in the "Hermanner

Volksblatt," the "Advertiser Courier," and "The Waterways Journal." Mary's journals, the newspaper accounts and her son's stories are interwoven, creating a three-sided view of events. It is a story told by those who were there, recorded here by the granddaughter Mary Miller Heckmann never knew.

Mary preserved that brief moment in time when the Missouri River and its tributaries were the scene of a true steamboat dynasty, founded by her husband Capt. William L. Heckmann and carried out by his sons. The majority of the steamboats during the period of 1870 to 1930 had a Heckmann on board, at the wheel or in the engine room. To a lesser degree, the rivers were home to Heckmanns until as late at 1950, with another generation taking over beyond that date.

In later life a different side of Mary Heckmann emerged, as she began to explore her own feelings and convictions. A resurgence of religious fervor resulted in her enthusiastic embrace of the cause of temperance. She became an active member of the WCTU (Women's Christian Temperance Union) and was jokingly—and perhaps not so lovingly—called "Carry Nation" by some of her offspring because of her efforts to enforce Missouri's Sunday Blue Laws. She wrote copiously and stumped the state on a lecture tour. The success of her efforts earned her the everlasting censure of her fellow citizens. The closing of the saloons in Hermann on Sunday was not popular, but she did her duty as she saw it. Her efforts to keep her family "dry" may have had some effect, since all of the Heckmann sons while not "dry" were amazingly temperate. Whatever the outcome, Mary Heckmann had established that she was something other than a woman in the shadow of her husband.

In addition to quotes from the diaries, many steamboat stories have been included in unaltered form. The stories from the "Hermanner Volksblatt" in German and the Hermann "Advertiser-Courier" in English were written by bilingual reporters for both newspapers, adding extra flavor to the writing. These are the stories of some 30 steamboats that ran out of the Port of Hermann, Missouri. All were locally owned, usually by the Wohlt and Heckmann family interests, most frequently by the Hermann Ferry and Packet Company, which also was largely owned by the two families. The diaries and the stories tell of rollicking good times and hardships beyond belief. They tell of rivalry and jealousy, of money made and money lost, driving ambition and pure brute strength.

This is a story of one of the most shining periods of small steamboat operation ever recorded in such detail. The period from 1870 to 1930 was the heyday of steamboating on the beautiful Gasconade, the Osage and the wild Missouri rivers. The echo of those melodious little whistles will never be heard again.

CHAPTER 1

Mary

October 23, 1866—Letter from Mother. She says we are going to Missouri till spring. It cost me some tears. —Mary Louise Miller

*I*t was a gloomy day in January. The station platform at Mechanicsburg, Pennsylvania, had only one occupant, a young Mennonite girl whose black dress and shawl, white apron and cap added no color to the bleak landscape. Aunt Sarah and Grandmother Miller had brought her to the station, but with a skittish team they were obliged to leave before the Iron Horse arrived.

The few leftover leaves of autumn that scudded across the platform and the lonesome whistle of the approaching train did nothing to dispel Mary Miller's somber mood. Her hand clutched three letters in her apron pocket. One was from her mother telling her to come home to prepare to move to Missouri. The others were from two young suitors.

She was 19 years old and had just reached marriageable age. Her parents upheld the tradition of seeing that their daughter went to "meetings" in Mennonite homes over a considerable distance, thus giving her full exposure to eligible young men. Lengthy stays with relatives had brought her closer to Christian Hershey and Henry Strickler, two young men who were showing an interest. She wrote in her diary that she had been having a *very good time*.

The Miller home was near what is now the town of Hershey, Pennsylvania, and Christian Hershey was a member of the family of later chocolate fame. Mary would one day tell her daughters, *had I but stayed in Pennsylvania you would all have been chocolate drops.* Henry Strickler went on to become a prominent figure in the Mennonite hierarchy. Years later, when news of his death reached Missouri, Mary wrote in her diary, *to think that if I had stayed in Pennsylvania I might now be the widow of a Mennonite bishop!*

What Mary Miller could not know as she left Pennsylvania was that she was heading pell mell into a great love affair. She was destined to become the wife of a colorful steamboat captain and the mother of a rambunctious family of 14 children. Her new life in Missouri would be a world apart from the serene childhood she had known on a wonderful Pennsylvania fruit farm, fittingly named Calmdale.

Samuel Miller, Mary's father, was a prominent horticulturist, famous for having propagated the Martha grape. George Husmann also was a well-known propagator of grapes, who later would become a founding father of the California wine industry. He traveled to Pennsylvania to persuade Sam Miller to join him in an ambitious new winery project at the tiny settlement of Bluffton, Missouri, on the north bank of the Missouri River, a few miles upriver from the German community of Hermann, which was situated on the south bank.

After two trial visits to the Bluffton site, Miller announced to his family that they would leave Pennsylvania and move to Missouri. Mary Miller was the oldest of the Miller offspring. A baby boy, named George Husmann Miller, arrived shortly before the family departed for Missouri. This baby was the ninth child in the family—two more children would be born in Missouri.

Leaving Calmdale Farm was wrenching for all the Millers. Memories of her childhood days never left Mary—a lingering nostalgia pervaded her reminiscences. She later described the beauties of Calmdale in a story about her father that was published in "Colman's Rural World":

In 1852 he bought the property two and one-half miles from Lebanon, a half mile from what was at that time Avon Station, on the Lebanon Valley railroad. There, on our small fruit farm and nursery, the writer spent her childhood. While I write every tree, shrub and path comes distinctly before my eyes. Father and mother both loved roses and many are the huge bouquets we gave our friends who drove out from town during the summer. There, too, grew the strawberries, that seemed to me to be ever on the list for weeding. In this place is where the Martha grape originated, and which was named for my mother, whose name was Martha Isabella. How often I think of the beautiful apples, peaches and grapes I helped my father gather on this same place!

Mary returned home to Calmdale in time to help get ready for a sale preceding the journey to Missouri, and Sam Miller rejoined his family in Pennsylvania. On March 23, 1867, a large gathering of friends and relatives assembled at the train station at 2 a.m. to bid the Millers farewell. The family arrived in Pittsburgh at 2 p.m. the same day and boarded the steamer Ezra Porter for Cincinnati, where they arrived at 2 p.m. on March 25. Mary wrote that they boarded *the cars* at 7 p.m. and arrived in St. Louis a day later.

In handwriting that was cramped and tiny to fit her small diary books, Mary meticulously recorded the bare facts of the journey. But she did not write what she felt and saw. Did the river interest her? Was she awed by the noise of the machinery—the liquid sound of the whistle, the splashing of the great wheels? She only mentions that they *found* their own breakfast and that the steamers provided their dinner.

Mary Louise Miller

The family tarried awhile in St. Louis while *Mama and Papa bought our things.* They left St. Louis the morning of March 28 on the steamer Post Boy and ended their long journey at 5 p.m. that afternoon at the Bluffton landing. There was a chute between Bluffton and an island in front of the town that could accommodate steamboats only during periods of high water, so the steamboat landing was usually on the south side of the island. Disembarking passengers walked across the island and picked up a skiff ride to the mainland.

By the time the Miller family arrived, the brand new town of Bluffton was fairly well-established. Mary reported, *Everything is better than we expected.* In a later diary entry she again referred to the arrival in Bluffton. *We had been having the best of living aboard the Post-Boy, however, soon after we were called to supper at Eatons. We had stewed potatoes, cold water biscuit and bacon. I remember yet, it seemed to me the best supper I ever eat.* The Miller home in Bluffton was a large, double two-story house with a breezeway connecting the two sides.

Samuel Miller's daughter, who shared his love of plants, found the Bluffton landscape bleak and bare until she discovered wildflowers. *Papa, the boys, I and*

3

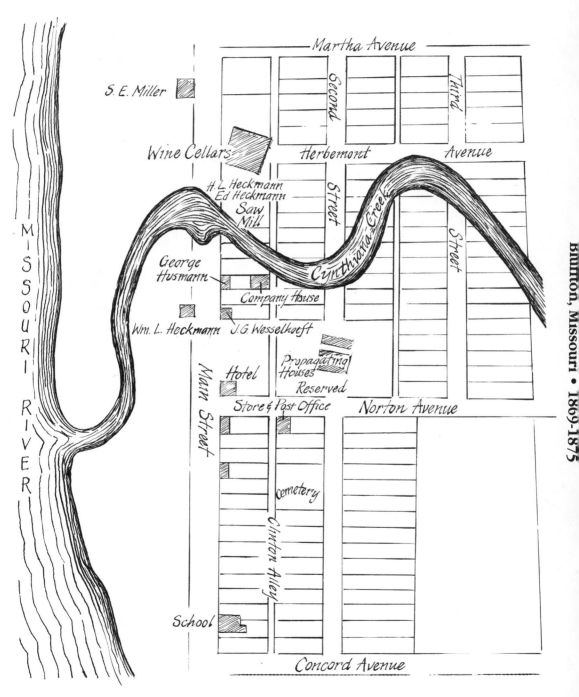

ILLUSTRATION BY LINDA HECK

others went to the cliffs. Were gone from early in the morning till noon, Got some beautiful flowers. Mary also wrote of excursions into the surrounding countryside for mushrooms, and by May she was taking walks alone and *got lots of flowers.*

In her diaries Mary noted the first steps of the little boy born just before the Miller family's exodus to Missouri, along with the passing of various steamboats. *Post Boy went up. George begins to walk. Dictator went up, Zephyr went up. The Isabella, Post-Boy, Kate Kinney. The Clara, Columbian, Yellow stone went down. Catons went to Portland in a sail boat.* Evidently some enterprising soul thought a sail beat oars for getting about on the river.

The new winery was off to a promising start. By the end of 1868, six propagating houses, 100 feet by 10 feet each, were doing well, as were three smaller propagating pits. These facilities had been built at a cost of $20,000, and that year the propagating houses alone brought in $10,000 in revenue. There also was an experimental vineyard, and two large houses had been constructed for the officers, along with a stable, blacksmith shop, a well-house and other facilities. A store, post office and hotel were doing a thriving business, and a crew of seven hands was employed at a salary of $35 to $50 a month. The railroad had not yet reached Bluffton, but a skiff ferry could transport passengers and goods across the wide Missouri River to the little town of Morrison and the Missouri Pacific Railroad tracks.

Having already built a large underground, arched cellar at his vineyard east of Hermann at a cost of $10,000, Husmann tried an experiment at Bluffton. Rather than blast out huge underground cellars, he developed a method of building double-walled, above-ground "cellars," backed into the bluffs and insulated with six inches of sawdust. Such a cellar, he reported, could be built for $2,000. Fermenting rooms occupied the warmer second story of the structure.

The entire operation was a huge undertaking for its day and time. The winery had been organized in the spring of 1866, with capital stock of $150,000. A total of 1,500 shares were to be sold for $100 each. Husmann, with 101 shares, and his partner, a Mr. Wesselhoeft, with 75 shares, were the two main promoters of the winery. The initial purchase of land was 1,772 acres, at an average price of $15.50 per acre.

In February of 1868, the Bluffton Winery issued invitations to 500 guests to an "Inauguration of the Cellars." The steamboats must have done a land office business transporting state legislators and other dignitaries to Bluffton. Numerous toasts were drunk and responses made. George Husmann reported in his "Grape Culturist":

It was a very pleasant affair; We were glad to see such a number of the friends of good wine, desirous of putting the native wines to the test. ... As to the quality of the wines, their rapid disappearance, we think was the best proof that the guests found them palatable. Among the wines which seemed to be especially appreciated, were the Catawba of 1867, which everyone seemed to enjoy, the Cynthiana, Herbemont and Norton's. Missouri Port also found its admirers among those whose taste leads in that way. From 11 o'clock in the fore-noon until dark the Cellars were constantly filled, and the guests seemed to take a reluctant farewell when they did go.

The cellars lighted up to their full length, with the jovial faces of the visitors, who thronged them, presented a very animated scene, and the large and smaller casks filled with the greatest assortment of American wines, comprising about 30,000 gallons, gave evidence of the importance which this branch of domestic industry has already acquired.

Husmann reported that Gen. McDougal, medical purveyor for the army, *expressed himself very favorable on the Norton's Virginia and Missouri Port, and assured us that he was gratified to see them introduced for medical purposes.* Many others expressed themselves favorable. *Even the chiefs of our importing houses, whom we were glad to see among our visitors, were well pleased with what they saw and tasted.*

When the guests departed, the Husmann-Wesselhoeft-Miller team breathed a big sigh of satisfaction. Little did they know that uninvited visitors would arrive the next day. George Husmann tells the story:

The next morning we were agreeably surprised by a delegation of ladies, the representatives of the agitation for women's rights and female suffrage. Mrs. Elizabeth Cady Stanton, Mrs. Phelps & Miss Cozzens, escorted by the Hon. H. T. Blow. As these ladies also advocate the cause of temperance we consider it very appropriate that they should visit this, as we flatter ourselves, one of the most active temperance institutions in the State. We are sure that they would have concurred with us in this opinion, had they met with as many of those who were at the cellars the day before, and had seen them all good natured and joyous, following their every day occupation, a sure sign that good wine is a promoter of health as well as happiness.

The Miller family certainly was not inclined to preach temperance, but this encounter with the leading feminists of the day may have made a lasting impression on Mary. In her later years she became a staunch advocate for the cause, stumping the state for the WCTU and writing copiously for various magazines and newspapers.

By the end of 1868, the value of the Bluffton Winery holdings was listed at $122,713.97. Spirits were high, a dividend of 15 percent had been declared, and the investors were happy. But the winds of change were blowing.

CHAPTER 2

William

I can't guess who you are, but whoever you are,
you are a handsome man. —Mary Louise Miller

A good-sized crowd had assembled on the Hermann wharf to await the arrival of the steamer Post Boy. While no longer a novelty, steamboat landings were always an exciting show. The Post Boy's landing whistle made a thrilling sound, gut-shaking, liquid and full-throated. It was the true Missouri River landing whistle—one medium-long blast, two short blasts, one extra-long blast and, finally, two short "whuff, whuffs."

The hail blown as the steamer rounded Teubner's Bluff (now known as Kallmeyer's Bluff) was a signal to all interested parties to get to the wharf. People meeting disembarking passengers, those receiving freight, departing passengers and local river buffs all hurried to watch the exciting drama of the landing of a big steamer.

From her vantage point aboard the Post Boy, Mary Miller watched a tall young man who stood out in the jostling crowd. With a jaunty cap perched on his curly head, he had teasing eyes of bright blue and a "take-charge" air. A crowd of boisterous young men seemed to hang on his every word. Laughing and joking, the crowd on the wharf pushed closer to the landing stage. To Mary's delight, the handsome young stranger came aboard.

It seems only fitting that Mary Miller and William Heckmann should meet aboard a steamboat. It was 19 years before Mary recorded in her diary that first encounter with the handsome, charming and utterly bewitching Will Heckmann.

Today is nineteen years since I, with the rest of my father's folks, landed at Bluffton. Sometime after dinner the steamer Post Boy stopped at Hermann. William Heckmann and some others for Bluffton got aboard. While he talked to mother, never noticing me once, I stood behind mother, and in my mind I said, I can't guess who you are, but whoever you are, you are a handsome man.

Mary Miller's tranquil childhood at Calmdale Farm was a far cry from that of

The young Will Heckmann cut a dashing figure.

her husband-to-be, who grew up with steamboats and a railroad in his front yard. The rough and rowdy Hermann riverfront was pure heaven for a boy, especially a boy like Will Heckmann.

As a youngster he would fill his skiff with garden produce and fruits and row out to peddle his wares to passing steamboats. Usually, the pilot let him ride along for a few miles, sometimes even permitting him to hold the big wheel. When the captain put young Will off the boat, he would row or float back to Hermann. The rowing skills he learned as a boy would serve him well the rest of his life.

William Lewis Heckmann was born at Hermann, Missouri, on February 7, 1845, the son of John Henry and Justina Rewald Heckmann, who had arrived in Missouri in the spring of 1838. A carpenter by trade and one of Hermann's first elected aldermen, John Henry Heckmann built a home facing the Missouri River on one of the prized Wharf Street lots.

The oldest Heckmann daughter, Rosalina, had been born in Volkmarsen, Hesse, Germany. Two more children, Louise and Henry, were born in Pennsylvania. Soon after the family's arrival in Hermann, a deadly cholera epidemic claimed young Henry's life. When another son arrived in 1841, he also was named Henry. Two more sons followed, William in 1845 and Edward in 1847. A daughter, Caroline, was born in 1852.

Created by a society called Die Deutsche Ansiedelungs-Gesellschaft zu Philadelphia (the German Settlement Society of Philadelphia), Hermann was intended to be a truly German city where the German immigrants could keep their language and customs, while still being good citizens of the United States. This euphoric notion was beautiful on paper, and the idea sold. Shareholders provided the funds to acquire a tract of land, with the understanding that shares could later be traded for a lot in the new town.

Scouts were dispatched, and upon their return George Bayer was sent to act as the society's agent to view proposed sites and purchase the most suitable tract of land. Bayer stepped off a steamboat and saw the lovely setting of what today is Hermann. He imagined the Rhineland of his homeland and looked no further.

The wilderness Bayer purchased was not at all what the first arrivals had been led to expect. Bayer cannot be entirely faulted. The mass migrations to the United States from Europe that began in the 1830s were strongly influenced by emigration literature, glowing accounts written by travelers who had experienced the New World. These tracts were particularly popular in Germany, where more than 150 examples of the genre were published between 1827 and 1856.

Gottfried Duden had written persuasively of a utopia in Missouri in his "Report on a Journey to the Western States of North America." He lied, or at least greatly exaggerated. But the optimistic Germans, Bayer included, took the flowery prose as gospel truth.

And so it came to pass on a wintry December day in 1837 that 17 eager settlers arrived at Hermann on the last steamboat of the season. They had no livestock, few tools and no idea of where food could be found. Instead of paradise, the new arrivals, who spoke only German, found a wilderness with two one-room log cabins occupied by English-speaking people.

The shock of Hermann's founders is well-recorded, as is their hatred of their agent George Bayer. But how Willis Hensley and the widow Polly Phillips, the owners of those two little cabins, felt about having 17 German house guests for the winter can only be imagined. Many years later when William Heckmann's son and namesake "Steamboat Bill" Heckman was a pilot on the Gasconade River, he recalled that "Old Man Hensley," the owner of one of the cabins, met his boat one day and said, "*Captain, get that boat out of here. I have moved three times to get away from those damn Dutchmen and I'm too old to move again."*

For a man anxious to escape German immigrants, Willis Henlsey and his offspring certainly managed to stay in the local news. His son, "Tombstone Bill" Hensley, worked as a marksman on Gasconade River steamboats to keep meat on the table. His employment ended when he began stealing tombstones and trying to hide them in the hulls of passing steamboats. He went to the state insane asylum firmly believing that his hero, Capt. William Heckmann, would come to his rescue. Year later, when he finally did escape, he went straight to Captain Will's door.

In 1908 the name Hensley came back to haunt the town once again. Willis Hensley's descendants filed suit claiming ownership of the entire downtown business section of Hermann. They said Hensley had died intestate and that they legally owned the land. The suit was unsuccessful, but it gave the city fathers quite a jolt.

Those early settlers who descended on Willis Hensley and the widow Polly Phillips in the winter of 1837 were given all the comfort such circumstances could provide. But by spring they were in no mood to give a pleasant reception to their agent George Bayer. Writing in 1907, William Bek reported, *At any rate Bayer found them later, sound in body, though not quite contented in mind.* This was quite an understatement—they were furious. Their vindictiveness made life miserable for Bayer and eventually led to his death. No wonder Willis Hensley wanted to get away, far away.

Violent events seemed to abound in the young town. On July 28 of 1845, the same year William Heckmann was born, Hermann was the scene of a terrible steamboat accident. The "St. Louis Weekly Reveille" reported:

It becomes our painful duty, as faithful chroniclers of passing events, to record one of the most serious disasters that has occurred upon our waters since the explosion of the steamer Edna. The steamer Big Hatchie, Capt. Frisbee, which left our port on Monday last for the Missouri River, with some 40 passengers on board, in leaving the landing at Hermann about 1 o'clock on the morning of the 23rd inst., on her way to St. Joseph, burst her starboard boiler with a loud explosion, which forced it straight forward, the steam discharging itself aloft, carrying away the main cabin as far aft as the ladies cabin, making a perfect wreck of the boat, and spreading death and desolation among the passengers.

The Heckmann family had ringside seats for this and all other riverfront calamities. Will Heckmann grew up hearing tales of the Big Hatchie explosion, which killed 38 people, most of them German immigrants bound for Kansas.

The disaster was almost more than the tiny settlement could handle. Some of the scalded victims were placed on passing steamboats and sent to St. Louis, but many had to be treated at the site. Mid-summer heat and 38 bodies left no time for coffins or funeral arrangements. The dead were buried in a trench in the city cemetery, where an obelisk still stands as a mute reminder of the tragedy.

The coming of the railroad in 1855 was another source of fascination for inquisitive little boys. The Heckmann boys—Henry, 14, William, 10, and Edward, 7—were just the right age to thoroughly enjoy the building of the tracks right in front of their house. There can be little doubt that they were on the spot on Nov. 4, 1855, watching and waiting for the first steam railroad engine and train to pass through Hermann. Later that day, they would witness the aftermath of one of the worst railroad disasters of that time. The Hermann "Advertiser-Courier" published this account 53 years later:

At 9 o'clock that morning a train of ten passenger cars, crowded with specially invited guests, among whom were many of the best-known citizens of St. Louis, left for Jefferson City, and arriving in Hermann, took on another coach containing the local militia company under the command of Capt. Geo. Klinge, and many other of our citizens crowding into cars where room could be found.

The bridge across the Gasconade was a new one; consisted of six spans, two of 120 feet each, two of 140 feet, and two of 92 feet—the abutment, or shore spans, 130 feet each. The abutments were of stone, thirty-two feet high. Each of the five piers was also of stone. The abutments and piers were completed, but the superstructure of the bridge and its eastern approach were incomplete.

In order, however, to serve the purpose of commemorating the opening of the road to the State capital by an excursion, the bridge contractors had undertaken to build scaffolding on which to place the track of sufficient strength to pass the train in safety. This was sought to be accomplished by erecting trestlework on piles and mudsills in the line of the intended superstructure— the piles fourteen feet apart and stay-bracked longitudinally and transversly. The embankment on the east or Hermann side, not being finished about eight feet of trestlework were built from the solid ground of the approach to the finished abutment.

The excursion train, about 600 feet long came to the bridge by this approach. When the engine reached the front pier, the forward part of the train covering the first span of 130 feet, the span gave away, precipitating the engine, tender, baggage car and several passenger cars to the watery abyss below, some thirty feet, causing an immense loss of life and utter wreck of cars. The President of

*the road, Hudson E. Bridge and Thomas S. O'Sullivan, chief engineer, together
with a number of employees of the road, were on the locomotive at the time and
all of them went down with it and were killed, except Mr. Bridge, who miraculously escaped unhurt. About a dozen Hermann men in the forward cars were
hurt.*

*The dead, about thirty-three, were brought to Hermann where an inquest
was held the day following. Many of our old citizens who were children then,
remember how the town on that day put on its holiday dress, how, when the
excursion train arrived here from St. Louis, the darkened sky opened the flood-
gates of heaven making the streets look like rivers, many hearts with evil
forboding. And when the first news of the disaster reached here; words nor pen
can describe the heart-anguish of the remaining population concerned at the
safety of their own dear beloved ones.*

That same railroad bridge would be a constant source of difficulty for all the
later Gasconade River steamboatmen. Piloting a boat through either of the two
center spans, each of which was 92 feet wide, took a great deal of skill. The
wider side spans were over water too shallow to navigate except during flood
stage—and then a steamer could not pass under the bridge without taking down
its pilothouse and smoke stacks. A steamer with a tow had even more problems,
and many a tie raft broke up at this dangerous place. That original 1855 bridge is
still in use today—38 to 40 fast Union Pacific trains go roaring across it daily.

It is highly probable that one of the dignitaries aboard that ill-fated train
was Charles D. Eitzen, an opportunist of the first order who quickly grasped the
advantage of having his town on the river. Eitzen had arrived in Hermann in
1838, probably on the same boat as the Heckmann family. He was only 19, but
he immediately found work as a clerk in Wiedersprecher's general store. Two
years later he owned the store. He was a pusher, civic-minded and canny with a
dollar—a man who worked for the good of his community, as well as his own
purse. His ideas for the town usually were commendable, but conflicting opin-
ions did little to deter him. In fact, he allowed nothing to stand in his way.

Many of Hermann's first residents saw the river as a formidable barrier.
Charles Eitzen looked at the same river and saw rare opportunity. Pine lumber
was already coming out of the Gasconade River and its tributaries, and in short
order he had become the transshipping agent. As the rafts of lumber came into
Hermann, he either took care of shipping the lumber to another port or, more
often, simply bought, stored and sold it himself. At times he had as much as
200,000 board feet of choice lumber piled up along Wharf Street, which he sold

for $4 to $5 per thousand feet.

In 1846 Hermann was about eight years old, and its inhabitants were building houses and commercial buildings as fast as possible. New settlers were still pouring in, so the lumber was most welcome. The business activity in Hermann even drew the attention of the St. Louis newspapers. The following is a translated version of a story from the "Hermanner Wochenblatt" that was reprinted in "Die Deutsche Tribeuene."

> The wharf in our Hermann has been so bustling for such a long time one might think our town was a great commercial center. There is a scurrying about like in an ant hill. This activity occurs just now because of the log rafts coming down the Missouri from the Gasconade where the only available pine lumber is being cut. Most of this is shipped on to St. Louis. This year not an insignificant quantity was put ashore and sold in Hermann. Taking apart these numerous rafts and lifting the mass of timber out of the water gave our wharf the look of a lively place of business where a great number of inhabitants were employed.

A man of great foresight, Eitzen promptly became the town's steamboat agent. In addition to lumber, he handled shipments of iron "blooms" from the Maramec Iron Works near St. James, Missouri. He truly made money coming and going. The big ox-drawn iron wagons always returned to Stringtown at the Iron Works filled with the goods from his store.

In the two decades preceding the Civil War, a boom in railroad construction created a demand for ties, and sawmills scattered throughout the Gasconade River valley created work for many who otherwise hunted for a living. One year three million oak and walnut ties were rafted down the river to Hermann, where they were either shipped or simply bought and resold by Charles Eitzen, who held a virtual monopoly on wharf space for nearly 30 years.

The river had helped Charles Eitzen become a millionaire, a fact that was not lost on a young boy who made a pest of himself on the waterfront. Young Will Heckmann dreamed of becoming rich, too. Later, when he began to flex his muscles in the steamboat trade, he entered into a full-blown feud with the richest man in town over wharf rights. The Eitzens and the Heckmanns were neighbors for most of their lives, but they were never friends.

The Gasconade Bridge made news again during the Civil War. The railroad was a prime target for the Confederates, and rumors of plans to burn the bridge eventually became fact. Since Governor Claiborne Fox Jackson was a Confederate, many Missourians thought he had declared war on the United States. On

June 1, 1861, the "Hermanner Volksblatt" reported (translation from German):

The first heroic deed by which [Gov. Jackson] *began this war was the burning of the Gasconade and Osage railroad bridges, which he had done by his janizaries on Wednesday morning shortly after his arrival in Jefferson City. Eye-witnesses who were present at this act assured us that with ten good marksmen, who could have been stationed on this side of the Gasconade bridge, the entire band could have been driven off, but before the news of this intended misdeed had reached the neighboring farmers, the trick had been played and the perpetrators were on their way to the Osage bridge, where they repeated the same maneuver. An American who was present at the burning of the Gasconade bridge said that a certain here well-known secessionist by the name of Robert Heath, after the attempt of the arsonists to blow up the bridge failed due to their own clumsiness, furnished them a barrel of tar.*

Another news story about the bridge was reported Oct. 4, 1864, this time involving none other than Capt. Charles Eitzen, who was stationed at the bridge when news came that Hermann had *Gone up and the whole town burnt, and that a train with two cannons was then coming up to attack us.* The report was false—Hermann was undamaged—but Eitzen said it put his men into such an uproar that he was unable to control them. The official record of the Union and Confederate armies reported: *Captain Eitzen, Thirty-fourth Enrolled Missouri Militia, abandoned one of the block-houses at Gasconade Bridge and ran away.*

It may have been some consolation to Capt. Eitzen to know that the men guarding the Osage River bridge also deserted their post. But two new enlistees—16-year-old Will Heckmann and his brother Henry—who were guarding the Meramec River bridge, must have secretly, or perhaps not so secretly, enjoyed the wealthy man's disgrace.

One of the stories of the burning of the bridges involved the steamer Cora, a sternwheeler owned by Captain Joseph Kinney. Sternwheel boats were a brand-new idea, and the Cora caused quite a bit of excitement in 1860 when she landed at the wharf at St. Louis.

Having no confidence in the radical new design, the underwriters refused to insure her first cargo. They said they wanted nothing to do with that *wheelbarrow of a boat.* So Capt. Kinney personally insured the cargo for $62,000. But when the Cora made the second trip, the underwriters were only too happy to insure her. After the burning of the Osage and Gasconade bridges in 1861, the steamer Cora ran from Hermann to Jefferson City and cleared $40,000 in three months.

William L. Heckmann

William was discharged from the Union Army at age 18 with the rank of Sergeant Major. He and his brother Henry became ardent members of the Grand Army of the Republic and faithfully attended reunions for the rest of their lives. By the time he was 19, William had married. Within a year he was the father of a little girl, Justina, and a widower.

Following in his father's footsteps, he began working as a carpenter at Bluffton, erecting the winery buildings, the store, the hotel and homes for the workers, a fine position for that day and time. His brother Edward also was at Bluffton and, for a time, so was his brother Henry. The Heckmann brothers ran a sawmill that undoubtedly supplied most of the lumber for the new endeavor. William boarded at Bluffton, but often went home to Hermann where his little girl was in the care of his parents.

His providential meeting with Mary Miller came at a time when he was more than ready for another try at matrimony. He was happily employed as a carpenter, but he heard another siren song—steamboats. It is doubtful that he ever revealed the true extent of his ambitions to the girl he was courting. With Eitzen as his role model, he set out to become a rich man. He almost succeeded.

CHAPTER 3

The Dear on the Bar

*Full attention to those duties will secure you that
happiness and satisfaction which no success in life and no acquired wealth
can give, without which the walk through life, however otherwise smooth,
will be sterile and desolate. —Martin Schnell*

*C*ontrary to what Mary may have thought, William Heckmann most assuredly did notice the shy Mennonite girl aboard the Post Boy. According to family lore, he vowed on the spot to *get that cap off of her*. He courted Mary Miller the way he did everything else—full steam ahead. The Miller family arrived in Bluffton on March 28, and by April 2 William Heckmann had shown up to begin his siege for Mary's hand.

He did not come empty handed. Mary wrote in her diary that day, *Heckmann here for supper. He gave us 3 doves, had them for supper.*

From this time on, "Heckmann" appears in the diaries with great regularity.

Heckmann came home. … Heckmann went across the river to get the Clara to stop at Strecks, when he got over it was not the Clara. … He and Papa were out gunning, he shot 2 ducks, had them for supper. … Heckmann and twelve men went down the river in a skiff, no work done today. … Papa and Heckmann went to shoot wild turkeys this morning, got none. … The men all went to the Big Tavern Creek to fish, came home about 3 o'clock. I cooked, had wild ducks

17

for dinner. H. shot them yesterday.

The courtship was unusual. This giant of a man could row a skiff 12 miles upstream from Hermann to Bluffton in the turbulent Missouri River and still have energy left to take Mary out rowing on a date. The island just across the chute from Bluffton was about the only place a courting couple could go—a skiff ride over and back was a "date."

Mary still had an avid interest in her old life, and letters were flowing back and forth from Pennsylvania with great regularity. Fannie Hershey wrote of a serious accident to John Hershey and shortly thereafter reported that *John was better*. But life in Missouri was starting to take on new dimensions. *Mrs. H. came up*, meaning that William's mother had come to meet the new girl in her son's life. Shortly thereafter, William's youngest sister, Caroline, came for a visit and brought Tina, his little girl, with her.

Meanwhile, William was pursuing his courting with a lot of rowing. *Will took us out in the skiff to the Sand-bar.... Will Heckmann came home, took a skiff ride to the sand-bar. ...Willie H. and others went to Hermann in the skiff.*

The work of the Miller household—the washing, ironing and sewing—never let up.

August 22—*Clear and warm. Em ironed. Killed 11 chickens for dinner, boiled apple butter.* No water had been available, except from the river, so a well was dug. On September 6 the welcome news was *Water in the well.*

September 7—*Clear and warm. Em done the work. Papa went to Hermann to get ready for the St. Louis Pomological Congress.*

September 8—*Clear and warm. Billy came home at dinner with six squirrels and six ducks. Helped Em to clean them, took a skiff ride to the island, took a ride in the waves of the Clara.*

Sept 12—*Very sick all day, could not leave my bed. Papa at home a few minutes, went to St. Louis. He came for the Delaware deed, is going to sell the farm in Delaware.*

Sept. 17—*At supper Fred Teubner came with a dispatch stating that there are 40 men coming. Billy came home at 12, pulled up from Hermann.*

Sept. 24—*Em, Liz, Will, Julius, Ed and I went to Portland. Fished down, caught one nice one. I shot off a gun for the first time.*

Sept. 25—*Hung up the wash. Mother ironed a little, Papa and George Wunderlich made wine. Heckmann's gun went off prematurely, he might have shot himself or Em.*

By this time Ed Heckmann also was beginning to be around the Miller house courting Em, the younger sister. Mary reported that they made two pillows for Eddie Heckmann. Also noted was that the *steamer Washington went up and brought us furniture*, but no mention is made as to who ordered the furniture.

The well was not adequate for doing laundry, so it was necessary to dip water from the river. At one point a log rolled from under the girls engaged in this task and dumped them into the river. They could not swim but survived the mishap.

Bluffton had no doctor or dentist, so home solutions were used for all medical matters. *Papa tried to pull Em's tooth but did not get it out.* There also was no fire department. *Montgomery Hill on fire, a whole party went up to put it out. …The fire is coming up the hollow. After supper the men all went out to save our fence, we carried all the tubs full of river water.*

On November 25 Mary wrote, *about 11 o'clock. Marie came to tell that Eddie Heckmann fell from a horse and broke his leg. They brought him home after dinner, the Dr. came about 3 o'clock. Eddie suffers very much.*

A spirit of fun came into the diaries when Will Heckmann got into the book—his entries differed considerably from Mary's. Will's taste for the golden lager was already apparent.

Dec. 6—A.M. Pleasant. Went to Portland. Beer there first rate. Drank 6 glasses. Came back sober.—WLH. Perhaps only wine was available at Bluffton, the wine town.

Dec. 7—A.M. Ditto, Nothing of importance transpired during the day; but the night passed off agreeably. Felt rather loose, but nevertheless slept up all night with Ed.—WLH.

Dec. 8—A.M. Ditto. Enjoyed a good headache all day. Try all to kill geese but failed, seen a "dear" on the bar, but could not catch it. Experimenting on Ed's leg, are afraid it will get well too soon, before they will get their diploma. —WLH. William was not writing endorsements for the doctors treating Ed's leg.

Just why the entries for December 9 and 12 were cut out of the diaries is not explained. Perhaps William became a bit too rambunctious in his reporting. "Mother" Heckmann again came up to Bluffton on December 15, and William took her back in the skiff the next day. A December skiff ride on the Missouri River must have been a numbing experience.

On December 24 Will went to Hermann to spend Christmas with his daughter and parents, while the Miller girls prepared for Christmas in Bluffton. *I prepared turkeys, Liz and Ed were making music and the boys and Lerna dancing.*

Dec. 25—A.M. Clear and very pleasant. Had awful toothache. After supper Em, Julius Silber and I went to the hotel to a dance, stayed till twelve.

Dec. 27—A.M. Clear and quite warm. Baked and sewed. P.M. Julius sawed his finger off. Dr. here. Mr. and Mrs. Silber here after supper.

Julius Silber would soon marry Will Heckmann's youngest sister, Caroline.

With the final entry in 1867, Mary wrote a list of expenditures: *calico, $1.80; gingham, $4.00; gingham, $.50; shoes, $2.00; corset, $1.75; stockings, $.60; hair pins, $.05; shoes, $1.75; gingham, $.90; drilling, $.80; shoes, $2.65; calico, $1.80; drilling, $.80; socks, $.30; balmoral, $2.25; shoes, $2.25.* Perhaps she was making a record of her hope chest.

Will Heckmann continued to chase the "dear" on the bar until he finally caught her. Mary Louise Miller and William L. Heckmann were married on February 23, 1868, the same month the Bluffton Winery held its grand inaugural celebration. The ceremony took place in Warren County, 20 miles east of Bluffton at the home of Will's sister Louise and her husband Martin Schnell, who was a justice of the peace. The marriage certification includes the marriage sermon that Martin Schnell felt called upon to deliver for his relative:

> *Once more I am called upon to fulfill the duties of my office in tying the bonds of matrimony between a couple who are ready to join their destinies in happiness and sorrow. It gives me particular satisfaction to see in one of the parties one of my nearest relatives, and more so as I find in the other party a lovely, well educated girl who promises fair to fulfill the expectation of a happy and successful future matrimonial life. In this light young folks always see their intending career in matrimony, not being aware of the numerous inevitable trials which not seldom test the energy and steadfastness of the husband and the love and resignation of the wife to a considerable extent.*

> *The duties of matrimony will soon enough present themselves in their earnest as well as agreeable shape, and it is there where the mutual love of the couple, the energy of the husband and the careful tenderness of the wife will tend to strengthen the inner and stronger ties, which the law can only fasten as far as the community outer appearances are concerned.*

Women's rights had not yet entered into Martin Schnell's thinking. The wife was strictly to be a helpmate to her husband.

> *While the husband exerts himself in the strife of life to secure to his family an existence as far as possible free from care and if success follows him, a comparable independency, the fond wife at home tries her best to make it to him comfortable and attractive, so that he can there gather new strength to attend to the duties of his vocation. When the husband, as it often occurs in married life,*

or he is otherwise bodily or mentally fatigued, it is she, the wife who with the tender feeling of her soul, will remit him by providing for his comfort, by diverting his over burdened mind to agreeable and enlivening thoughts and strengthen him for the continuance of his daily strife.

But here your duties are not over, the most important will present themselves when you will to raise a family. Here not only your future happiness but the interests of the community demand of you the education of your children to useful members of society, to imbibe them with that mutual love among these lives and their parents without which real happiness in a family is impossible.

Full attention to those duties will secure you that happiness and satisfaction which no success in life and no acquired wealth can give, without which the walk through life, however otherwise smooth, will be sterile and desolate.

Mary, who would bear a child on almost every even-numbered year for the next 28 years, had a firm conviction that the Lord took care of such matters. Each woman, she believed, was predestined to have a certain number of children. Thirty years later, after the arrival of her 14th child, she began to wonder.

CHAPTER 4

Babies and Boats

Of all things I think for man and wife to be separated
is the hardest. —Mary L. Heckmann

*I*t could not have been a surprise to Mary Miller Heckmann that babies started coming with great regularity after the wedding. Her first child, William Lewis Heckmann Jr., arrived in the world on March 7, 1869. Steamboat Bill claimed that the exact place of his birth was somewhat disputed. His father said he was born on a steamboat between Hermann and Bluffton, but his mother insisted he was born in Hermann—and she is *the one who ought to know.* A second son, Samuel, who variously and confusingly came to be called Greeley or Cy, made his appearance on December 21, 1870.

Mary and her mother alternated having babies for several years, which later made for very convenient baby-sitting. Martha Miller, the mother, gave birth to a baby girl named Alice in 1868. Mary, the daughter, then had William and Samuel. Mother Martha produced Gertrude in 1871; the following year daughter Mary followed suit with Angela, whom the family called Annie. Mary also had several brothers and sisters living nearby.

The Bluffton Winery enjoyed another good year in 1869, but the following year wine prices dropped precipitously. By 1871 it was evident that the winery was in serious trouble. Samuel Miller left Bluffton to join George Husmann and

Fred Teubner in Sedalia, where they were propagating grape rootstock that would be resistant to the root louse phylloxera that had laid waste to French vineyards.

The disease had been introduced into France from grapes imported from America, where phylloxera is native. By 1870, the year of France's war with Prussia, it was said that phylloxera cost the French more than twice the amount that Bismarck demanded in indemnity. The plague was halted only when millions of acres of vineyards were uprooted and replanted with American rootstock onto which French vines had been grafted. The French credited the Americans with saving their vineyards, and horticulturists like George Husmann became national heroes.

Back home, however, the Bluffton Winery was forced to close its doors. With the winery out of business, there was little in the way of carpentry work for William, and business was slow at the sawmill as well. The newlyweds moved to Hermann so Will could return to his first love—steamboating.

He began short-tripping on the steamer Washington, a stiff-shaft sidewheeler. The pay was not steady, but at least he had no money invested in the boat—which proved to be a rare time in their lives, indeed. Will Heckmann was no novice in the pilothouse, but experience was still necessary before he could become a licensed pilot.

He learned his lessons the hard way. The Washington was notoriously hard to handle—piloting her was said to be akin to trying to steer a car today without a differential. Steamboat Bill later said he did not know what his father saw in the old tub: *She was no beauty, hard to handle and my Dad was the only one who ever made a dime off the old lugger.*

William's entrepreneurial instincts began to make themselves known. The steamer Clara, a 222-foot-long sidewheeler owned by the Star Line Packet Company, had hit on a snag on the Missouri River one-half mile above Ousley's Landing. William bought the wrecked steamboat for 50 dollars, dismantled her and hauled the pieces to Bluffton by barge. He then proceeded to use the lumber to build a home for his rapidly growing family.

Steamboat Bill reported that the gingerbread from around the pilothouse was used to trim the dining room and that the bells were used to call the Heckmann children to meals. The house still stands today, although not on its original site. It was moved to make way when the Missouri, Kansas and Texas Railroad tracks were laid on the north side of the river.

William also acquired his first piece of land during this period. With the money he had earned as a carpenter, he bought the island in front of Bluffton with the idea of developing a fine farm. Eventually, the chute between the is-land and mainland closed, and, like so many parcels of land subject to the vagaries of the river, the farm became the subject of years of litigation.

Mary thought her first years of marriage were wonderful. She was gay and carefree and, in her later opinion, not always as responsible as she might have been. But when steamboats entered the picture, the purse strings tightened, and her happy-go-lucky existence abruptly came to an end.

William and his brother Edward, who had married Mary's younger sister Emma, formed a stock company, which they christened the St. Louis and Port-land Packet Company. In 1874 the new company bought the steamer Dugan from Capt. Joseph Kinney of Boonville and entered into competition with the famous Missouri River Star Line. The Dugan, whose dimensions were 160 feet by 30 feet by 3 feet, was by far the largest steamboat to call the Port of Hermann home at the time.

Years later the oldest Heckmann son, Steamboat Bill, never one to pass up an opportunity to brag on his father, wrote about the rivalry that developed between the Dugan and the Mattie Belle.

The twenty years' period that included the Civil War and ended with 1873 was known as the "Golden Era" on the Missouri River. In the year 1874, through rebating and rate cutting by the Missouri Pacific Railroad, the packet boats were forced to carry freight for almost nothing. Still, at that time, the once-famous Star Line had some one-half dozen large steamboats in the St. Louis and Kansas City trade. In the same year, the sternwheel steamer R. W. Dugan, as an independent packet boat, entered the St. Louis-Portland trade in opposition to the Star Line. To compete with this boat, the larger company put their fast sternwheel steamer Mattie Belle in this trade to harass the newcomer and make her carry freight for practically nothing. There followed one of the most bitter rate wars ever waged on Western Rivers.

These two boats made weekly trips, both leaving St. Louis every Saturday night. The captain of the Dugan was a better navigator, a better mixer and a handsomer man than the Star Line could put on the Mattie Belle. But the Belle was a larger, faster and finer boat, a craft fully able to keep ahead of the Dugan, both upstream and down. Naturally, like Capts. Cannon and Leathers of the famous racing Queens, the Robt. E. Lee and the Natchez, these two men became bitter enemies. They looked forward to, and they welcomed, any opportunity to

The steamer Dugan with the little Light Western, left.

harass each other.

One of the big shipping points in this trade was Howell's Landing near the end of the St. Louis Olive Street Road at the banks of the Missouri River. Most all the boats landed there. A very pretty girl named Miss Coleman was a favorite and knew most all the crews that operated these boats.

One morning the Mattie Belle, piloted by E. M. Baldwin and mastered by Capt. Whitledge, came busting down the swollen Missouri, loaded flat and running a little late. Miss Coleman, herself a trifle late, rushed out from behind the warehouse and hailed the boat in. Now heavily loaded and coming down-stream on a swollen river meant a lot of effort and consumption of fuel to make this landing, even if Capt. Baldwin had received the hail in time to get ready. When he finally had rounded to and got back up to the landing it had been a real effort and a costly one, too. Capt. Whitledge then called to the girl, "Honey, what have you got to go?"

"I have a bouquet for you, Capt. Whitledge," the young woman replied. Capt. Whitledge left the roof and went down for his token. He thanked everybody's favorite and then he asked her if she knew Capt. Heckmann of the

Dugan?

"Oh, yes, he is the finest man on all our rivers."

Capt. Whitledge said, "Well, the Dugan is right behind us. Here is a silver dollar for your trouble. Make him up a bouquet, too, and hail him in just like you did us. Give him the flowers with my compliments."

A dollar was "some money" in those days, and the girl played her part well. Those bouquets cost each boat at least $20. The tale continues, as told by Steamboat Bill:

At the time the channel of the Missouri River came down on the right of Howell's Island. About two miles above was what they called Hamburg Chute. Nestled above the chute was the little hamlet of Hamburg, another shipping point. The boats could not get into the chute at the upper end of Howell's Island, but could come up from below. The Dugan came down the river and at the foot of Howell's Island the pilot looked up the chute and saw a hail. They turned the old boat around and steamed up the chute, only to find a big white horse flopping his tail to keep the flies away ... but the warehouse was empty.

The next trip down the Mattie Belle, as usual, was ahead of the Dugan. While she was loading freight at Hamburg, they told Capt. Whitledge how the horse had fooled the Dugan. So the captain got in touch with a shady character and gave him five dollars to again hail the Dugan into an empty warehouse. The shady character hailed the boat, and when she was close to Hamburg he took to the hills.

Capt. Heckmann found out what was happening and told Capt. Whitledge on their next meeting that the third time this happened would be the charm. "If you ever have anything more to do with my making a wild goose chase up Hamburg chute," he said, "they will have to begin looking for another captain for the Mattie Belle." Capt. Whitledge took him by his word and was more careful afterward. His opponent had the reputation of being a "he" man, not to be trifled with.

On one trip downstream when freight was somewhat scarce, the Dugan, through skillful piloting and by running after night (something the Mattie Belle's captain would not risk), passed the Belle and kept ahead of her rival all the way to St. Louis. The Dugan took almost all of the freight at all landings, leaving just enough that the Mattie Belle would be hailed in, causing her to land almost everywhere. Capt. Heckmann even bribed some of the landing keepers to delay the faster boat all they could.

When the Dugan came out of the muddy Missouri into the clearer Mississippi the crew could look back and see the Mattie Belle's black smoke. Immediately, there was a race to the St. Louis stock yards where it was always "first come, first served." Both boats reached the stock yards at the same time. But the Dugan was on the inside, and while the larger boat was turning around the Dugan made what is known as a French landing and Capt. Whitledge had to wait an hour for the rival boat.

When these boats arrived at their wharfs, the Dugan was loaded flat. The Mattie Belle, however, was almost empty and her captain was called on the carpet, but could not explain what had happened.

While it is true that the Dugan was forced to carry wheat sacks into St. Louis for three cents per sack, she also had some other problems. Steamboat Bill said anyone could see that *the Dugan was cramped in the stacks. ... It wasn't that Capt. Ralph Whitledge was a better pilot than that Dad of mine—the Mattie Belle was just a better boat.*

It was while William was on the Dugan that Mary began to feel the pain of not having a husband around.

May 9, 1875—William was here a few minutes. I wished so much he could stay here awhile, sometimes think I cannot bear it. Of all things I think for man and wife to be separated is the hardest. I envy the poorest man and woman around, first because they can be together and I must be parted from the dearest one, only to have a stolen moment with him now and then. The only hope I have is that I may have it better sometime. If I was not blessed with the sweetest baby, I do not know what I would do sometimes. These last few days I have felt so bad, I fear I may get sick.

A little while later she was somewhat more cheerful and noted that the boat was getting good loads. She also began taking the boat from Bluffton to Hermann and even made occasional trips to St. Louis and Jefferson City. Leaving the children was no problem with her mother and her sister close by.

June 14, 1875—Boat came by daylight. I went along. A party from Jones Landing, dancing all the time. Got to Jefferson City by 2 o'clock. Griffith's girls went along to Cedar City, when we got back, went to state house. We run up the river about twelve miles, got back by 2 a.m.

By September of 1875, she had missed her journal entries for a month.

Almost another month gone, it seems to me to be the shortest year I have ever known, although last year I cried many times thinking what a lonely time I would have without William. Sadly we have missed him, but the time has passed quickly. He was at home yesterday while boat went up, the children were all so happy while he was here. Now he talks of going South. I hope and pray something may turn up soon to benefit us and prevent his going, for I have sad forebodings about him and I know that the long winter nights and gloomy days will drag heavily, although I have plenty to occupy my time.

An avid reader, Mary found that books provided a wonderful escape from worries about steamboats and her absent husband. Occasionally, she gave her own version of a book review. After reading "We and Our Neighbors," by Harriet Beecher Stowe, she wrote:

Mrs. Stowe said woman has two vernal seasons in her life, one is the fresh, sweet-brier apple-blossom spring of girl-hood, dewy, bird singing, joyous and transient. I may add, careless (even when a cloud obscures the sky, it soon passes, leaving one the same happy creature as before). The other is the spring of young marriage. Before the austere labors and severe strains of real life commence, every word true. HBS, how often I think of my first and second year of married life, how careless, light-hearted and happy I was, and yet, I did not even then know, how truly I was loved, even when I had one babe. I was thoughtless and careless, after I had my second boy and he was taken sick, I then found that I had never known the good and true heart that was mine. He often lay for hours by the child's side because he loved him so dearly. That time is passed, the child is fast growing up, there are others too. It seems strange that a mother's love does not grow less as one after the other comes to claim her love, but it only seems to grow the stronger. Even now, I often think the hardest part of my life is passed.

In August, new worries came with the rising river. Mary wrote about the efforts of her father and brothers to rescue mules from the island.

Papa called us early, said the river rose five feet. John, Dave, Bob and Papa went over to the island for mules, but could not get them off. The house is in water up to the windows. Tonight it is within 1 foot of the edge of back at the warehouse and still rising slowly.

The next day a party *got the mules over, they swam. ... The boat came early in the morning, got all the children ready and went with it, got to Jefferson City by sunset. The boat nearly overrun with people there.*

The island farm always remained a great source of hope for Mary. She was delighted when William engaged Fred Moody to work on the farm. But in short order Moody took off for Portland with Mary's 15-year-old brother John and came home drunk, another reason for Mary to hate demon rum—or beer, in this case.

A third son—Julius Frederick Heckmann, who would be called Fred—had been born on November 25, 1874, bringing the count up to five children—Will's daughter Tina, Will, Sam, Annie and Fred. At times Mary waxed philosophical about her children.

Tina is growing to be a great help to me. Willie and Sammie can help themselves some. I sometimes feared Willie would not be as intelligent as Tina and Sam, but I find while it is natural for the others to show it, his lies latent. It is a pleasure to me when I am about my work and they do not know I am listening to hear them arguing different subjects. For instance, the difference in value of a steamboat and a farm. They always come to me to have it decided, and it amuses me to find what implicit trust they put into all I say. Therefore, it behooves me to watch and be prepared to answer all questions of reason and sense, as it does every mother.

To Mary's great relief, the much-discussed plan for the Dugan to go south for the winter failed.

William gave me good cheer, thinks the boat will not go South as he has been saying of late. It is what I have been hoping and praying for all the time. For it seems as though I could not bear it, to leave him go.

But her joy was short lived. By December Mary wrote:

William is still on the Dugan, she is on Upper Mississippi River, do not know when W. will be home. I know he wishes he had taken my advice last year. I wish he had never got steamboat on the brain, he has so much trouble and to me it is a plague. I have no comfort at all, some times I lose all heart and do not know what I am living for. I feel since I heard the ways things are going, like going anywhere. I do not know how I am to pass the time, with all the trouble on my mind, it seems like a constant nightmare to me. I only hope we may be successful next year with the island, maybe if we make something on it once he will try to content himself at home. His idea of getting rich is to take by one leap, mine is to go steady but sure. That is the only way to get rich, and then one knows how to value it too.

William returned home for Christmas, and the frozen river kept him there awhile. Mary even reported some domestic help from her husband.

He took the old cow and sold her for $90 and bought himself lumber for skiffs, and yarn, bacon, comb, tin bucket for us. Bought a lot of fresh sausage, the children run at it like starve. ... W. is lying around, he felt so stiff, the old cow led him such a dance. Went out in the evening and killed some game.

The work of the household was endless. A great deal of the family's meat came from wild game, and the dressing of the ducks, geese, rabbits, and squirrels was a big undertaking. Mary sewed dresses, waists and saques for the girls and suits for the little boys. For her husband she made and dyed overalls and knitted suspenders. She and Tina worked up rags from discarded clothing to be woven into rugs, an interminable task. No fabric was ever wasted—even Mother Heckmann at Hermann sent packages of clothes for carpet rags.

The rag carpets were important—they were the only floor covering the family could afford—but they also were a continuing source of work. After the strips of cloth had been cut, sewed together and wound into balls, they were taken to a weaver to be made into rug strips, usually 21-to-23 inches wide. The women sewed these woven strips together by hand to make a room-sized rug.

When the rug was placed on top of a layer of fresh straw and tacked along the edges, it made a wall-to-wall carpet that was decorative, easy on the feet and warm. But the rag rugs also became filthy with tracked-in mud, especially in winter and early spring. So periodically the women had to take up the rugs, unravel the laboriously sewn strips, wash them on a washboard, dry them on a line and then sew everything back together again.

Clothes, rugs and just about everything else were washed with homemade soap. Wood ashes from the stove were put into a hopper so the lye could be filtered out. Combining excess grease that had been saved with the lye made a good, serviceable soap. This handy commodity was a universal cleanser, used for everything from people to floors.

Despite the never-ending rounds of household chores, Mary still found time to write for numerous newspapers and magazines. No record exists as to what pay, if any, she received for her various writing endeavors. But there was a steady stream of requests. She "found" time to write by reserving Sundays for reading and writing. Since Bluffton had no church, this was her way of keeping the Sabbath—she did not consider writing work.

I finished reading Great Expectations, a book by C. Dickens. Liked it very well. The Author has a way of making the reader see his characters, they seem to stand before you, every motion his character has, that is peculiar, he can make you see and understand. Dickens was a deep thinker and great observer. He seen through many of the veils and screens of this world, that are too thick for most of us.

William and Mary Heckmann, two people as different as night and day, were nonetheless a devoted couple. Despite long absences from home, William was a loyal husband and father who took any opportunity to be with his family. In one journal entry Mary recorded, *William left this morning at 5 o'clock, it was terrible dark, he went down in the skiff.* To a man who was alone and in the dark, the Missouri River must have been a fearsome place. When William sent word that he wished his wife to join him, as he frequently did, not once did she demur. For Mary, being ever at the ready to leave home and children—or to take them with her—was a small price to pay for a few hours with her husband. Usually, she described the trips in some detail.

The boat put off a lot of apples for us. I went along and had a pretty good trip, but the river is so bad it takes time. We were on a bar about 4 hours at Boonville on the down trip. Got to Bluffton on Friday, Nov. 19, in the afternoon. Found things at home much better than I expected.

Bluffton still had no firefighting equipment, and fire remained a dreadful foe. One night at 11 p.m. the family received word of a fire. The next day Mary wrote in her journal:

By the time I was dressed and got out the blaze was striking out of the store door and window. I found all the children out of the house, already. The old bar-room also took fire and in one hour, both buildings were down to the ground. Wrights can give no account whatever for the fire, his loss is something like 2 thousand if he gets his insurance.

Thanksgiving that year was not celebrated in the expected manner.

We did not keep much holiday. In the afternoon I took all the children up to the big rock to see their Papa when he stopped off. We were caught in a rainstorm as

we came down in the skiff. The next day William went up to meet the boat, she
went down after dinner, landed about 1/2 mile from Bluffton, got some corn
from her. There is a bar just opposite the house nearly closing the channel.

In December the ice was running thick, and all Mary's plants froze in the greenhouse. William returned home Christmas morning, and Mary had dinner almost ready when *a dreadful chill* put her to bed. The ever-present malaria, no respecter of holidays, was so common as to be an expected ailment. Cures ranged from the practical to the ridiculous.

The next day Mary was feeling better, and the entire family gathered for supper, singing and parlor games. The Heckmanns always had a piano in the house, and everyone sang. *Had lots of fun singing and trying mesmerizing, excitement got pretty high.*

Mary closed the year 1875 with a final entry.

Let us hope with the new will come better times than we have had the past few
years. The Centennial which is creating a stir all over the world, will perhaps
bring some life, energy and money into this country.

January of 1876 was bitterly cold. The peaches froze, a second try at flowers in the greenhouse froze, and Mary wrote that she was entirely *disgusted with it. I believe I may as well give up all thoughts of doing anything to earn a little money, for everything I try with the best will is sure to be unsuccessful.* The hunters continued to bring home game—five ducks one day—and even the family rooster found his way to the dinner table. *Plucked old Tilton yestereven, had him for dinner today.*

In March of 1876, after two years in the packet trade, the Heckmann brothers sold the Dugan back to Capt. Kinney for $8,000. It is doubtful if any of the stockholders ever received a penny from the sale. Capt. Kinney continued to operate the Dugan, but after two years he, too, gave it up. Even the mighty Star Line eventually was forced out of business by the railroads. Will's nemesis, Capt. Whitledge, took a berth ashore as a steamboat inspector. Steamboat Bill said they were all *kicked to death by the Iron Horse.*

Mary restrained herself by not mentioning a word of the sale of the Dugan in her journal. If she was sad at the loss or relieved to have her husband out of the steamboat business, she does not say. But financially, the family hit rock bottom. Steamboat Bill, a writer with a penchant for embroidering a good story to make it better, told this tale about one of the tough winters the family endured in Bluffton:

During one of the winters that we lived in Bluffton, my mother and I formed a company. We plucked wild geese that my father killed and dried a lot of fruit. Spring came and there was no market on the north side of the river, so we had to take our winter output across the river to the little town of Morrison, two miles across a big river bottom.

One of my uncles ferried us across the river in a skiff. When he put us ashore he said: "I don't see how you two ever expect to get that stuff to Morrison. The roads are bad and muddy."

We had a monster sack of wild goose feathers and a sack of dried fruit that weighed about seventy-five pounds. In my long time on the river it has been my pleasure to handle many difficult kinds of jobs and my misfortune to dabble in many that cost lots of work and turned out to be failures, but never have I slaved as we did with that sack of fruit. However, we got to Morrison and sold our products.

In after years when going seemed impossible and everything looked lost, my memory would go back to that first delivery of the Heckmann Feather and Fruit Co. and I would say to myself, "Buck up, Old Boy, this is not half so hard as getting that fruit to Morrison."

In making that trip, my whole energy and strength were devoted to the fruit. Several times, if it had not been for mother, the feathers would have been ditched. As it was, we had to double trip over lots of the worst places in the muddy road.

On the way back home mother asked: "Will, what do you think we made?"

"Oh, there's no telling," I replied, "but if it hadn't been for those darned feathers we would be home long ago."

"We did pretty well with the feathers, but we didn't get much for the fruit," replied mother. *"We got twenty-four dollars for the feathers and only a dollar sixty for the fruit."*

Forced by circumstances to be more of a farmer than a riverman, William bought a pair of mules, but the owner refused to give them up. It was nearly a month before Mary reported that *William got the mules.* Inspired by a break in the weather, Mary had planted potatoes, peas, radishes and lettuce on February 13. But by April she was once again dismayed by her garden.

My early gardening has been to no purpose, everything dead, even the lettuce.

Chickens are doing better now, but still nothing to boast of. Had an adventure yesterday while hunting a turkey's nest, seen crows whipping a hawk, were close on a flock of quail. George scared up a rabbit on a grave, it ran over the bluff! Willie and I seen it go under the tie-pile and just then William came along and he caught it after I pushed it out with a rail. Tina and Annie found the turkey nest today with 2 eggs in it.

Garden produce was important to the family, so Mary tried again. *Planted cabbage, cucumber and other seeds on island. Planted a lot of truck here too this week. Set out my house plants and sowed the seed. ... Since last writing, have made a strawberry bed on terrace and planted cabbage between the rows. Planted 10 acres of corn on island. ... I have been helping down home, sewing, tying grapes and planted potatoes and corn. ... The Centennial opened as promised on the 10th of May. ... Planted lima beans, sweet corn, popcorn, bunch beans, squashes and potatoes. ... I planted early watermelon out of the greenhouse, planted in a box five weeks ago.*

That fall, another baby girl was born to the Heckmann family.

October 1, 1876—*On Friday Sept. 22 William was here a few minutes in the evening of same day I was taken sick. On the morning of 23rd Sept. I waked brother Bob up early, sent for Mother and Mrs. Coleman. They were with me all day and at 4 o'clock there was a little girl baby here, got along quite well. When baby was four days old, William came home to find his new baby safe by my side. Today I have been up all day for the first time. On Thursday I had a severe pain in my chest, put on mustard freely and by evening did not suffer any more, but the blister annoyed me very much on Friday night. Dr. Thompson here the past week, went home yesterday. Think we will call baby Mary Elizabeth and call her Lizzie.*

In November Emma and Eddie Heckmann had twin babies, a boy and a girl. But Mary wrote that the little boy, who died when he was four days old, *did not seem right from first. "The Lord giveth and the Lord taketh away."* The sad story drew to a close on November 27.

Em's little girl was taken with spasms and continued to have them until last Sunday night about 12 o'clock when she died. It suffered very much and was as it seemed dead at least ten times each day. It was astonishing to see what a struggle for life such a little being could make, everyone who seen it after having a spell thought it was dead. M. Glover made the coffin here on Monday, they took up the little boy and buried them in one coffin. The little girl looked so pretty, looked like a wax figure.

In preparation for Christmas, William rode one of the mules to Loutre Island and from there made his way across the frozen river to Hermann. Mary recorded that he:

Brought shoes for each of us, cups, saucers and knives and forks for me, dress and slate desk for Tina, a wagon for Will, wheel-barrow for Greeley and rocking-chair for Annie, a little wagon for Fred, a picture for Willie and Greeley. Willie kindly gave his picture to Annie and he said he had "Charlie" the horse. My Christmas was passed working all day and having a sick spell (cholera morbus) on 23rd.

December 31, 1876—Thus ends the Centennial year for me. The political state of affairs are in a terrible muddle, the election of Nov. 7th is still undecided. Each party accuses the other of fraud. God only knows what the next year will bring forth, let us pray for Peace, Prosperity and Plenty.

During the fall there were terrible complaints about the grasshoppers in Minnesota and Iowa, the suffering in many places cannot be told, in many villages the people were entirely destitute. So that suffering will be terrible to contemplate this severe winter. Those having enough of healthful food to eat, plenty of clothes, and plenty of wood to keep them warm are surrounded with great blessings, compared with the hoppersufferers.

Little Lizzie laughed loud for the first time last week, she is growing so fast and is as fat as can be.

CHAPTER 5

For Better or for Worse

The pretended preacher failed to put in an appearance. Souls are of
no consequence in rainy weather. —Mary L. Heckmann

*A*s her 30th birthday approached in 1878, Mary was the busy mother of
five children. She had adjusted to the irregular schedules of the little steamers
and was more content knowing her husband would not be away from home
very long at a time. Both husband and wife worked constantly. A typical day for
Mary: *Washed, ironed, baked, washed two pieces of carpet, got wood on island. Dipped*
river water for wash, started soap, worked in the garden.

When Will was not aboard a steamboat, he was building a skiff, salvaging
wire out of the old vineyards of the Bluffton Wine Company, rowing around
with Will Jr. salvaging ties and even tie hacking sometimes. On occasion, he
found time for a playful entry in his wife's diary. February 29, 1878—*This day does*
not come this year.

Mary, whose mind was occupied by other matters, did little reporting about
the boats. At one time she wrote, *Will thinks he will get a berth on the "Yellowstone."*
Late one year she recorded, *Will home for good. They think they can get along without*
him on the Washington. But by March 12 of 1878, the Washington was running
again, with Will at the helm. *Washington here a few minutes. W. is pilot on her, a*
party of Hermanitz have bought her, J. Silber one of them. Mary also reported that her
father was home from Sedalia and that Tina, who had been doing much of the
daily work, had gone with William to go to the Hermann school. *I do not miss her*
much, only in the way of company.

On April 19 Mary *kept a holiday. It was Good Friday, the day of all days on which we should feel our humblest to our Lord and Saviour. On this day He finished and ended the long list of sufferings and pain. He suffered for our sakes.*

The next day found her preparing for the children's Easter. The chickens were not supplying enough eggs, so she dispatched nine-year-old Will Jr. across the Missouri River in a skiff to get eggs. A little later she again sent over to Morrison for supplies and reported, *Greeley let 50 pounds of sugar fall in the river. We saved some of it.* Greeley was only seven at the time.

Mary spent Easter Sunday reading and going for ferns to press, a commodity for which she had found a market—she traded with a pen pal for Spanish moss. The next days were rainy, and she *done some fixing up of drawers and over haul papers. Ducks coming out, been painting pottery preparatory to decorating. One of the hobbies of today.*

Another side of her sociable husband was coming to light in the diaries. On Independence Day Mary stayed home with the children while Will and Dave Miller, her brother, went to Metzler's Park after the noon meal. *W. came home at mid-night.* The next day, *W. has been sleeping nearly all day. I done some mending.* Another day Will crossed the river to Morrison, leaving Dave Miller on the island. Again, Will did not return until late. When Dave grew tired of waiting for him to return with the skiff, he simply swam across the chute and came home.

Mary was less delighted by the lively steamboat excursion parties than the "Advertiser-Courier," which reported: *An interesting little race took place yesterday afternoon between the steamers Light Western and Washington. The latter had the start of our little Ferry boat but soon the Light Western showed her heels to the Washington much to the chagrin of W. L. Heckmann who is pilot on her.*

Mary's journal told a somewhat different tale. *Last week, the menfolks, the would-be aristocricy of Hermann chartered the Washington to make an excursion to Augusta, a trip exclusively for the men. The Ladies, nothing loth, very quietly went to work preparing also for a trip to the same place. They chartered the Light Western. When the Washington had been gone, the Western followed. Both parties took each a band, many of the men had heard that the ladies were to follow, but neither one knew whose really would be along. I suppose each one wished theirs would stay at home.*

During the warmest part of the late summer, Will and most of the children contracted a severe form of malaria. Mary, still on foot and nursing the lot, gave up on home remedies. A doctor was called.

As the time for the delivery of another baby drew near, Mary was busy canning and drying peaches, sewing, writing and using her new Spanish moss to make *a fancy hanging basket*. William was not quite recovered from the sick spell and continued to have fever, but he did feel up to going hunting on September 19. The next morning Mary *fixed a nice breakfast of squirrels and pigeons. By 5 o'clock I was suddenly taken sick, went for Mrs. Melins about dark, she came and staid all night.*

On September 21, 1878, Mary gave birth to her sixth child, Martha Eveline. *Mrs. Melins thought she knew better than I and left this morning, promising to come in the afternoon again. I depended on her word, and waited too long, so luck would have it, Mrs. Colman stopped in at two o'clock. Mother was here at 3. There was a little girl born, a large nice baby.*

Two days later Mary was suffering with chills and high fever. On September 28 she had *a frightful headache and dreams last night, took a chill again this morning and suffered until evening with a fearful headache. W. does not come home this week. Lizzie missed her chill today for the first time in about three weeks, has had them every day.* Two days later she *spent nearly the whole day sleeping. I took quinine in whiskey all day yesterday and it made me a kind of drunk.*

This was a nursing mother, and she reported that *the baby is having trouble with its little seat, it is all chaffed.* Mary was also suffering with diarrhea and piles. Everyone seemed to have a remedy for her, from oatmeal to white oak bark. Finally, William brought medicine from a doctor at Hermann *that done good.* But when the family went for persimmons, Mary ate a few and promptly became worse.

By November 8 William went to Hermann to meet the Light Western and *got his money from Wohlt.* He also was involved in a lawsuit about the title to the island and was making frequent trips to Danville, the county seat of Montgomery County.

Hogs were butchered, sausage, pudding and pan hus had to be made. Family tragedies continued. On November 20 word came that Ed and Emma Heckmann's little boy was sick with the croup. A doctor was called, but *poor little Eddie died this morning at 11 o'clock. Did not suffer much at the end. Ed came home the next day and found his boy gone.* Eddie was buried the following day in the Miller family cemetery at Bluffton.

Sewing was an ongoing project, and Mary could complete dresses with great speed. *Finished my dress and put it on much to the astonishment of the whole family.* She also was a good sewing machine mechanic.

Christmas preparations were meager. Mary made a horse for Greeley and a pin cushion chair for Annie, a stuffed horse, dog and rabbit for the younger children. *Expenses for Christmas have been fifty cents. … We enjoyed it about the same as other years, although we had no presents, no tree, and nothing extra. I enjoyed it more than last year when I was sick.* The day after Christmas Mary wrote articles for "Colman's Rural World," the "Journal of Agriculture" and the "Western Farm Journal."

The Heckmann children attended the Bluffton school, which closed January 8, 1879, after a four-month term. *W. and I attended in the afternoon, left Sammie, Lizzie and Martha to keep house.* Sammie was 8 years old, Annie was 6, and Martha was just a baby. *Willie got a silver quarter dollar for head marks in his spelling class, the children all got pretty pictures.*

William kept meat on the table with his gun. In the back of Mary's diary, he recorded a total of 129 kills for the month of January—36 squab, 24 geese, 40 rabbits, 24 squirrels, two turkeys, two doves and a pheasant.

Mary's home doctoring skills were often in demand. *William was very sick. Had intended to send for medicine, but gave up the idea and gave him salts and senna, which done him good.* When Gert, Mary's eight-year-old sister, cut her finger with a hatchet, *we closed it up with fresh carpenter glue.* About the same time little Annie Heckmann *went up to the ties and fell hurting her lip badly and her finger. I pasted a cloth wet with glue over the outside of her mouth and now she can scarcely open her mouth wide enough to eat, has to take soups. She complains most with the finger.* When Martha Miller, Mary's mother, came down with what Mary diagnosed as Erysipelas, iodine was the favored remedy.

A new journal book was not available right at the first of the year, so Mary copied from Tina's journal. *I find she had made a mistake so that I have been cleaning the chicken houses on a Sunday, which is a mistake as it was Saturday.*

Mary celebrated her 31st birthday in 1879 by cleaning a goose, ironing and taking up the carpet. The February weather must have been mild because *I took the first skiff ride of the season.* A stranger came to her parents' house, billing himself as a revivalist, but Mary was unimpressed. *Will and I went through darkness and rain to the schoolhouse this evening, but the pretended preacher failed to put in an appearance, souls are of no consequence in rainy weather.* The next evening she and Will tried again and *heard what I call a poor excuse for a sermon.* The preacher remained in the area for a week. After his departure two showmen arrived. *Tina and Will went to the Panorama this evening.*

With the demise of the winery, Bluffton was rapidly losing population. Ed and Emma Heckmann joined the exodus in March, moving their possessions to Hermann on the steamer Washington. *The big Company house is empty now,* Mary sadly noted.

The river traffic was observed: *Fannie Lewis went up, first boat of the season.* Tie cutting must have been going on at Bluffton. At one point Mary mentions that the *steamers Kate Kinney and Durfee were here for ties, both full of colored people moving to Kansas. They buried a little darky in the graveyard off the Durfee.*

Mary and her friend Amelia, who lived on the island across from Bluffton, often traded work. At times Amelia would bring her little ones over and Mary would help her with sewing. At other times Amelia would row over to help Mary with the wash, boiling soap and other chores. *Amelia pulled over from the island,* Mary wrote, after which she and her brother Sam *walked down with Amelia to see her cross, got home by dark.*

The nearby Miller household was equally busy. Five of the younger children were still at home, and the Millers had taken over the Bluffton hotel business. On April 2 the weather was *cold, cloudy and windy. Papa and Mother went to Hermann on the Light Western. I kept house for mother. There was a fearful wind about 3 o'clock. The two tie inspectors came down home to stay all night and a peddler too. I got supper for all. Sam got Colman's mare and took her and Jim, the mule, down to get Papa and Mother. The mare tore the bridle and started home, so Sam followed with Jim and left the folks at Jones's. As I had to get breakfast for all, we went to bed down there. About 12 o'clock in the night Papa got home, he had walked up. Our skiff got off, we got it again.*

Later that month news was received from Sedalia that Mary's sister Liz and her husband Fred Teubner had lost their young son, Joe. The child's body was returned to Hermann for burial. *Little Joe was buried on the graveyard reserved on the Teubner place. Thus one after the other is taken from this world. For many years Death had been a stranger in our family. Now he makes frequent visits; five short months ago little Eddie was laid beneath the clay, now the little pet at Sedalia is taken away. Poor broken hearted mother. God give her strength to bear the trial.*

Game was a staple of the diet, but fish are rarely mentioned. One memorable fishing trip to McGirk's Island did prove worthy of comment. *Brought home a ton of all sizes. The greatest fish haul I ever seen. All fell to work cleaning fish, sold some. And prepared to take a load to Montgomery City. … Did not go to bed until 2 o'clock this morning when the fish men got started cleaning fish all day and eating much of the time. …William and Henry got home at midnight last night, very tired, only sold about 200 pounds of fish. We cleaned and salted all that were not yet dressed. Henry took a box full along over the river.*

Gardening was Mary's domain, but occasionally help was available. *The whole family went to the island. Planted potatoes, beets, parsnips, cabbage, corn and beans.*

This photograph of Hermann's Wharf Street was taken about 1910. The Heckmanns lived in the two-story frame house in the middle of the block (fourth house from right), next door to the Charles Eitzen home, which is set back somewhat from the street. The family later moved to the Peter Miller home next to the White House Hotel, the large building at the far end of the block.

Got home by dark. A few days later Mary took the two little girls—Annie, 7, and Martha, 1—to the island and *cut stalks all day, did not quite finish.*

In May of 1879, William bought into the Hermann Ferry and Packet Company, thus acquiring a financial interest in the Washington and the newly built Light Western. In short order the family made plans to move in with the senior Heckmanns at Hermann. There was even discussion of selling the island, but nothing further was reported. Mary was busy *collecting things together for moving, selling most of our old truck. A terrible hail storm caused some peculiar freaks, on the Experimental here, it cut up John Sutter's wheat awfully, while at the Company house at the creek and at Colman's it did not hurt a straw. Some of the hail stones were very large.*

When the family arrived in Hermann, more bad news was waiting. *Took dinner with Mother H. Lizzie's here. She came down yesterday with her little baby, buried it along side of her little Joe. Lizzie seems so much distressed.*

John Henry Heckmann, William's father, was failing fast, and many family members came to help and pay their last respects. On January 2, Mary wrote,

Grandfather died at half past eight this evening. Lena had just called in Dr. Smith, he said grandfather would only live fifteen minutes, and in fourteen minutes he was dead. He was carefully washed and layed out by Lena and Rauss. Henry Rauss's and ourselves staid up part of the night. Telegraphed to Ed. Shubert brought the coffin and put grandfather in it.

Wrecked by ice, the Light Western had reached the end of her earthly journey, as well. *All worked at the Western until noon, they have to wreck her. Funeral took place at two o'clock. Mr. Rose, the teacher, spoke at the grave. Ed came down last night, Louisa Schnell, Henry, Emma and Tina here, left again right after the funeral.*

Less than two months later, the family assembled again for the death of Will's mother, Justina Rewald Heckmann. On February 29 Mary wrote, *Between 10 and 11 o'clock our poor old Grandmother fell into the sleep that knows no awakening. Since last Monday she has been in bed, failing very slowly until Friday night when she was very fretful all night. Yesterday all day she lay quiet and unable to speak more than few words, she only wished to rest last night. We watched, thinking every moment would be her last, but she lived until today.*

CHAPTER 6

Melody in the Ozarks

*The only trouble with going upstream with a flatboat
was that you had to take the boat with you.*

*S*teamboating on the beautiful Ozark stream called the Gasconade River was largely wishful thinking until 1874 when a man of vision appeared. Henry Wohlt, who was born in Germany in 1833, came to the United States as a lad of 10 with his mother and stepfather to settle on the Gasconade River at First Creek. To him goes the credit for putting the melody of the little steam whistles into the Missouri Ozarks.

The Wohlt family arrived at Hermann by steamboat, but transportation up the Gasconade River had to be on the Jug Line, a flatboat that was really two barges hooked together and steered with a sweep. This contraption floated downstream, but the upstream operation took men with poles and ropes—the cordelle—pushing and pulling the boats. Because of the strenuous labor involved, it was claimed that each man kept a jug to ease his aching muscles. Someone dubbed this outfit the "Jug Line," and the name stuck.

Young Henry Wohlt dreamed of finding an easier way to get about the river. After the Jug Line, steamboat transportation must have seemed wonderfully easy to him. One commentator claimed, *The only trouble with going upstream with a flatboat was that you had to take the boat with you.* But steamboats faced other difficulties. When the Gasconade was at low-water stage, pilots reported that navigating it was like *putting a steamer on dry land and sending a boy ahead with a sprinkling can.*

The Maramec Iron Works at St. James produced heavy blooms of iron ore that had to be transported to the Hermann landing for shipment to St. Louis. Flatboats, keelboats and steamboats had been tried on the Gasconade River with varying degrees of success—in the case of the steamboats, no success at all. Heavy ox carts also pulled the blooms over an overland route—the Iron Road—that connected St. James and Hermann.

The Iron Works built a road to Paydown on the Gasconade River in the hope that steamboats could pick up blooms there. But all the boats imported for this work—the Iowa, Howard, Dart and Chastain—were forced to turn back 25 miles short of Paydown Landing.

The mere fact that these little steamboats even attempted the trip may have been an inspiration to Henry Wohlt, who in 1872 succumbed to steamboat fever and began building a little steamer he called the Stem. He was a married man at the time, with two sons, a shoemaking business and big dreams. The best summary of his early efforts appeared in his obituary in the "Advertiser-Courier."

Capt. Henry Wohlt who died last Thursday, was a shoemaker by trade who did not stick to his last, but who done better by commencing to run a small boat propelled by steam, on the Gasconade river to Hermann in the early seventies. Wohlt's neighbors at Fredericksburg knowing his scant resources and inexperience were profuse in their predictions that he would never succeed, and that he was fooling away his time instead of mending shoes.

The writer of this well remembers when Capt. Wohlt made his first landing at this wharf: his craft was a very primitive affair, the only prominent feature about it being that the whistle was so big that every time a signal was given it required so much steam of the propelling power as to stop the boat. Capt. Wohlt's industrious habits soon attracted the attention of Hermann people, with their assistance he built and operated a ferry boat at this point which enterprise became the nucleus of the present Ferry Company, proving profitable to himself and associates as well as to the town.

Other reports about Henry Wohlt's first boat include one by Steamboat Bill. *The first we heard of the Wohlt family was in 1872. In that year Capt. Henry Wohlt, who lived on a farm some 12 miles up the Gasconade River, built the steamer Stem. Herman Kaiser, a fine old man who worked for the Hermann*

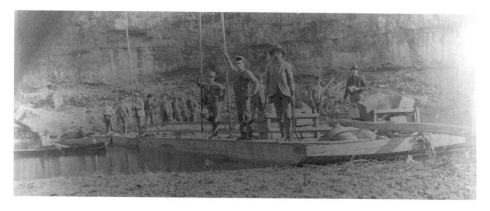

A rare early photograph of the Gasconade River "Jug Line."

Ferry and Packet Company for over 35 years says: "The Stem was not much of a boat; she had a beer keg in the engine room for a water feed heater, she had no rudders but used a raft oar for steering purposes. She was very slow, but 'got there just the same' and was the forerunner of a tremendous business that developed later on this stream." Captain Henry Wohlt and his son, August, operated this boat. August had to stand on a box or beer keg to answer the bells and son Gustave handled the lines.

This was an exaggeration, but help did start young in those days—Gustave Wohlt was 12 and August was 19. Bill Lalk, a Gasconade River farmer, was a partner in this first endeavor. There is no record of what became of the little steamer Stem, but we do know that she did make it to Hermann because the "Hermanner Volksblatt" reported: *Der Dampfer Stem, zu deutsch Stiel, von der Gasconade Packet Linie, liegt im umserem Hafen.* "The steamer Stem, in German Stiel, of the Gasconade Packet Line, lies in our harbor."

While the Heckmann brothers were getting their first taste of steamboating with the Dugan on the Missouri River, other Hermann interests were in search of a reliable ferry service—something that had been a priority for more than 30 years. Hermann's first settlers had looked longingly at the Loutre Island settlement, which had been established across the river in 1799. The river was a barrier that prevented them getting to the people and supplies they so sorely lacked.

The settlement at Loutre was well established by the time the first steamboat, the Independence, came up the river in May of 1819. The event was reported in the "Montgomery Standard."

Those who were not frightened at its appearance flocked to the riverside to see
the phenomenal "critter." A portion of her cargo was put off at Loutre and in
the lot was ten barrels of whiskey for a man named Mills, who evidently realized
the danger to which the inhabitants were subjected by the prevalence of rattle
snakes.

George Bayer, the agent for the German Settlement Society, had eyed the
little settlement of Loutre and noted the need for a boat in his first letters back to
Philadelphia. In short order, he traded a lot in the new town for a skiff. In 1839
when Hermann was incorporated, the board of trustees were granted the *exclusive*
power to license and regulate ferries in the town. Two years later, two residents were
licensed to run a ferry for five years, but no description of the type of boat used
was recorded. The "Advertiser-Courier" later carried a story that referred to
Hermann's first steam ferryboat.

It was built by Mathias A. Klenk, was 40 feet long, made of two barges, 3 feet
apart, held together by iron bars and heavy chains, the entire space covered by
flooring except the center which was left open for the wheel, boiler and engines,
two small smoke stacks and pilot house were in front of the wheel, while the rear
was left open for freight. There was no cabin. This unwieldy craft was demolished
by ice at the mouth of Frene Creek.

The town's next ferryboat was a sidewheel steamer, the W. A. Knapp, owned
by Jacob Graf Sr. *This boat had cabin, tubular boiler and was 100 feet long, made trips*
up the Gasconade River and did a general ferry business on the Missouri prior to and
during Civil War days. The Knapp probably was used to move women and children to Graf Island in the Missouri River when word came of Marmaduke's
advance toward Hermann.

By the early 1870s, Hermann was ripe for a solution to its ferry problems.
Providentially, one soon appeared. Having cut his nautical teeth on the Stem,
Henry Wohlt set out to build a bigger and better steamboat—the Light Western—at the Fredericksburg landing on the Gasconade River. This time he approached the Hermann Board of Aldermen with a proposal to bring his little
steamer to Hermann and run a regular ferry service in exchange for $650. Offi-
cial records show the Light Western valued at $1,250. Where he found the other
$600 to build his boat was never explained.

It took incredible imagination and gumption to build a steam vessel without
plans or even any knowledge about how to run a steamboat. To make matters
even more difficult, there was no mail, railroad or steamboat service to

Fredericksburg to deliver the machinery necessary for such an endeavor. But Henry Wohlt prevailed.

By early 1875 Hermannites were eagerly awaiting the arrival of their ferry-boat. The "Hermanner Volksblatt" reported the arrival of the little Light Western at the Hermann wharf in March of 1875 in typical flowery German prose. The boat arrived after *much hustle and bustle and was masterly built.* The announcement ended with the admonition, *Ever forwards!*

As soon as the Light Western arrived, a town meeting was called. The newspaper reported: *There will be a meeting of citizens interested in the ferry-boat this evening at the market house, to discuss some important measures in regard to the ferry. Mr. Chas. D. Eitzen will leave Jefferson City so as to be here in time for the meeting.* Eitzen by then was a state representative but still very involved in Hermann affairs.

After a lengthy meeting, a contract was drawn up with specific provisions as to what the town and Wohlt could expect.

Mr. Wohlt shall have leave to be absent from this landing from Saturday evening until Monday noon, and on Wednesday morning he shall make a trip to Kalmeyer's and other landings he choose, so as to enable him to be back to Hermann by 11 o'clock A.M. and ferry here from then until 3 o'clock P.M. when he shall bring the passengers he brought to town on his morning trip to their respective landings. The other days he shall ferry regularly at Hermann and make at least four trips per day. He shall also be at liberty to make such side-trips as will not materially interfere with ferrying at this port. ...Mr. Wohlt will begin ferrying on Monday, June 7th and keep the ferry in operation for the term of two years from said day.

When the chairman asked Mr. Wohlt when he could begin the regular trips, he said he did not know exactly, as he had to go to St. Louis to secure his license as pilot and have his boilers inspected, but that he thought he could manage the June 7 date. Apparently, he was not too worried about these details because in the same paper he advertised a "Grand Excursion"—an all-day affair to a picnic grounds on the Gasconade River.

There'll be a grand excursion on board the steamer "Light Western" to Onckens Grove next Sunday morning. The boat will leave Loutre Island at 6, Hermann at 7 and Gasconade City at 8 o'clock A.M. Round-trip tickets, 25 cents. Kropps Brass Band has been engaged for the occasion.

The town loved the social possibilities of having a boat available—picnics, excursions, baseball games, fraternal organizations and Grange meetings all were waiting to use Wohlt's little boat. The newspapers had a field day, reporting outings in great detail. Citizens could read about the exploits of local steamboats in either German in the "Hermanner Volksblatt" or in English in the new "Advertiser-Courier."

The grand excursion of May the 30th, was in all respects a very pleasant affair so far as the trip going was concerned. But on arriving at the pic-nic grounds, the Oncken Grove, all hands went onshore, for the purpose of inhaling the pleasant country air, which was delightful. The pic-nic, so-called, was a failure but as the beer kegs rolled about there was evidence that there must be another nic, which is properly termed a drink 'nic in which all seemed to take a part, even to the magnificent Steamer itself.

When leaving Hermann in the morning of the beautiful day of the 30th with colors streaming, the Band making sweet music, above all the sound of the base drum could be heard, above the din. But, after the day was spent at the nick and the time for returning to our homes had arrived, the whistle blown and all in readiness for the trip there seemed to be something wrong, when on making inquiry it was found the base drum had taken so much of the splendid beverage that it was unable to sound. Mr. Oncken thought there might probably be some sound in the instrument, so giving it a considerable blow, the head bursted and the music was spoiled, nevertheless the band did their best and made considerable noise until the Steamer grounded on a sand bar on the Montgomery side of the River when in the excitement the sound of music died away, and it was found that all the instruments were blowed out—that is, had too much sodawater.

Other social events associated with the little Light Western followed. In September the dedication of the new church at Morrison caused quite a pilgrimage from Hermann with both the little steamer Light Western and the noon train carrying 500 people to the celebration. But along with the fun of the little steamer came an element of danger. The same issue of the paper reported another event, a tragic one, the drowning of Dan Skinner.

Mr. Dan Skinner, who was very well known to a great many of our readers, was drowned on Friday of last week under the following circumstances.

Mr. Skinner boarded the "Light Western" at Hermann to make the trip to

Kalmeyer's Landing and return on her. As usual, he seated himself on the guards of the forward part of the boat. Capt. Wohlt remonstrated but Skinner payed no heed to his warning and said he was all right. When the boat had got about opposite of Mr. Con. Riek's place, the captain saw Skinner lose his balance and fall into the river. He at once gave the bell signal to stop the engine, but as the boat was under full headway it was impossible to stop her before she went a considerable distance up stream, passing over the unfortunate man, who came up a short distance behind the boat.

A life float was at once thrown out and passed very near to S. who was swimming against the stream, but it seems that the shock he received by the boat passing over him in part stunned him and his hair hanging down over his face partly must have blinded the poor man or else he would have either swam toward the float which was only a few yards distant or grasped the planks which floated by him. When the Light Western, whose engine had been reversed was about 10 feet from the swimmer he suddenly sank under and was seen no more. All efforts to find his body have failed.

A month later, the newspaper's account of the sad story was concluded. *Last Monday Coroner Ettmueller was notified that the body of a dead man was found near the point of Rush Island. The Coroner summoned a jury and held an inquest on the body which proved to be that of Daniel Skinner, whose death by drowning we announced in a former number of the Advertiser. An attempt to recover the body, which had lodged on a limb of a tree lying in the river proved unsuccessful as it fell from its position into the river whose swift current took the body under a large rack heap, after which it was not seen again.*

Always quick to seize a new opportunity, Charles Eitzen immediately saw the advantage of having a ferryboat at Hermann. Henry Wohlt needed to supplement his ferry income by hauling produce out of the Gasconade River. Many would have declared that stream unnavigable, but Wohlt was willing to try, and Eitzen was willing to exert his influence to help him. The newspaper reported:

Last Wednesday morning the Bill introduced by Hon. Chas. D. Eitzen, in which Congress is requested to make an appropriation for the improvement of the Gasconade river, was passed in the House by a unanimous vote and has been

referred to the Senate. We are informed that Senator Read will exert all of his
influence in favor of its passage.

The wheels of progress ground exceedingly slowly. Not until the end of
1880 did any work on the Gasconade begin. The "Vienna Courier" reported:

The work of removing snags from the Gasconade river, for which purpose an
appropriation was made by Congress last session, has been commenced. The
work was begun at a point on the river known as Deer Slough and the snags
and obstructions will be removed from there down the river until the money
appropriated is expended. This will prove of great benefit to the rafters, who
have experienced much difficulty in running rafts down the river during low
water.

By the time his two-year contract was up, Wohlt was in trouble with the
town fathers. He wanted more time off from ferrying. But when he had new
posters printed stating his new schedule, the objections were immediate. Tech-
nically, Wohlt had kept his word. But the townspeople felt he owed them a debt
for their aid in building his boat. While this controversy was simmering, Wohlt
took off up the Gasconade and came back with a good load, including 50 barrels
of whiskey, just to show the town fathers what he was talking about.

While Henry Wohlt was running the Light Western, Will Heckmann was
piloting the Washington and other steamboats. Steamboat Bill wrote of his father
that *the largest boat ever in his charge was the steamer Collosal, 210 by 44 by 5 feet. He*
was also in charge of the E. Hensley, the R. W. Dugan and the Washington before he
began navigating the Gasconade River with the Wohlt brothers of Hermann. He made
one trip as pilot with Capt. George G. Keith on the Dacotah, known as the "Big D." A
boat with six letters in her name was considered unlucky so an "H" was added to the
name.

In 1877 Capt. Wohlt took the Light Western back to the Fredericksburg
landing to place her in dry dock and give her a thorough overhauling. The move
may have been prompted by an incident in which a woodpile near the Light
Western's boilers caught fire. The boat was saved when several boys came aboard
and poured pails of water over the flames. The "Advertiser-Courier" reported:

Capt. Wohlt intends to change the Light Western to a side-wheeler in a few
weeks from now. The change will compel him to lay up about one month. He
also intends to make the boat 10 feet longer than she is at present. The captain
thinks the boat will be much easier to handle after the change has been made.

An 1869 photograph of the Steamer Washington

During the Light Western's absence, a skiff ferry ran between Hermann and Loutre Island, and the steamer Washington, often captained by Will Heckmann, carried heavy freight and animals across the river twice a week. True to his word, Capt. Wohlt returned to the Hermann wharf with the Light Western, which now measured 80 feet in length and was outfitted with a new and larger boiler. The "Advertiser-Courier" joyfully reported:

> *The sound of the Steam Whistle of the Light Western is again heard in the land and gladdens the heart of the people who wish to cross the Big Muddy. The Steam Ferry Boat will now make its regular trips again as it done before the alterations were made. The boat has a much finer appearance than formerly and the new machinery works to the satisfaction of Captain Wohlt.*

Capt. Heckmann was enjoying having a son old enough to go with him on the Washington. The Washington was Steamboat Bill's first boat—almost akin to his first love—and he spent every spare minute on her. Memories of that boat surfaced throughout his life, and he wrote about her often.

> *One moonlight night this craft was steaming up the Missouri below the mouth*

of the Gasconade River when she picked up a cottonwood tree in front of the port wheelhouse. It went straight up through the lower guard, up through the boiler deck, then through the hurricane roof and then up along the port side of the pilothouse. It knocked all the sash out of that side of the pilothouse and then broke off near the water with a report like an old Civil War musket. Wood and glass were scattered all over the occupants of the pilothouse.

We had four rafters going home to Portland, Uncle Pete Miller and myself were sitting in the far corner on the safe side. Dad, bespattered with glass, never rang a bell, and went on up the river.

Another story by Steamboat Bill appeared in the "Advertiser-Courier." *One of the most comical incidents on this river happened on a trip of the old side-wheel Washington when she was in charge of my father and was the first steamboat to go above Cooper Hill, Mo. They went up near Rich Fountain and loaded the old boat down flat in the water with wheat but before starting back downstream the river commenced to fall fast, and they made haste to get away. At that time just after you entered Pryor's Bend coming downstream there stood a monster gatepost right in the middle of the river, a very swift and dangerous stretch of river to navigate. The Washington was a ferryboat and had bull railings all around her outside to keep cattle, horses, hogs and even drunks from falling overboard.*

Before getting to this place, my father in the pilot house rang the big bell to sound the water. Fred Koeller, one of the deck hands climbed up on top of the bull railing with a big pole to sound the water. A monstrous big fat girl was standing wild-eyed on the river bank in a field of corn. When just opposite this girl, the stern of the boat hit the big gate-post. Koeller, knocked off balance, made a mighty leap right towards the girl and started to swim to shore.

Dad, with always a joke up his sleeve, cried "Run girlie, he is coming after you." The big fat girl turned and ran for home. Dad said no human being ever knocked down more growing corn than this 350-pound gal, and when she did get home, she did not stop to open the door of her house, but busted the door off its hinges and fell in a faint on the floor.

The steamer Washington was in the Hermann ferry trade on Monday, Tuesday and Wednesday, after which she made a round trip in the Portland and St.

Louis trade. The long trip occasionally produced some good stories, such as this one by Steamboat Bill.

My father was considered the best lower Missouri River pilot in the 195-mile stretch from St. Louis to Rocheport. This was not because he was a better pilot than many others, but because he was always posted. One fall, about 1872, the river was dead low and Green's chute and Catfish Island were very shallow places. Dad came down the river with the Washington loaded with apples, the guards dragging in the water and with a barrel of apples on each corner of the pilothouse. At the head of Greene's chute he found seven mountain boats tied to the bank for lack of water (so their pilots thought) for them to get through. Dad told the pilots to watch and he would show them how to get through. He said he would wait for them at the foot of the chute and they could follow him into St. Louis since there was more thin water on downstream.

Greene's chute ran down to the left of big Bonhomme Island. At the head of the island, to the right, was a small towhead. Dad took the Washington down the right of this towhead. He then turned back upstream until he came to a narrow, snaggy chute that led into the bight of the bend in Greene's chute where there was good water. Dad waited until all seven of the boats got over the bad water and they then followed him all the way to St. Louis.

The captains, pilots and owners chipped in and bought my father a new suit of clothes and all the trimmings from head to foot. He was six feet tall, weighed 200 pounds and was as straight as an Indian chief. One of the pilots objected to chipping in for Dad's suit, saying nobody but a fool Dutchman would look for deep water in that kind of a river.

Jealousy has followed the Heckmann clan ever since that date. Dad later heard what the noted pilot had said—and happened to meet him one day on the St. Louis levee.

"I heard you called me a 'fool Dutchman' and refused to chip in on my outfit."

This pilot was also from Hermann and knew of Old Rough Head's reputation as a scrapper. To avoid any trouble he said that he had bought the cap that my Dad was wearing. Dad grabbed the pilot around the neck, pulled the cap off his head and rammed it halfway down his throat. He kicked him in the fantail and

53

told him never to cross his path again. This man and my father spent a lifetime on the river but never worked on the same boat.

Will Heckmann was a better river pilot than businessman, a fact recognized even by his admiring son.

Long about 1873 a fine little sternwheeler steamed out of St. Louis for Fort Benton with a valuable cargo. She had lots of trouble getting over the lower river and when just below the mouth of the Gasconade River, one of the pilots ran her up on a big flat rock. The river was falling and something had to be done right away. They sent to Hermann for help and Old Rough Head took the Washington to the rescue. The whole cargo had to be shifted to the Washington before the steamboat could be pulled off the rock. The owners were aboard and were disgusted. They offered to trade boats even up. Dad refused. Whether he was too honest or too ignorant we do not know, but all through life he refused to make deals like that.

Capt. Joe Kinney was ahead on that score, in fact he was a much better businessman. He built one of the first sternwheelers for the Missouri River. In a very short time the sternwheel boats had run the sidewheelers out of the mountain trade.

At that period Missouri Point, below St. Charles, with its immense crops of wheat and corn, was practically without transportation. After harvest, the farmers at Missouri Point had to wait for months at a time to get rid of their crops. Father said that on many occasions he saw over 100,000 sacks of wheat and corn waiting at Cul de Sac, La Barge, Black Walnut and Yellow Dog landings waiting for transportation. Had he quit trying to operate the Washington and placed his new boat in the Black Walnut trade, he would have become a very rich man.

The fun times with the two boats were reported in the newspaper with considerably more gusto than the cargo and ferry trips. Outings by the Harmonie, a men's singing society, always made good copy.

The excursion of the "Harmonie" took place Sunday, the two steamers Washington and Light Western being chartered for the occasion. Although the weather was propitious, the attendance was not as large as expected; the hail storm on Saturday evening having changed the mind of many who intended to participate.

The Miller's Landing Brass Band and the Harmonie Amateur Band made things lively near the Wharf, and the gay and festive youths with "their sisters, their cousins, and their aunts" were seen tripping towards the boats, ready for the fun.

The trip from Hermann to Onken's Grove, music, singing, fishing and refreshing the inner-man was the order of the day, sociability and good cheer prevailing through. About four o'clock the excursionists proceeded up the river and the music discoursed reverberating from hillside to hillside astonished the natives.

The party arrived at Hermann about dark in the best of spirits.

Weather was a constant peril on the river. The "Advertiser-Courier" reported: *The steamer Washington got into a very bad fix last Saturday during the heavy gale. She was coming down stream, when the wind threw her with such force on the bar just above town that she could not get off again. The boat at the time had aboard about 40 hogs and several hundred sacks of wheat. Yesterday the Light Western took off her cargo, after which the Washington was able to get out of her disagreeable position.*

Ice also posed an enormous hazard for steamboats and was a subject of intense local interest. During the winter of 1879, the "Advertiser-Courier" reported: *Last Sunday night the ice crust over the Missouri, between the Little Blossom and Coles Creek broke up, but could not make much headway as the ice below was perfectly solid yet. Monday night about 11 o'clock the ice opposite town began to move and the proprietor of the Washington informed the people of this long expected event by sounding the steamwhistle, which induced many, who had already retired for the night, to go to the river and witness this grand spectacle, but were doomed to disappointment, as they could only hear the noise made by the moving ice, but could see very little on account of darkness.*

The ice came down the river in immense cakes, crushing and breaking each other as they were brought into contact by the strong current. The barricade built for the protection of our Steam Ferry Boat proved to be very efficient and there is no doubt, the boat would have been seriously injured, if not wholly destroyed, had not the huge timbers broken the large ice-cakes as they attack it and turned the pieces out into the current beyond the boat. About midnight the river was clear just above the wharf and no ice came down on this side until about 5 o'clock in the morning, when the ice began to move down again and has been coming down pretty lively ever since.

Ice was the undoing of the Light Western. On December 31, 1879, the "Advertiser-Courier" reported:

The steamer Light Western, which was moored at the point of the Hermann Island, was considerably damaged last Saturday afternoon by a huge cake of ice which struck her with such force that one of the planks in her hull was staved in causing a leak about twenty feet long, through which the water rushed in and in a short time filled the hull, sinking the boat to her guards on one side while she remained on the sand bar on the other. It was at first feared that the hull could not stand the strain thus put on her and would break, but by the aid of braces, etc, this danger was averted.

Mr. Predick from Washington, who has raised quite a number of boats in a similar condition to that of the Light Western was engaged and under his directions the work of stopping the leak and pumping out the boat is now proceeding. The leak has nearly been stopped and today the wrecking crew is condemned to inactivity as the river rose considerable last night and this morning the water was running over a part of the deck, so that pumping is of no avail. As soon as the river falls work will be resumed and the boat soon afloat again.

But it was not to be. A later edition of the newspaper reported:

The Light Western has been dismantled and the hull taken below the point of the Island, where she will lie high and dry after the river falls. The proprietors of the boat intend to use the hull for a barge and will as soon as practical begin to build a new hull on which the machinery and rigging of the Light Western will be put. The new boat will be larger than the Light Western and the mode of power be a "stern wheeler."

The steamer Washington was aging, and the inevitable bad news was bound to come. Mary Heckmann wrote, *Washington inspected, will pass for one year yet, and then her doom is sealed.* The end came even sooner than expected. On April 14, 1880, the "Advertiser-Courier" gave the local version of the final demise of the steamer Washington. Will's brother Henry Heckmann was at the wheel.

Last Friday afternoon as our ferry boat, the steamer Washington, was making its regular trip from the Loutre Island Landing to this place, the wood, which was stored aside the boiler, caught fire, and before it was noticed the whole front part of the boat was enwrapped in flames, which spread rapidly all over the boat.

Capt. Heckmann, endeavoring to save the lives of those on board, tried to steer the boat to the shore, but all in vain; the fire had made such rapid progress and destroyed the steering apparatus. The destructive element, fanned by the strong wind, which was blowing at that time, soon reached the cabin and the passengers were compelled to seek another place of safety. All rushed forward to the bow of the boat, but here the heat was so intense that it was impossible for them to remain there and in their despair jumped into the Missouri, but thanks to the heroic conduct of Mr. Henry Maushund, who had noticed the distress of those aboard the Washington from this point and quickly rowed to the place of disaster; the passengers and crew were saved from a watery grave.

Unfortunately, however, it occupied too long a time for Mr. M. to pick up those who were despairingly struggling with the waves and before assistance could be rendered one of the passengers, Mrs. Redhorst, who jumped into the river to escape falling a victim to the fire fiend was drowned.

Mary's journal was more succinct.

While making the afternoon trip from the other side, she took fire and before Henry could get her to shore she was in flames. Four men and four women were aboard, all had to jump into the river to get away from the heat. One woman drowned, they found her floating body the same evening.

Steamboat Bill later said two of the women who jumped were quite stout with plenty of petticoats, so they floated like corks. The drowned woman, he said, was skinny and sank like a rock.

With the Light Western wrecked by ice, the Washington burned and neither boat insured, the Wohlt and Heckmann interests should have been out of the steamboat business. Instead they were making plans for a new boat.

CHAPTER 7

The Little Steamers

They separated the men from the boys at the mouth of the Missouri River, the men went up the Missouri River and the boys went up the Mississippi River.
—Steamboat Bill

*A*nd they made another cut when they reached the mouth of the Gasconade River. It took real he-men to conquer that beautiful and convoluted stream, which Steamboat Bill later claimed was the smallest river ever navigated by steamboats.

The Wohlt-Heckmann team had decided there was no point competing with the Star Line on the Missouri River, but they had great ideas about using the Gasconade River as a money maker for little steamers. (See Gasconade River map and landings in Appendix.) The Light Western had hardly been wrecked before Henry Wohlt and Will Heckmann were making plans for another boat. The newspaper told of the final dismantling of the Light Western on January 7, 1880. By January 21 the paper reported:

> *Messrs. Wohlt and Heckmann went to Louisville, Ky., last week for the purpose*
> *of inspecting and purchasing a steamboat, suitable for the trade at this point.*
> *They selected the steamer "Hope," for which $3500 was paid. The boat is expected*
> *here on Monday next. Messrs. Wohlt and Heckmann deserve credit for their*
> *enterprise and we hope they will meet with deserved good success.*

Steamboating was finally beginning to agree with Mary, and she maintained a faithful vigil for the new boat.

January 18—*William went to Louisville, Kentucky.*

January 20—*Heard they bought the boat.*

January 21—*Boat left Louisville this morning.*

January 22—*Did not hear anything of the boat today.*

January 23—*Boat passed Evansville, Ill. today.*

January 24—*Bought a paper but seen nothing about the boat.*

January 25—*Bought another paper. Steamer Hope passed Grand Tower yesterday. Got a dispatch this evening, boat is in St. Louis.*

January 26—*Boat advertised to leave this evening.*

January 27—*We are looking for the boat.*

January 28—*Hope arrived at 4 o'clock.*

The newspaper completed the story.

This afternoon the Steamer Hope which was purchased by Messrs. Wohlt and Heckmann for the tie-trade at this point arrived at the landing. Quite a number of our citizens turned out to see the new acquisition. The boat is as good as new, having only been used a few years, but stands badly in need of a coat of paint. She has some powerful machinery and made good time coming up the river. We hope the expectations of her owners may all be realized and enough freight always be on hand for them to carry.

So great was Mary's enthusiasm for the new boat that the morning after its arrival in Hermann she packed up three of her children and boarded the steamer Hope to visit her parents in Bluffton. Her return trip to Hermann by skiff was not so pleasant.

Clear, cold and windy. After dinner Brother Bob, the children and I started down the river. Were so near froze we stopped at Spaires. They were very kind, gave us wine and coffee, then we started again and got to Hermann at dark.

The town welcomed the new boat in the customary manner—an excursion. The "Advertiser-Courier" reported the story with its usual flair.

Availing themselves of the kind invitation of Capt. Heckmann, about twenty members of the Harmonie Singing Society boarded the Hope last Saturday evening about 8 o'clock for an excursion trip up to Graf's island, there to pay their respects to Mr. Joe Leising former ink slinger of this paper. A run of about 20 minutes brought them to the landing on the island where they disembarked, shouldered a keg of Kropp's "lemonade" and marched up to the castle, a distance of about half a mile.

His grangership had already retired for the night and by vociferous snoring was keeping time to the chirping of the cricket on the hearth and the hooting of the owl in the adjacent woods. A few strains from the visitors put a sudden termination to this music of nature, and Joe, disregarding the deranged condition of his toilet, rushed out to greet his friends and in his great joy humbled himself low in the dust in their midst.

The fun then commenced, and singing and talking and eating and drinking and smoking were kept up the greater part of the night. Towards morning a few expressed a willingness to retire provided the hotel accommodations were sufficient to admit of such a performance. The host conducted them to the hay loft, tumbled them in and the show went on.

A serenade to the sleepers was of course soon in order and was given, much to the disgust of these individuals and not until Capt. Heckmann threatened to turn the hose loose and drown them out did they desist. Morning came without further accidents, except that some base wretches stole Philip Kuhn's bottle of cock-tail while he was asleep, drank the contents and filled it with beer and replaced it. Philip says he can whip any ten men who would do such a thing.

Most of the crowd returned to town in skiffs at day light while some went on up to Portland with the Hope and returned Sunday afternoon, all looking fresh and happy of course.

Mary, meanwhile, made no mention of the Harmonie trip. The principal excitement in her life was her discovery of a new labor-saving device—the wringer for a wash tub. She borrowed one and reported how wonderful it was and how the clothes dried so much faster. Later she heard of and borrowed another modern marvel, the wash boiler, or steamer, as she called it. She put clothes to soak and the next day washed a large wash and cleaned cellars and closets.

Washing heavy long skirts, pants, bedding and even the rugs from the floors and then wringing them by hand was an enormous job, and when it rained drying the clothes was next to impossible. Water was scarce, so clothes were washed in river water, which had to be dipped and carried up the bank and across the railroad tracks to the Heckmann house. Sometimes Mary simply took the washing down to the boat, often taking two days to get the job done.

An 1878 photograph of the Steamer Hope

Mary also helped out with the family business. *Had 17 men for dinner and 16 for supper. Hope went to Portland and left half the crew here to load cars.* Occasionally, she packed up her brood and went to cook on the Hope. She voiced no complaints about the extra cooking, although it was summertime and she was cooking on a wood stove in a sweltering kitchen. *Hot enough to kill!*

She was, of course, pregnant again. Her seventh child, Charlotte, would be born in August. She and all of the children were very ill with red measles that summer. William, unfortunately, was not around to help out. But except for recurring malaria and the bout of measles, the family remained healthy. Others were not so fortunate. Next door, two of Charles Eitzen's children died. Typhoid fever, diphtheria and rheumatism were listed as causes of death for many other children in town.

As always, Mary patched up minor ailments with glue and home remedies. *Willie got a fish hook in his thumb. W. took him to Dr. Ettmueller, had it cut out. He has very little pain. ... William came home with a bad hand, he was capping the gun, it went off, and a wire on it tore open his hand badly. I put glue on it.*

When young Will hurt his leg, she applied a poultice of camomile and flax-seed.

Carpentry work was not outside the realm of the housewife. She and William bought the house in which they were living from his father's estate for $1,170. She immediately began making improvements, installing several window-panes and generally sprucing up the place.

Located next to the railroad tracks and the river, the Heckmann home was a great target for tramps. Mary always fed these "Knights of the Road," but sometimes her patience gave out, especially with a "high-class" beggar.

Found a charity seeker at home, a Mr. Brunner, a German gentleman, too proud

to beg, too good to steal, but not too independent to take board and shelter for

nothing. He has been sick and has no money.

When their boarder left several days later she wrote, *Mr. B. took all of our kindness as a matter of trifling importance.*

The Concert Hall was located just behind the Heckmann house, and occasionally Mary accompanied William to special performances or parties. One Saturday night they stayed until 1 o'clock. The next day she wrote, *William asleep until 3 o'clock, when a "mob" came along and he had to go along out to the wine cellar, came back by dark. I took a walk, for fresh air, and got some.*

By the next Sunday she could no longer contain her disapproval of the Harmonie.

William went out with the Singing Society to visit Mr. Poeschel and then stopped

at the hall when they came back. I regretted for the hundreth time that he joined

that "Farce Club." He was elected President at their last meeting and I would

have been well pleased if they had expelled him for some trifling cause.

It was unlikely that her wish would come true. In fact, the Harmonie came up with a special event to honor the popular captain. The "Advertiser-Courier" reported:

That Medal

Quite an interesting little episode occurred at the meeting of the Harmonie

Singing Society last Wednesday evening. It was the presentation of a leather

medal by the Society to Capt. William L. Heckmann, one of its worthy members

for gallant conduct in saving the life of a fellow mortal, Mr. A. C. Leisner, from

a watery grave. The medal had been prepared with great care by one of the best shoemakers in town. It was about 5 inches in diameter. The field or background was of nice white leather, around the outer edge of which was a ring of black leather about 1 inch wide. On the background of white leather, was drawn in a very high style of art, a picture representing Capt. Heckmann in the act of pulling Mr. Leisner out from the mad waves.

At the appointed time for the presentation ceremonies, Col. F.L. Wensel, who had been selected to deliver the address appropriate to the occasion, escorted Capt. Heckmann to the center of the room, (who, by the way, had heard nothing of the intended honor up to this time and was completely overcome) and in presenting the medal said: "I have the honor of presenting you this slight token of esteem and grateful remembrance, to say to you in behalf of the members of our honorable society that they, recognizing your brave and valorous conduct in extending a helping hand to a drowning fellow man, the elements of a great hero, desire me to present you this medal—this leather medal.

"They have also suggested that I should suggest that while this leather medal is not as artistic in design and as perfect in execution as some leather medals might be, it was nevertheless conceived by loving hearts and wrought by faithful hands, and is good enough for all practical purposes. Yes Sir, I say its good enough for anybody. Why Sir, your admiring friends here desire me to inform you that George Washington, Julius Caesar nor Gen. Grant nor Kaiser William nor Hancock not any other man never, no Sir, never, wore such a medal as this. (Applause)

"Take it and may it adorn your manly breast through all the trials and tribulations of this vale of tears and or running a steamboat."

Capt. Heckmann bore his blushing honors like a genuine hero and said he could not make a speech, but that he felt very happy; and that he had never thought that too much water was good for a man, and that he would "set 'em up" if any of the gentlemen present ever drank.

Mr. Wensel said he could only speak for himself, and winked at the President. The President said he was willing to adjoin for a few moments. Later in the evening Capt. Heckmann and several other gentlemen visited Mr. Leisner. When that gentleman saw what honors had been bestowed upon his deliverer, his feelings overcame him and, as he wiped the big briney tears from his eyes, he stammered out: "Boys, what'el you have?"

Mary was beginning to realize that she had married the Pied Piper of Hermann. With increasing frequency, her daily entries noted that as soon as he came home William headed for the Concert Hall, where he usually remained until very late on Saturday night, sleeping most of Sunday. Gradually, his wife became more of a familiar convenience. She treasured his companionship, but it was seldom available.

A convivial man who thoroughly enjoyed the company of his friends, Will Heckmann had a large following and enjoyed being the center of attention, a trait he would hand down to several of his sons. A nephew, Henry Schnell, writing for the family genealogy, explained the lure of the saloons.

Uncle William was remembered in the 1870s as being an unusually agreeable companion; he had many friends and was popular in the community. When he came into town after a boat trip, things began to happen as he made the rounds of the hangouts to treat his friends. He was the center of good fun and joking. Henry and younger friends followed along so that they could see and hear the fun. He was called a "good feeler."

Captain Heckmann's popularity carried over to his steamboats. This was particularly true of the Hope. Arriving after the loss of the Light Western by ice and just before the loss of the steamer Washington by fire, the Hope was a godsend to the community. The little steamer went to work immediately, trying to do the work of two boats, but she was not a ferry. So while Capt. Heckmann was running the Hope, the Wohlt family was busy on the Gasconade River, using the machinery from the wrecked Light Western to build another fine little steam ferry. The "Advertiser-Courier" had a terrible a time with the name of the new boat.

The new steam ferry-boat, "Faith" is rapidly nearing completion. Both decks will be completed this week. Capt. Wohlt promises to have her in running trim during the first week in June. It is said she will be a daisy.... The steamer Hope has just received a new coat of paint and a general repairing. She and the newly finished "Favor" form a little flotilla which is a source of just pride, not only to their owners but to the town in general. ...The new steam ferry boat "Faith" got up steam and made her first trial trip last Saturday afternoon. As she steamed up past the town she and her builder and master, Capt. Henry Wohlt, received many compliments and expressions of "faith" in a prosperous future for her

The Wohlt family built the steamer Fawn from the wreck of the Light Western.

and her owners, from the crowd of spectators along the shore. She will ply as a ferry-boat between this point and the north side of the river and will supply a need that has been a source of great inconvenience both to our people and our friends on the other side since the burning of the Washington. May she enjoy a prosperous career.

By August the newspaper finally got the hang of it, and the name of the new steamboat appeared correctly. *Captains Heckmann and Wohlt will be on an excursion up to McGirk's Island with the Steamers Hope and Fawn next Sunday. Leaving Hermann at 7:30 a.m. they will return at 7 p.m. Here is fun for everybody. Round trip tickets 25 cents.*

Times and boats were changing. The newspaper kept track of the number of sacks of wheat carried on the various boats. *Capt. Heckmann brought the Hope into port last Sunday morning laden with 2,200 sacks of grain. He also had two nice little catfish, one weighing 50 lbs. and the other 56 lbs.* The little Light Western had been put to shame when the Washington came in with 900 sacks—the largest load ever brought out of the Gasconade River at that time. In July the Hope came down the river with a record 2,562 sacks of new wheat aboard.

Life on the steamer Hope was not always peaceful. The newspaper reported a labor problem. *The colored population employed on the Hope struck for higher wages last Saturday morning but most of them returned to work in a few hours. The only harm done was that Capt. Heckmann docked them for the time lost.* On a happier note, two of the black workers were married aboard the Hope.

Last Monday morning Judge Oncken united Mr. Lee Bowen and Sarah Smith in the holy bonds of matrimony. The ceremony took place on board the steamer Hope where the two contraction partners had been engaged as cooks. They left yesterday for Maj. Johnston's camp on the Gasconade River, where they will be engaged as cooks for the men employed on the river improvement.

After the incident in which the ladies followed their men in a second steamboat, the Harmonie welcomed the ladies to join its next expedition. An advertisement was placed for *an excursion of the Harmonie to Augusta, Mo. August 15th, 1880. Tickets for the round trip, for members only, 50 cents. Steamer Hope leaves Hermann at 5:30 a.m., on return leaves Augusta at 6 p.m.* The newspaper reported the event in grand style.

To Augusta

Last Sunday morning at six o'clock the Harmonie Singing Society of this place, numbering about forty members, with quite a number of ladies, and the Harmonie brass band boarded the Steamer Hope and started for an excursion to the rugged and hospitable little town of Augusta in St. Charles county, about 45 miles below this place.

The morning was beautiful and the air fresh and vigorating. The music from the band rang out upon the waters, in the morning air, with an unusual sweetness, and all was joy and good cheer. The trip down the river, a run of three hours, was exceedingly pleasant, the time being mostly passed in singing, "playing" on the band, promenading, etc.

In Augusta our party was met at the landing and received by the citizens en masse, accompanied by the Harmonie brass band of Augusta. Conveyances were in waiting to take the party to the Harmonie Park, a most charmingly situated and well kept place, where the day was to be spent, and here again was extended another very pleasant and agreeable reception in the way of an invitation to everybody to step up to the refreshment stand, and take a cool, delicious, foaming, tempting glass of beer, which was most heartily accepted.

About noon the cry rang out: "Hermann Harmonie come to dinner," and the Hermann Harmonie was escorted into a large hall, the walls of which were beautifully decorated with flags, mottoes and evergreens, and the floor still more beautifully decorated with three long, well filled, tempting tables, to which it is needless to say, the Hermannites, with their proverbial love of good things seated themselves, and did justice to the most sumptuous feast before them. The Hermannites involuntary exclaimed "Splendid" and went to business, and the unanimous verdict was that the Augusta people entertain guests in a princely fashion. Their open hearted kindness and unfeigned hospitality make every one, friend or stranger, feel comfortable.

We only fear that when our Augusta friends come to see us, we, with all our boasted hospitality, will fall short of giving them the warm and generous reception they deserve, but we will do our best.

About 3 o'clock in the afternoon a Steamer from Washington arrived, bringing a large number of ladies and gentlemen from that place. They too have an excellent band, and with three good brass bands and two or three singing clubs on the grounds, of course there was no lack of good music.

At 7 o'clock p.m. the Hope started on her return and arrived at Hermann at 2 o'clock the next morning, bringing as woe-begone and dilapidated a looking set as one ever sees, but all cherishing vivid recollections of a most pleasantly spent day. Capt. Heckmann stood at his post all day and all night and as he always does, did everything in his power to make his passengers enjoy themselves.

Mary, who would soon give birth to her seventh child, was less impressed. Her cryptic comment: *Hope returned by 2 o'clock, all had enough of Augusta.*

August 23—Very warm. Mrs. Gensert and Mrs. Soissong here at half past 3 o'clock a little girl was born, I am doing well.

August 24—Annie's birthday. Baby came one day too soon. It is a very good child. Mrs. Everson here washing.

Aug. 26—William in St. Louis, came home last night. Annie had a few school mates here to drink lemonade and eat her cake. She could not have a party as the baby was too young.

Mary's social life was picking up. *A whole crowd of gay women here to see me last evening.* Mother Miller and the youngest Miller sister, Gertrude, came down on the Hope. *I am getting about quite lively, baby is good. Mother went home on Hope this afternoon.*

In October Mary hustled about at an even livelier pace getting stoves ready for winter, putting children's clothes in order and sewing a new dress for herself in preparation for a trip to Sedalia to visit her sisters, Emma Heckmann and Lizzie Teubner. She boarded the noon train for the four-hour trip to Sedalia on October 7 and returned four days later. *Pretty tired. But for me the whole trip was a very pleasant one. Children were tolerable, the weather was fine and the treatment exceedingly good.*

In November the steamer Hope was hauling ties, and the ladies of the household were busy making carpet rags. Town, state and national news occasionally made its way into Mary's journals. The election of James A. Garfield as the country's 20th president was a joyous time for traditionally Republican Hermann.

> *The election is over and the returns prove the Republicans victorious all over the land. Here the Independent or "Don't care a darn what you call it so I get an office" or The People Party got most of the County offices.*

Later, Mary wrote of a *grand torch light prossession, cannonnading, and sky rockets. All the Republican houses illuminated. It was quite a grand affair for Hermann.*

By December the Heckmann hogs were brought down from the island and sent to the butcher. The meat was worked up, sausage was made and hung up, and the pigs' feet were pickled. The steamer Hope was aground, and cold weather was coming. But the river was rising, and the Hope got off just in time to escape damage from ice. The crew made the most of the grounded time by taking down the old pipes *because they were burnt out.*

Christmas was a happy time that year. *When I compare it to last Christmas day, we were in double trouble then and today nothing seems wanting.* Friends came to call, and the Heckmanns kept a baby for one of the visiting couples so that they could attend the New Year's Eve Ball at the Concert Hall. *I went to back door, heard the dancers, the church bells, and the shooting of the old and new year, then went to bed.*

Hopes were high for a prosperous 1881. The boats had plenty of work, and William finally got around to acquiring his pilot's license. Mary wrote that he had been called to St. Louis *on account of steamboat laws.* There was even a rescue. In May the newspaper reported the sinking of the steamer Durfee.

About 7 o'clock last Monday morning the Capt. of the steamer Hope received notice that the steamer Durfee had gone down in the Missouri river at a point just above the mouth of the Gasconade river. In a few minutes the Hope was steaming up to the scene of disaster. Our reporter visited the wreck and from Capt. Keith learned that about 6 o'clock on Monday morning, the lost steamer which was loaded, struck a snag and almost immediately commenced sinking. There were but few passengers on board who together with the crew were safely landed.

The cargo consisted of 250 head of hogs, 60 head of sheep, 1,050 sacks of wheat, 6,060 sacks of corn, 21 boxes of Glassware, 10 sacks of wool and 350 miscellaneous packages, all of which, with the exception of about 125 hogs, a few sheep and six hogsheads of tobacco, was a total loss. The Hope succeeded in saving a greater part of the boat furniture and a few sacks of grain. The Durfee was estimated to be worth about $14,000 or $15,000 and was insured for $9,000. We also understand that there is insurance on the hogs.

About a month later the Wohlt interests wanted out, and the Hope was sold. Capt. Henry Wohlt was building another boat and may have wanted money for that enterprise. The local newspaper reported: *The steamer Hope has been sold to the "Steamer Hope Company," a company duly incorporated with capital stock of $5,000. Bankcroft, McDaniels and Heckmann are the incorporators. The Hope will still continue in the tie trade at this place under the command of Capt. Heckmann.*

The tie business was a brutal one—the men often were in the water fully clothed. Mary complained that William *wet two suits today* trying to save ties.

Mary arranged for the three little Heckmann girls—Annie, Lizzie and Martha—to pose for a photograph as a birthday present for their papa, but she gave a dour account of the day itself. *Bad luck today, and Wills birthday. He is 36. Snow, sleet, but not cold. I was going to crochet, lost the needle, wanted to cut out some sewing and could not find the scissors, baked two cakes for Will's birthday, burnt them, started the barrel of molasses and left some run over.*

After the birth of her baby, Mary had to have a lot of teeth extracted and happily reported that she had her new teeth. Her offspring, as usual, had some minor ailments. *Will has a cut foot, Sam has a stiff neck, Lottie a swollen hand.* August would bring a return of the ever-present malaria. Tina became ill at Sedalia, where she was visiting, and Annie and Martha had fever at home. Later that year smallpox was raging. All the children were vaccinated, and all developed very sore arms.

At one point Mary skipped an entire month of journal entries. Her husband had left with the steamer Hope, and little Sam was very ill. *I have been having so much care I could not write. Sammie has been sick four weeks on Friday, his spleen and liver are so swollen, he is very weak, yesterday and today.*

Henry Heckmann's baby became very sick and died. *It suffers so terribly.* There was grave national news, as well. *President Garfield was shot by an infernal fool. ... There was great suspense and excitement endured in those days, but at present after a severe relapse there are good prospects of the President getting well.*

In September of 1881, Mary learned that her brother, Dave Miller, was ill, and by the end of the month there was yet another death to record.

Just as I was cooking dinner John Sutter came in. I asked about them at home, and he tells me, so unexpectedly, that they brought poor Dave home and buried him, he died of brain fever. It seems so strange that I should know nothing of it, but Mother instead of getting the dispatch on Sunday only got it on Monday afternoon in time to get the grave ready, they had to bury poor brother by the light of lanterns.

In a box set apart on the page and outlined in black, she also recorded the death of the assassinated president.

The people of Hermann made quite a fine display, in honor of Garfield, who died of his wound on the 19th of September and was buried at Cleveland, today, September 26th.

The Heckmann farm holdings were increasing, to Mary's great delight. But the drinking associated with Hermann bothered her more and more. Trains, as well as boats, now offered excursions. After a crowd of 300 people visited Hermann on the Missouri Pacific train, Mary wrote that *it was a shame to abuse such a beautiful day with so much drunkenness.*

Mary recorded the birth of her eighth child, Robert Evans, in May of 1882.

Once more I take up my journal to chronicle the past weeks. One great event has taken place, on the 18th the same day as the school picnic at 3 o'clock in afternoon, God sent a little white, blue-eyed boy to look to a mother for care and love. May the good Father who sent him, (On the same day the Savior ascended to heaven) also give me guidance to lead him in the paths of goodness. The rest of the children enjoyed themselves very much, and were much pleased to find a new baby. Old Mrs. Kizer is staying here to look after me and baby, she is real good.

June, 1882—Yesterday a lot of fellows for the lack of some useful employment, chartered the Vienna and went to Gasconade to fish, have not returned yet.

July 2, 1882—Today one year ago, the wires flashed the news that our newly made President had been shot. He suffered untold agonies and died. On last Friday, June 30th the wretch who fired the shot died on the scaffold, thus ending a wretched and misguided life. What, oh what was it all for?

August 1, 1882—Time passes so quickly, another month begun and I can scarce realize that Autumn is fast approaching. Our boy is getting so fat and sweet. Hope busy carrying wheat and ties....We have the house nearly painted and finished, have an iron pot walled in and a nice little bake oven, done a nice lot of baking on Saturday.

August 9, 1882—Rain prevented the men from finishing painting they were here today, painted the upper porch and keep us in a "stew" keeping clear of it. On Sunday Hope made an excursion trip to Round Island, and back, quite a nice crowd went along, got home by dark. William went to St. Louis last night, had four of the Hope's men for meals today.

August 27, 1882—The past week we uncanned all that we canned the week before. It looked as though it was not going to keep so I took and preserved the peaches, and heated the tomatoes over. There was a ball on Saturday night, a Concert in afternoon on Sunday and a ball again in the evening. I heard the band play before it left at the depot, they are considered very fine musicians.

September 10, 1882—Hope not doing much of anything. Our Annie took the private premium for best writing in Second Class, $1, she is to have $1 from Uncle Lorenz Rauss, 50 cents from Papa. I did not go out at all to the Fair, to me it is nothing but a farce. Tonight the Harmonie is fixing up another spree. How I wish and pray that soon I may see these things put to an end, they are sickening and disgusting to me. When I do mix in them, I feel myself mean, small and low. I think something like a man feels after doing an awful deed.

The steamer Hope took out one final excursion party and then in September was sold to outside interests. The "Advertiser-Courier" reported:

The steamer Hope and Barge was sold last Monday to Capt. C. B. Tilden for the Robert B. Brown Oil Co. of St. Louis for the sum of $4,800. The Hope will be

used by its purchasers to carry Cotton and Cotton Seed from the South to St.
Louis. The steamer Hope made her last trip under the command of Capt.
Heckmann on Monday last.

The sale of the Hope was sad news for Mary.

Friday at noon the Hope blew her last whistle and left for St. Louis. From there
she goes to run from New Orleans up the Mississippi carrying cotton seed. I
felt almost like crying to see her go, it seemed like bidding adieu to an old friend.

This should have been the last news of the Hope, but the fates decided otherwise. Julius Silber, husband of Caroline Heckmann, Will's youngest sister, went
with the Hope to New Orleans as engineer and remained with the boat instead
of returning home. He contracted yellow fever, and on December 3, 1882, Mary
wrote:

What sad, sad words I must chronicle again, a dear brother is lost again, for he is
indeed lost, his grave is nearly a thousand miles away, among strangers. Julius
Silber left here with the Hope as engineer, he intended to stay a month, every letter
he wrote he promised to come home soon, yet he staid, and just seven weeks from
the day he left Henry got a telegram, saying, "Julius is very sick, come immedi-
ately." William left immediately, had but five minutes to make the train. On Sat-
urday, the 25th, we got another dispatch saying, "He is dead. Will send the body."

Henry then telegraphed to William, and he, under the impression that the first
boat up the river would take the body hurried back from Vicksburg to Memphis,
only to find that it had been impossible to bring the body. As the quarantine rules
are so strict, the officers of the boat had advised Tilden, the Captain of the Hope, to
bury Julius where he died, at Butcher Bend, about 60 miles above Vicksburg. Poor
Caroline is broken hearted, and we do not know what to do, we have not yet heard
from Tilden since the last dispatch.

The final chapter was written in early January after Henry Heckmann brought
the exhumed body back to Hermann for burial. Mary reported, *Caroline is more*
at ease now. Years later a Hermann steamboat would be named for Julius F. Silber.

CHAPTER 8

Steamboats 'Round the Bend

Indian Summer in the Ozarks is a gift
from the Gods. —Steamboat Bill

*A*fter Henry Wohlt built his first little steamer up on the Gasconade River, the idea caught on, and a flurry of boat building ensued. William Lalk built the steamer Georgie Lee in 1878 and promptly sank her on her first trip. Rhey McCord, George Gore and Dick Vaughn also built little steamboats, the fates of which are unknown. What is known is that the competition did not faze the Wohlts. They kept right on building more boats.

Located 60 miles upriver from the mouth of the Gasconade, the Vienna landing was the head of navigation on the Gasconade River for all practical purposes. Steamboats ran there regularly and even carried the mail.

Henry Wohlt purchased the steamer City of Plattsmouth and rebuilt her on the Gasconade. In February of 1881, the "Advertiser-Courier" reported: *Henry Wohlt's new steamboat built especially for the Gasconade river trade will be launched in a few days, and will be completed about April.* The newspaper later reported, *The steamer Plattsmouth was launched today. It is to be rechristened the Vienna, so our Vienna friends may listen for her whistle soon.* The Vienna ran on the Gasconade but also short-tripped to ports on the Missouri River.

Two other novice boat builders, Boeger and Heidbroeder, built the steamer Dora at Boeger's Landing on the Gasconade River. Steamboats sometimes took on characteristics strangely similar to people, and the accident-prone Dora generated numerous stories. An early incident reported in the "Advertiser-Courier" set the stage.

> Mr. August Boeger's new steamboat, the Dora, was considerably damaged by the breaking up of the ice on the Gasconade River. The force of the ice coming down stream tore the boat from its moorings and carried it along several miles, at several places it was carried under trees along the banks and very much damaged. We learn however that no damage was done to the machinery or the hull. The smoke stacks and the pilot house were completely torn off and will have to be replaced before the boat can be used.

Work was proceeding on the Gasconade River, and the channel was improving.

> Maj. Johnston, who had the work done on the Gasconade River last season has again been entrusted with the management of the work to be done for the improvement during the present season and work was taken up on Monday last. Mr. Johnston intends to remove all obstructions from Vienna down to the mouth and to deepen the channel at Round Island so that boats can get above that point at low water. Major Johnston has 22 men employed on the Gasconade River improvement and will considerably increase his force soon.

The steamer Hope was still running during the summer of 1882. With the addition of the Dora, the Vienna and occasionally the Fawn, the Gasconade had quite a busy season. But by September, when the Hope was sold, things were not so rosy. Warehouses all along the river were filled with wheat that could not be shipped because of low water.

With the coming of cold weather, the boats had to be readied for winter quarters. The newspaper reported:

> The steamer Fawn was taken to the Gasconade last Saturday by her owners to remain there until the river is clear of ice and will be brought here again, so that communication with our neighbors on the north side of the river will be regular until old Boreas puts in another interdictment and stops navigation. ... The steamer Vienna left our port last Thursday for a trip to Portland but the drift ice coming down the Missouri in such heavy masses suggested the advisability of going into winter-quarters, and Capt. Wohlt concluded to run into the Gasconade and lay his boat up until there was less ice in the Missouri.

Ice was truly a threat to steamboats, and the Dora was by no means the only victim. The steamer Emma, owned by Missouri's ex-governor McClurg, was a casualty of ice. Torn loose from its moorings, the boat came down the Missouri River and was caught by Messrs. John and Otto Miller and J. Frey, who received $187.60 in salvage. This same trio caught the barge belonging to Capt. Lohmann, who paid them $22 salvage. The "Franklin County Observer" reported the tugboat Petrel was pulled from its moorings, turned almost completely around and capsized near South Point.

Mary also made note of the ice in her journal.

A steamboat and three flat boats were caught here, they had all got loose when the river broke up and were drifting with the ice. William, Will Rauss and Lullie R. took after one, and before they got back the ice came so thick that they had to stay on the other side from Thursday evening until Sunday noon. They got the flat anyway. ... This afternoon is beautiful, sun shiney, cold, calm day. Like a stately, calm, cold, beautiful woman. Last evening the mercury stood at zero by 5 o'clock.

By 1883 young Bill Heckmann was working on the boats, cubbing in the pilothouse and doing general roustabout work. Writing as Steamboat Bill in his book "Steamboating Sixty Five Years," he remembered:

About half of my time while "learning the river" on the beautiful Gasconade was spent under Captain August Wohlt. He was a man just the opposite of my father, slow to act, slow to make a promise and slow in handling a boat. But he was a real man who accomplished things and got there just the same. He was not an extra good shot and did not get the satisfaction out of the success or disappointment of steamboat fishing and hunting that my father did. Still he was willing to let others enjoy this and no matter what you killed from the deck of a boat, he would spare no expense to pick it up. He allowed nothing to go to waste. No work was too hard or too long for him to help get a boat to a turkey roost or to a lake where all could enjoy a few hours hunt.

Capt. Wohlt was a great weather prophet. On a snagging trip up the Gasconade one fall he worked a big crew of men in clearing the river of overhanging timber and snags. Early one morning he got up and predicted rain within twenty-four hours. He did this every morning for a solid month and it never rained a drop. Like lots of homemade weather prophets, he had run into a flock of Indian summer so we blamed him not. Indian Summer in the foothills of the Ozarks is not a sin but a gift from the Gods.

Eager to get out on the river, young Bill Heckmann had no objections when his father took him out of school at age 13. He loved to tell tales of those early learning years.

The Gasconade River empties into the Missouri 127 miles up river from St. Louis. At times it comes down through the Ozark Mountains in a hurry. In fact, all mountain streams are the most rapid when bank full or just before they are high enough to spread out over the bottom lands.

In the spring of 1883 my father was running the steamer Vienna on this stream and his oldest son, Bill, was his champion roustabout, deckhand, hog catcher, steersman, game driver and devoted offspring. No task, no work, or no command was too big an order for Capt. Heckmann's boy Bill, and the older man expected and made his boy take chance after chance that he would not ask or could not expect of any other member of his crew.

One night we were slowly making our way up stream on this picturesque Gasconade River with the old Vienna. The night was pitch dark, the river bank full, and the old boat was laying low in the water with all kinds of merchandise for the merchants and farmers along the upper reaches of the stream. All went well, dad was sitting back on the bench in the pilot house, his eagle eye catching all mistakes of the young navigator who was steering this old craft under the kindest, sternest and most skillful master and pilot I ever saw. We had just pulled out under Scott's Island when a mighty rumbling like thunder was heard in the engine room and the engineer called up that both big drive chains had run into the river.

Dad jumped up and said: "I'll stick her nose in them big willows at the foot of the island; get below and jump on one of those willows right now with a line. Get it fast in a hurry and tell them lunkheads not to check this boat up too soon and part the line." Dad got her headed into the willows while his boy grabbed a line and made his leap correctly to light in a big willow and get the line made fast all right. But a loaded boat in a current like we had in the river that night will not hold her headway long. She glanced off the willows, her head hit the current, and the men held the line too tight on the bitts; it snapped and almost

The Steamer Vienna

threw me out of my perch on the tree. Before they could heave the anchor over-board the Vienna had drifted downstream out of sight and hearing.

Scott's Island was all under water and midnight found me hugging my friendly tree. Under the island was some dead water but on both sides of me this little river was sure in a hurry to reach the sea. On the bluff side of the river a catamount was letting out some bloodcurdling cries; on a nearby tree on the island a big horn owl was giving a concert; and over on the bottom side of the river some 'coons were fishing and letting out their strange language to furnish their share of this night's show. This with the surging waters rushing through the tree tops made the young pilot rather nervous and he thought of ma and the kid brothers and sisters in their snug beds at home.

Did you ever spend six hours in a tree top away out in what was then a wilderness, with blackness all around you? If not you have no idea how this 14-year-old boy felt. My feet and clothes up to my waist were already wet from making the line fast to this friendly tree, and along towards morning I felt something slimy trying to share this tree with me which felt so much like a snake that I let all holds go and swam to another tree close by and waited there—all wet, shivering and scared—for daylight, knowing that nobody, not even dad, would venture out on such a river and night with a yawl or skiff to rescue a sweet water sailor like myself.

With daylight two men in a skiff came and took me back to the boat, and after a big breakfast I was ready to row father back to Hermann, Mo., our starting point, 65 miles down river, to order a new set of chains. The good old Vienna was out of commission 10 days, and this was an early lesson on geared machinery for Steamboat Bill.

The newspaper never missed a chance at some unusual bit of steamboat happening. The steamer Vienna, the F.F.F famous fishing club and the townfolks teamed up for a reporter's delight.

The great annual excursion of the F.F.F. Club of Hermann, consisting of about twenty Hermannites and four gentlemen from St. Louis, left town last Saturday morning on the steamer Vienna for the Gasconade River with Capt. Heckmann at the helm.

The trim little steamer was neatly decorated with flags and streamers and well loaded with boxes and baskets of refreshments and barrels and bottles of bait, etc. Oncken's lake, a few miles above the mouth of the Gasconade River was reached in due time and the remainder of that day and night and the greater part of the Sunday were devoted to fun and fishing—principally the former we suppose. But they claim to have had plenty of fish to eat while there and a few to bring home, and of course we accept their statements without question.

About noon Sunday their friends in Hermann began to think of and look for their return. Some of the more thoughtful suggested that a delegation should go to the landing to receive our absent friends. It was then proposed that some means of hauling up the fish should be provided and that wheel-barrows should be used for that purpose.

The idea took at once and all hands started off in search of Irish buggies. They soon began to come in from all directions and by two o'clock such an array of wheel-barrows and hand-wagons, as was strung out in front of the Concert Hall was never seen in Hermann since the days of railroad building—there were twenty-three in number as well as we could count. Such an imposing procession as this must, of course, be accompanied by music, which was soon forthcoming in the shape of Christ. Winter's organette band, consisting of one instrument for the operation of which Christ himself did the Circular work.

This band was mounted on Oscar Merten's band wagon, which like all the wagons and wheel-barrows, was appropriately decorated with a few smoked herrings suspended from slats nailed to the sides. There were also other decorations, such as flags, mottoes, pictures of fish, frogs, etc. and everywhere appeared the magic letters "F.F.F."

Thus equipped the procession patiently awaited the sound of the whistle of the Vienna that would herald the return of the wanderers. A juvenile watchman had been stationed up the railroad to report the first sight of their coming. The unusual demonstrations had in the meantime excited the curiosity of the entire town and men, women and children, were seen flocking to the river bank by the hundreds.

At last the word rang out "They are coming" and in a moment everything was in motion and the procession was formed and just as the boat swung around to land, the novel procession moved out, headed by the band wagon above mentioned and marched down to the river in single file, just in time to meet the boat as it landed.

At first sight of this extraordinary demonstration, it was but natural that the F.F.F.'s should be a little dumbfounded, but they soon caught the joke and all joined in the laugh. They then invited the reception committee up to the Concert Hall and set up a keg of beer.

The whole thing was pronounced by all to be a splendid but innocent joke, well carried out. It will be a long time before the reception of the F.F.F. Club by the wheel-barrow brigade will be forgotten. It is such things that make Hermann famous as a fun making and fun loving town.

The next year the fishing excursion of the F.F.F. Club again chartered the Vienna, but the affair could not top that of the previous year. They actually fished! About the most exciting news to report was a race with the little steamer Troy, with Mr. Spery and Mr. Metzler and their families on board. *The Troy started out a few minutes ahead of the Vienna and showed us her heels for quite a distance before the larger boat was able to pass her.*

There was always news when the F.F.F. Club announced its annual trip. In 1885 the newspaper reported:

At a called meeting of the "Finney Tribes" in the Gasconade Hall last night the following resolutions, offered by Whale and seconded by Bluefish, was unani-

mously adopted and directed to be engrossed on Ocean sheets and deposited in coral archives: Resolved, that we regard with regret the contemplated action of the F.F.F. Club to carry the war of extermination into these waters and therefore decline to bite at any bait or hook on the 6th.

The departure was noted thusly:

Last Saturday the steamer Fawn was gayly decorated and festooned and streamers with the ominous letters "F.F.F. Club" waived fore and aft, giving due notice that Hermann's famous fishing club was again on the war path against the finny tribe and this time would direct its crusade against the inhabitants of the Gasconade River. A large supply of provisions, refreshments, camp outfit, in fact everything that could add to the comfort of the men—about 22—were put aboard and away they steamed amid huzzas and strains of music. From what we could learn there was 36 hours of uninterrupted fun and Mr. August Begemann, who caught the first fish, was awarded the Champion Anglers Badge inscribed as follows;

This is the bait the fishermen
take, the fishermen take,
the fishermen
take when they
start out the
fish to
wake so
early in the
morning. They
take a nip before they go,
a good one, ah! and long and
slow for fear the chills will lay
them low early in the morning. Another when they're on the street which
they repeat each time they meet for luck
for that's the way to greet a fisher in the
morning. And when they are on the river's
brink again they drink without a wink—
to fight malaria they think it proper in the
morning. They tip a flask with true delight
when there's a bite if fishing's light they
smile and more till jolly tight all fishing
they're scorning. Another nip as they
depart one at the mart and one to part,
but none when in the house they
dart expecting there be mourning.
This is the bait the fishermen
try who fish buy at prices
high and tell all a
bigger lie of
fishing in
the morning.

Mary, who was busy with other matters, largely ignored the various excursions. The boats were doing well, money was no longer so scarce, and she was beginning to get about town more, calling on people, attending birthday parties and seeing to her children, who, counting step-daughter Tina, now numbered 10.

With the death of Julius Silber, Will's sister Caroline and her five small children were left penniless. Mary and Tina helped her establish a store in the two lower rooms on the east end of the Leimer/Heckmann house. The newspaper gave Caroline a good write-up.

Mrs. Caroline Silber will open her new millinery store, in the Heckmann building on Wharf Street tomorrow. Mrs. Silber is a practical milliner and dressmaker and will always aim to keep a well selected stock of all articles required in the makeup of ladies toilets on hand, and ladies will find it in their interest to give her a call and examine her stock of goods and learn the prices, before they make purchases elsewhere.

In June Mary again chronicled the death of a family member, Lena Rauss, Will's oldest sister.

On Thursday evening about 7 o'clock Julia Eberline came over hastily to tell us that Lena Rauss was lying in an unconscious condition. I went over to find her still breathing, but after all doing what we could for her, she died at 1/2 past 8 o'clock Friday, May 31st. She was buried yesterday, Saturday, June 2nd. Aged 52 years, 5 months and 5 days. She had taken a hoe and gone up to Mumbrauer's lots (she had rented a small piece of ground from him, and was going to surprise her husband when it was growing) so she was at work alone when Mr. Mumbrauer got up there some time about 5 o'clock and there was Lena, lay on a heap, not quite unconscious, but in a very bad condition. By the time any of them got up there or the Dr. was called she had fallen into a stupor from which she could not be aroused.

More bad news followed. *On the 5th of June a mob came to town and lynched the prisoner, that was here in jail charged with the murder of young Buchard. It is shameful!!!*

June also brought a big flood, with the river cresting on June 23 almost three feet higher than the flood of 1876. Mary went along on the boat to see the effects of the flood.

Many predicted a 1884 flood, but it looks almost beyond comprehension to think of it. Many people have been driven from their homes, and others are staying in their houses, surrounded by water. At one house we passed there was a girl in the door, bare-footed, all she need do was to put her foot down one step and it was in the water, another house had only a small spot around the house, still another was in water up to the windows.

When we got to Thee's the wind blew so hard, they were unable to make a landing at the only place where the horses could be got out—that is what they went up for. The boat could land on the wheat field, but the ground was soft and there the horses would have mired, so we came away and left them, promising to go up immediately if the river should rise more. ... We seen a small sternwheel boat or a skiff, running over the wheat field, coming toward us, it looked more like a reaper than a skiff. Up to last Sunday it rained nearly every day, and we had some fearful storms.

William, the children, and I keep a skiff at Bluffton, and left the Fawn to go on home. We staid at Mother's for dinner and supper and came down the river. When we started it was so pleasant there were light clouds over the sun, and it was about one hour of sunset. After we had passed Coles Creek, the clouds became black and thick. Hurrying to the northeast, before we got to Hermann, the rain was coming from the north. William pulled for dear life, and we just got into the house, before the rain came down in torrents, and the wind blew awfully. That was the last rain we had. The past week has given the farmers a good chance at their wheat.

This was a daring undertaking—rowing downstream on a flood-swollen river with night coming on.

September 9, 1883—*Today is a boisterous day for Hermann, not the weather, for it is breezy, sunshiney and very pleasant, but this is the last day of the Fair here, and a long train has come up from St. Louis. As a rule they are all folks who are not over particular about their conduct, there is singing and music over at the Concert Hall while I write. Altogether there is a fearful crowd for this place. I staid at home, preferring a quiet day at home to the noise and confusion of the Fair grounds.*

Now that the boats Fawn, Dora, and Vienna were running out of Hermann, Charles Eitzen surfaced, and a pitched battle over warehouse rights ensued. Capt. Heckmann wrote a vigorous letter to the editor explaining his side of the argument.

A Reply to Mr. Eitzen

An article in your last issue in regard to the Warehouse on the wharf, prompts me to reply to a matter, which I thought was satisfactorily settled. Since, however, Mr. Eitzen had found fit to stir it up again, I think it my duty to give the citizens of Hermann an insight into the true inwardness of this business. I went before the board of trustees and obtained permission to build a warehouse on the wharf and as soon as Mr. Eitzen got wind of this he circulated a petition objecting to it. He secured the signatures of about ten of our businessmen, some signed it because it was Mr. Eitzen who presented it, and some because he represented to them that the principal object of the petition was to call a special meeting of the board for a reconsideration in this matter.

Now in this same petition were embodied twelve reasons why the warehouse should not be placed on that particular spot that was designated by the trustees. Some of these reasons were too silly to talk about and could only originate in a brain like Mr. Eitzens, muddled with too much Heckmann. Not one of the signers of that same petition but what will admit that the ware-house is a great necessity, and would have been on our wharf long ago had it not been for Mr. Eitzen's opposition. A few fees connected with the ware-house, that will now go to some other pocket is what hurts. So it was with the gravel on our streets. Had it not been for Mr. Eitzen making some money off the limestone macadam in the shape of selling the town fuse, powder, etc, we should have had the gravel years ago, which, by the way, does not cost as much as this same macadam did. So it is with all things. The allmighty dollar and Heckmann are at the bottom of everything. This all should not be thus.

There was a time, when Mr. Eitzen ran this town to suit himself, but thank the Lord, that time has passed; because Mr. Eitzen said at the election in which he was defeated, that if defeated then, he would never run again. (No, Never, that is hardly ever.) If Mr. Eitzen would have made his word good with me once, there would be no occasion for him running anymore, but as it is, I have my doubts about it. This world is very fickle and we do not know what might happen at a given time. He might find a small town some place that he could buy and run to suit himself.

Wm. L. Heckmann

The fight with Eitzen was an ongoing one. Will had a lot of company since Eitzen was usually fighting with others. Photographs of the waterfront show a warehouse was built, but whether it was built on the site the trustees had designated is not clear. It was not quite in front of Eitzen's home.

In June the "River News" contained a whole column of news of steamboat movements out of the Hermann port.

> *The steamer Troy in command of Capt. Chas. Sperry arrived at this port last Saturday. It is a little floating palace—perfect in every particular. We wish Capt. Charley success. ... The people are justly proud of the four daily packets which are now plying between this point and Sperry's Landing, Portland and the Gasconade River, respectively. ... Capt. August Wohlt went up with the Vienna to the Gasconade River this week and brought down a load of gravel for our streets. Capt. Riddell ran the Fawn during his absence.*

Other news in this column was of the passings and landings of the Missouri River steamers. The reporter for the Gasconade River News had some choice tidbits of local interest:

> *Dull times along the river since harvest.*
>
> *Corn is looking well, now if the chinch bug will let us alone.*
>
> *One of our farmers cut 165 dozen large bundles of oats from 2 acres of ground. Who can beat that?*
>
> *Mr. John Gaither is in town today from high up the river. He says crops have turned out beyond the expectations of all. Mr. Gaither has cleared about $600 on ties this year.*
>
> *There was a mysterious looking moving outfit came down the Gasconade River one day last week in a skiff, claiming at Fredericksburg to be bound for Kansas and at Gasconade they said they were going to Mississippi. It is quite probable that some old man has lost his daughter.*
>
> *We learn that the Gasconade City Hotel has lately undergone a thorough re-fitting and re-furnishing at great expense to the proprietors. The straw ticks have been emptied, burned and re-filled, the quilts have been turned over, and some coal oil put on the bedsteads.* (Hopefully, that got the bed bugs!)
>
> *The Gasconade River has been on a big rise lately, but has fallen two and a half feet, so we see the tie rafters again coming into Gasconade city, and we will soon see the boys on their regular trips down the river. Some of the tie men have*

had the blues for several days past. Other business at this burg is generally dull. The boss merchant is doing a good business with his saw-and-grist mill.

In January of 1884, Henry Wohlt again wanted out of the company. In a parting of the ways that was not entirely amicable, he sold the Fawn and the Vienna to William Heckmann Sr. and George Hale Talbot for $6,100. Mary reported that the boats were both running as soon as the ice left the Missouri River.

By March the social life began picking up again. The Chamois newspaper reported:

Our town was visited last Sunday by an excursion party from Hermann, consisting of a large crowd of the inhabitants of that town. They came up on the Steamer Fawn, landing here about two o'clock in the

GRAND
EXCURSION

next Sunday, August 19, 1883
on the
STEAMER FAWN
up the Gasconade river to
Onckens Grove.
The celebrated
APOSTLE   BAND
will entertain the participants dur the entire trip. Dancing and fishing will be the order of the day.

Refreshments and eatables of all kinds to be had on the boat and picnic grounds.

Round Trip Tickets 50 Cents.
Tickets for sale at Geo. Kracttly's store only.

Everybody is cordially invited.

LOUIS RINCHEVAL.

afternoon. Louis Rincheval with his famous Apostle Band was among the excursionists. The excursion party immediately repaired to Shobe's pasture, where the grounds had been prepared for the occasion and a game of base ball between the Hermann and Chamois nine, was begun. The game was rather interesting so far as it was played, yet it was not played out. The boat whistle sounded about 5 o'clock and put an end to the game. The Hermann boys had played three innings and the Chamois two. The score stood as follows: Hermann 9; Chamois 15. As the game progressed the band played several pieces of nice music.

Life on the boats could be hazardous. In August Mary wrote, *On Tuesday Frank Thomas done some "cut-up" on the Vienna, held a pistol at William's head and at the cooks. Cook had him arrested, but they have settled it. Frank had been on a four-days spree, he sobered up after William knocked him into the river.*

To Mary's regret, William was up the Gasconade on his birthday in February of 1884. They had now been married 16 years. Illness struck the family again. Bobbie had scarlet fever, Tina had diphtheria, Sam had diphtheria, then pneumonia, and finally typhoid fever. He was quite *out of his mind for four days, then hung between life and death, but gradually recovered strength.* Mary commented on the great love and care her husband had shown in his concern for this child's illness.

With both the railroad tracks and the river literally at their front door, it was inevitable that the Heckmann children would wander into danger. Two such incidents were reported in the newspaper.

Last Saturday afternoon while some children were at play in a skiff at the wharf, Annie, fourth child of Capt. Heckmann in attempting to climb on the steamer Vienna fell into the river, but was rescued from a watery grave by Charles Greene.

A few days later the newspaper had another frightening tale to tell.

Last Sunday afternoon while several little girls were standing on the railroad track on Wharf street, the construction train came down the road and noticing the little ones on the track, the engineer gave the signal with the steam whistle to call their attention to the approaching train. Hearing the whistle, the children turned around and when they saw that the train was so near to them, they became perfectly paralyzed with fear and could not move from the spot. Fortunately the train was not under full headway and the engineer succeeded in bringing it to a stand before reaching the terrified little ones, who were lifted off the track by the train men and told to run home to mamma.

Mary mentioned not a word about these two well-documented cases. Perhaps her mind was on other matters.

July 7—On the stroke of 5 o'clock p.m. there was a little boy born to us. He is to be named Edward.

Of all of the Heckmann children, Edward was the only one with just one name. In later years he came to resent this and took Rewald, the surname of his paternal grandmother, as his middle name.

The newspaper recorded this event:

"Ship Ahoy!" was the cry in Capt. Heckmann's family Monday, but Mrs. Roethemeyer who is an experienced pilot, pronounced it a boy. The captain is correspondingly happy.

Caroline's children developed whooping cough that summer. Living in the same house, it was inevitable that the Heckmann children would have it, too. *Martha has it, Bobbie and Lottie are beginning with it.* The fear was that the baby would take it also.

In September school had started and the annual Fair was held. Caroline Silber and little Annie Heckmann upheld the family honors in the premium department. *Caroline took a premium for best display of merchandise, also for a quilt and some other things. Annie Heckmann got $1.00 for the best writing. All passed off nicely as far as my own were concerned, but some others had several hot political arguments and mixed in some hard names.*

William and his new partner Mr. Talbot bought the steamer Dora from Boeger and Heidbroeder, with Heidbroeder to stay on as pilot for a while. The newspaper was, as usual, enthusiastic in its coverage.

Messrs. Talbot and Heckmann have purchased the steamer Dora, and will run the same in addition of their other two boats, the Fawn and Vienna. These gentlemen are good business men and river men and will put the boats to profitable account.

The new arrival was heralded on Oct. 29, 1884:

The steamer Dora arrived at our wharf last Thursday and looks as neat as a pin. Considerable improvements have been added and she is in first class order for business. She will run on the Missouri River until opening navigation on the Gasconade. When in connection with the steamer Vienna they will make regular trips, the steamer Dora running from Aug. Boeger's warehouse to Hermann and the steamer Vienna from the mouth of the Gasconade to Vienna in Maries, Co. This will accommodate all shippers and they can depend on getting their wheat to market in good time. Capt. Henry Heidbroeder will command the steamer Dora and Capt. Wm. L. Heckmann the Vienna.

Steamboat Bill later wrote about the adventures of the Dora. One of his tales included the steamer General Meade, a chain-driven boat better known as the "Old Gutshaker" for reasons obvious to anyone who ever took a trip on her. The chains would fall off the sprockets with a mighty clank—a real gutshaker. Steamboat Bill claimed the "Gutshaker" also was owned by the Hermann Ferry Company, but this is in error. In fact, the Hermann Ferry and Packet Company was not formally organized until 1890. In his book and in the "Waterways Journal" Steamboat Bill wrote lengthy and entertaining accounts of Capt. Sterling

Dodd as a pilot on the Dora.

While I was aboard the Vienna under Capt. Wohlt, Captain Sterling Dodd was master and pilot on the Dora running the Gasconade. Sterling Dodd was the youngest of the renowned Dodd family of Osage, Gasconade and Missouri River pilots. In my time on this river, Capt. Hal Dodd was the greatest character on the Western rivers and I saw most of them in flesh and blood. Brother Sterling Dodd was destined to be an even greater character, had death not taken this blonde giant after thirty-five years had failed to put a tan on the rose-com-plexioned, round-faced boy that would today take Hollywood by storm.

In dress and habits, Sterling Dodd was careless to a degree beyond de-scription. His high topped shoes were never laced, he had no use for the buttons on his vest or coat, his shirt was always open down to his belt.

Dodd took the Dora to Cooper Hill, Mo., and loaded her out flat at that landing with wheat, walnut lumber, eggs, pumpkins, etc. He started down the creek and came to Pryor's Bend, three miles of the swiftest, crookedest river that man ever saw. One of the best pilots on the river rang three hundred bells bringing a loaded boat through this place. Only one man ever took a loaded boat through this bend after night, downstream bound. [Bill's brother, Greeley Heckmann.]

When Dodd sighted the head of Pryor's Bend he told one of the owners, George Talbot, to go down to the engine room and tell the Dutch engineer to answer the bells just as Sterling rang them, to answer them quick because he was going to show old Bill Heckmann how to run Pryor's Bend with a steam-boat.

In pointing down the head of this bend you have to drive a boat through the first crook, and then set her back hard. Dodd drove the Dora down too far and before he could check her headway she went head-on into the big clay banks. The walnut lumber in the deck room skidded forward, scrambling a big pile of eggs, penning the fireman in the fire room, fouling the whistle valve, and scraping the clay off the top of the boiler. Some of the timber went halfway into the five hundred sacks of wheat piled in the forecastle. Cargoes have not infrequently been known to shift, but this one skidded, and no worse mess was ever unloaded from a Gasconade River packet.

When Dodd hit the river bank, off came his cap which he stamped upon. In the next crook, he kicked off a shoe. He just missed the big gatepost out in the middle of the river by inches and down came his suspenders. Next, off came his top shirt, then another shoe which he threw at Talbot to chase him out of the pilothouse. In the dead eddy he kicked himself out of his pants. He treaded the old pilot wheel (and it was a big one) next to the hub, next to the circle and outside the circle on the handles. He kicked two spokes clean out of the wheel as he spit chewing tobacco all over the front of the pilothouse and down on a pile of pumpkins in front.

He flanked the Dora out of the foot of Pryor's Bend in his underwear and stocking feet with perspiration dripping off his face like the big scattered raindrops that fall in Chariot Creek in April when the croppies bite the best.

He went to bed with nothing to say, but early the next morning he was ready for battle again since Pryor's Bend was behind him. As Talbot came out in front of the pilothouse he said: "By the gods, George, I painted your pumpkins and I brought your old saw and hatchet waterlogged Dutch pinochle of a boat down through that bend just as good as Bill Heckmann ever did in his life."

Pryor's Bend got its name from the first pilot ever to run the bend, Buel Pryor, who did not know how to flank a boat. He did not have much luck and did not last long; only made a few desperate attempts and quit when his boat sank further down the river.

Old Bill Heckmann, my father, was the King Bee of them all when it came to a rough and dangerous piece of steamboating. He would come into Pryor's Bend with an overloaded boat and the pilothouse full of shippers. He would pilot, maneuver and talk. The only times that he got into trouble were those in which he would be explaining just how and why the boat should be handled "this way." Capt. Greeley Heckmann, my brother, was the only man who could run Pryor's Bend with a boat and two loaded barges while telling stories, shooting ducks and lighting his own pipe.

While Sterling Dodd was piloting the Dora he had Will Kay, son of that great boatman, Perrin Kay of Jefferson City, Mo., as engineer. At the time my father was running the "Gutshaker"—the General Meade. One night they both landed at the same woodpile at the foot of the longest, deepest and straightest

89

"Old Gutshaker," the Steamer General Meade

stretch of the Gasconade. Both boats were loading cordwood for the fuel and both boats were headed upstream. It was two miles to a narrow shoal at Brown Shanty where the river was too close for two boats to run abreast.

We were loading hickory and ash split fine and seasoned just enough to make plenty of fog. The Gutshaker was not a slow boat, she had geared machinery that connected with cog wheels, bull wheels and every other kind that continued back to the wheel with long steel chains. These chains when falling off the sprockets onto a smooth running board, made a mighty racket, especially when the old boat was being crowded.

Dad had as his engineer, Bill Lalk, a pioneer Gasconade River boatman, who was afraid of the Gutshaker's complicated but powerful machinery. Still he was working for Old Rough-head and he had to obey orders. Someone suggested a race between the two boats and dad offered a keg of beer as a prize to the crew of the winner.

Both boats eased out into the middle of the stream and when abreast of each other, they turned them loose. The Dora had large machinery for her boiler power and was a hard boat to fire. The Gutshaker had plenty of boiler power and steamed like an aluminum kettle on a hot stove. The Gutshaker, with plenty of steam was soon out ahead before they could get the Dora warmed up. This boat was cramped in the stacks, made a mighty noise and had a draft that would almost pull a stick of cordwood out of your hands when you opened a fire door.

When Kay saw the Gutshaker leaving them and the steam not getting up to where he wanted it, he went out to the fireroom where a man called Bottlehead Joe was firing. He said, "If that boat beats us to Brown Shanty I'll knock you in the river with these fists." (His brawny arms were hung with two menacing *hams.)* "Throw two lengths of cordwood in and throw two shovelsful of coal in each door and get some steam."

Kay went back to the engine room, pinched the stems and adjusted the machinery as only one who had learned under Captain Perrin Kay could do. The steam commenced to come. The Dora was coughing in her stacks and throwing sparks with pieces of burning cordwood heaven-ward. Most of the crew were up on the roof keeping the sparks from burning this sky-rocket up. She began to crawl up on the old Gutshaker.

My dad ordered his cub pilot to "Take the wheel. This boat is not moving. Them young pups are going to pass us up. I'm going down to the engine room and if that hard headed engineer does not give this boat all she's got I'll break his neck."

All the difference this made in the Gutshaker's engine room was to make the chains rattle some harder, but to no avail. The Dora passed the Gutshaker and nosed ahead into the narrow channel of Brown Shanty. No one thought to keep the time on this race but it must have set a record. The natives living along this stretch of water still talk about that race.

Dad did not break the engineer's neck. That Hoosier, too, was a hard man. It has often been speculated upon whether Will Kay would have knocked Bottlehead Joe into the river if the Dora had lost. Bottlehead was a fine specimen of young manhood, whose fists had shown skill and power when in use. Will Kay was a well-known prize-fighter as well as an engineer. It would have been a real battle.

The boats Dora and Vienna were both undergoing repairs for several weeks at the season's end. Mary reported, *Times are awful dull, the election is decided, Cleveland is the President-elect. I hope and trust that all will be well. Christmas passed off for us very quietly. We have a tree, but few presents, owing to close times, not hard times, for the boats have done well and if all goes well, we promise ourselves good times next year.*

The weather was turning colder, and winter quarters were in order for the boats. Capt. Will tried to make a trip with the Vienna, but the wheel froze up and he had to tie up. Both the Dora and the Fawn were in safe harbor at Gasconade.

Dec. 27, 1884—*W. run up to look after ice for Kropp's Brewery at Gasconade, a little too late. In afternoon he sent word for Will and George Talbot to come up to "man" the boats, as it rained all night and the ice has been softening. This year has been a troubled one for us, and I suppose it will continue until the end. When I look at others, I am thankful it has been no worse, we had such sickness, but all recovered.*

Dec. 31, 1884—*The old year passed away in gloomy silence, good bye to 1884 with all its cares, its pains, deaths, sickness and sorrow. Many are the hearts that have ached, many are the care worn who have lain down their burdens forever and passed to the great future, never to return. Yet the world goes on, with the same inhumanity to one another as ever. Could we all "do to others as we would have others do to us" how peacefully would we live together. We have seen much trouble, and yet I feel thankful, that all our children are spared to us and are all well again. There are only two families who have passed through trials equalling ours in this town, but they too were all spared.*

CHAPTER 9

Friends and Foes

They have killed the goose that laid the
golden egg at Hermann. —Capt. Archie Bryan

*R*iver ice was a killer for boats of any size, making the winter months an anxious time for steamboat owners. Since worry was a major occupation during this time of greatest danger, the men wisely found something else to occupy their minds and hands.

When the boats were in safe harbor, Capt. Will organized hunts that sometimes extended as far as Arkansas. Local hunters would be joined by St. Louis men, including Col. Norman Colman, publisher of "Colman's Rural World." One such expedition brought back 11 deer and large quantities of smaller game. Ice fishing also was a popular diversion, as reported in the "Advertiser-Courier" in 1884.

A "Gar" Picnic on the Gasconade River

While the Gasconade River is covered with ice it is fine sport to "gig" gars through the ice, and your correspondent in company with several other parties went up from here last week and had some rare sport. There were probably twenty other persons at the place when we arrived there and the ice was already covered with a wriggling mass of gars. We were not long selecting suitable places and cutting holes about 2 by 4 feet through the ice. We were soon at work and during a few hours, killed about 200 gars. There were from 2,500 to 3,000 killed that day and at least 10,000 during the winter at this one point. When we consider that the gar is the greatest enemy of all small fish, there certainly is some satisfaction in seeing them exterminated at this rate, and besides the sport is quite exciting.

Imagine about thirty men on the ice, each standing at an opening with his fishspear intent on taking as many gars as possible. This fish at this season of the year travels in schools and at times as many as ten or twelve appear below one of the openings and as the holes are close together, say ten or fifteen feet apart, you can imagine what an excitement such a school of gars will create when they appear, everybody killing as many as possible and the scenes are sometimes ludicrous in the extreme. Sometimes as many as three are taken at one throw of the gig and often 100 in a single hour out of one hole. When they have passed one lot of holes everybody runs to the next lot, probably 100 yards up or down stream, according to the route taken by the gars, and then the fun commences again.

The gar is not considered very good eating, but does very well for a change, and farmers are coming miles to enjoy this rare sport and taking off wagon loads of these fish. Every fisherman knows what a gar is, knows his qualification for stealing bait and killing small fish and therefore will hail with pleasure anything that will help to diminish their numbers, and if this war of extermination keeps on we will soon have plenty of good fish in the Gasconade River. It will not be necessary to enact laws for the protection of fish if we attend to the gars.

Winter also was a good time to attend to legal matters. Gustave Wohlt, who was courting Julia Heckmann, daughter of Capt. Henry Heckmann, left for St. Louis to be examined for his engineer's license. *We wish him success,* said the newspaper. The Henry Wohlt family experienced a tragedy in the loss of little Willie Wohlt, age nine, to typhoid.

A week after the death, the Wohlts announced plans to build another Gasconade River steamboat. The newspaper reported, *This will give us four steamboats at this point, for which there will be an abundance of work during the next months as but little corn or wheat has been brought to market from the Gasconade and Missouri River country.* On November 26, the newspaper announced, *The new boat built by* the Wohlt brothers has been christened "Royal" and will make its first trip in a day or two. The government inspectors were here yesterday and after careful examination of the boat and its machinery, pronounced it a safe vessel and issued their certificates of inspection to the proprietors.

For reasons not given, the parting of the Wohlt and Heckmann interests had not been friendly. The two factions entered into an intense rivalry, which prompted Capt. Archie Bryan, a respected pilot, to remark, "They have now killed the goose that laid the golden egg at Hermann." Bryan's dire prediction did not come true. After a period of bitter and hectic competition, the Wohlts and Capt. Heckmann rejoined forces.

A spell of mild weather in December brought the boats out of their winter hibernation. On the last day of the year Mary wrote, *Just five minutes before 12 William came in, he had come down from Gasconade, on train, to attend to some business. Dora and Vienna were unloading at Gasconade.* Over the next few days she noted that the Fawn, the Vienna and the Dora all were running, and she heard the whistle of the Royal, the Wohlt's new boat. But a mid-January cold snap caught the boats out of their winter harbors.

January 16—4 A.M. Zero! 4 P.M. Zero! Snowing and blowing all day. Sewing. Chatwick around the house keeping up the fires, about 6 o'clock p.m. I went into the kitchen and there stood William, nearly froze to death. He had walked from Oldenburg, the Vienna froze in there and the Dora in Lost Slough 40 miles up the Gasconade River. The Fawn is below the bridge.

Whether Will had walked 40 miles is not certain, as the location of Oldenburg has been lost. The next day word came that the Dora had worked herself down as far as the Vienna. After a brief rest, William took the train to Gasconade and then trudged through snow and zero-degree cold to the icebound Vienna. Mary wrote, *William kept me in a stew yesterday and last night. He went up to the boats, and was coming back this afternoon and did not come until the 10 o'clock freight.* When all the boats at last had been moved to Gasconade, the family breathed a sigh of relief; all was safe, and life could return to normal.

A month later Mary wrote about an unexpected outing.

At breakfast William asked me whether I would like to go along to Gasconade to the boats. I thought he was joking, but at 9 o'clock he asked me again, and I slipped on a dress and was ready. Borrowed Fritz Ochsner's sleigh, and went on the ride over hills and dales I shall not soon forget. The snow is a foot deep and the poor mules were nearly played out when we got back at 5 o'clock. Took dinner on the Dora. Boats are both in good water. It snowed until 3 P.M.

This was a nursing mother with a seven-month-old baby. No account is given of how the girls at home fed the baby. The day after the wild sleigh ride, the family celebrated William's 40th birthday with eggnog and cakes in the evening.

Social events helped the winter months pass more quickly. Mary permitted Tina, now 19, and Annie, 12, to go to the Masquerade Ball. *Instead of Tina coming home early as she promised, she staid until 2 o'clock.*

William's sister Louisa and her husband came to visit, and the Heckmanns went by train to Sedalia to visit Mary's sisters. Company or not, the eternal washing went on. *Greeley and I dipped water for washing down at the levee on the Vienna. Commenced washing, as our cistern is empty we took the wash to the water. The old cook helped me wash.* The cook, no doubt, was female. Men did not do washings.

Louis Rincheval was a fat, jovial fellow who was always getting up an excursion or dance. Jumbo, as he was called, converted the Rotunda building in what is now the city park to a roller skating rink. For a town whose citizens loved dancing, roller skating caused quite a moral uprising. The newspaper countered with a tongue-in-cheek editorial.

Last Saturday evening Mr. Louis Rincheval inaugurated the roller skating seating season at the Fair Grounds, and quite a number of children and young people of both sexes enjoyed the sport very much. There is a great difference of opinion about the moral status of roller skating rinks, but where is the opponent who can certify, on his own knowledge, that he ever saw anything shocking or demoralizing occur in one of them?

The whole thing in a nutshell is this: The amusement is a pleasant, healthy, graceful exercise, toning up both body and mind; but, of course, may be carried to excess. Constant exercise strengthens and develops the part of the body exercised, as has been elsewhere demonstrated, and it may result in an entirely different shape of the human figure in this country, bearing but little resemblance to the Apollos and Venuses now considered the type of physical perfection. The shoulders and bust will gradually grow less and less, and the hips, legs and feet assume abnormal proportions, or what would now be considered as such. It is not pleasant to contemplate. Pope says, "Whatever is, is right," but smart as he was, he got left on that statement.

With the coming of warm weather in April, Mary and three of the children went along on the Vienna to Round Island to get gravel for the town. Upon their return they found an angry mob waiting at the Hermann wharf to prevent the Dora from landing with a load of infected cattle.

Came home to find the river bank one black mass of people, they were ready to stop the Dora as she was to come in with cattle from Calloway County. Up to the present there has not one step been taken concerning the cattle disease to be prevailing in said county, but they took a sudden jump at it later. … Bob Miller took midnight train to stop the Dora from bringing those cattle, but he missed it and the cattle were stopped about 1/2 mile up the river and taken back.

The newspaper gave a longer account of the story.

Considerable feeling was manifested by our town people here yesterday forenoon when it was learned that the steamer Dora had left for some point up the river to get a cargo of Calloway county cattle and unload the same here to be forwarded by train further east. The more the matter was talked over and the danger to which cattle on this side of the river would be exposed, the more the conviction and determination made itself manifest on the part of our citizens that the landing of the cattle should be prevented at all hazards.

As the day was drawing to a close and the boat was likely to arrive at any hour, the feeling of indignation became more intense and Messrs. Kropp and Robt. Robyn suggested a citizens meeting at the Market house, to take the necessary concerted action. The ringing of the fire bell which never fails to attract attention, now had thoroughly alarmed the people, and at the unusual hour of six o'clock a large, earnest and determined citizens meeting was in progress.

Mr. Joseph Leising was called to chair and after explaining more fully the object of the meeting, Mr. Clark addressed the meeting and read a communication from M. R. P. Slocomb, the Depot Agent, wherein he stated that he fully sympathized with the people in this matter and that he would not receive for shipment, or permit the use of the railroad stockyards, any cattle which came from the infected district.

Resolutions were passed requesting the boat owners not to land any cattle from Calloway county at this wharf; also to disinfect the boat if they have had cattle from Calloway on board and landed the same somewhere else.

A committee of twenty was appointed to proceed to the wharf and await the arrival of the boat and notify the owners of the action taken by the meeting, and prevent the unloading at all hazards. Up to a late hour this morning the boat had not arrived, and gave color to the rumor that a message has been dispatched by the steamboat company to meet the boat and countermand the order of landing here.

During the summer months Mary accompanied the boats more often. Eddie, the baby, was walking, and she was trying to wean him. Watching a toddler on a steamboat was a chore, especially for a mother who was usually cooking on the boat.

I went with the boat to Berry's Landing, had all the children along.... I went along to First Creek, had a good time. I had forgotten my work and we took the skiff and pulled up and down the creek. ... I took Annie, Bobbie, Eddie, Fred and Sam along. We went first to Fredricksburg, on the Gasconade River, then to Avans creek for sacks, then up the Missouri to Bluffton at 1 o'clock Saturday morning, staid there to load some ties in the morning. I cooked dinner on the Vienna.

At home Mary complained that *washing, ironing and baking is about all we get done. The house is full of children from morning till night. It is nothing for six strange children to be playing here most of the time.* A conscientious housekeeper, she nearly always "done up the work" the first thing in the morning and was chagrined when caught less than neat.

Mother was down on Thursday, we left all the work lay, had Mary Dame to help and began on cellar, got it all done by dinner. Mealys and Mrs. McClotchey found it convenient to take dinner here, so I felt pretty cheap about the house being topsy turvy.

Illness was an unwelcome caller.

William has been very sick, he first took Cholera-morbis, and now his liver is the worst. In fact, he first took liver and kidney trouble and neglected it until the stomach trouble brought it all to light. Yesterday at one time I thought he was dying. Last night Siedler and John Sutter nursed him and I had a good nights rest, he is much better now. I have been polticing his liver since 4 o'clock yesterday afternoon. I am writing because I feel too bad to do anything else.

William recovered from his ailments, and the family took in the exposition in St. Louis—*Everything there is lovely*—and prepared for the wedding of Tina and Robert Miller, Mary's younger brother. After the ceremony the newlyweds left immediately for Bluffton *there to make their home.* This marriage posed some odd problems for the Heckmann children. Their half-sister had married their uncle—did this make him a brother-in-law or an uncle? Things became even more complicated when Tina had a baby—was she a cousin or a niece?

In November Mary noted that *William and Will have been running the ferry boat. Vienna came down with a load of the everlasting wood of Gasconade, cut winter before last off Neuhans and William's land.* The meaning of "everlasting wood" is not explained. Was it wood that seemed never to come to an end or a particular type of long-lasting wood? William was buying up land, a fact that received only oblique references in Mary's journals.

Winter returned, with all its worry, and the river closed in December. Mary wrote that the portly Louis Rincheval *caused an excitement by trying the ice. He was nearly to the sandbar, but after going in up to his arms twice, and breaking in with one foot four times and falling everytime he came back, he would surely have drowned if Frank Rebsamen had not helped him out the last time. He had the big head and wanted to show people he was "no coward."*

Mary concluded 1885 by saying "goodbye" to her old journal and "hello" to a new one.

> *Goodbye old book. With the old year I say good-bye to you too. In your place I have a shiney new one, but never-the-less you are still dear to me, with all your mistakes and blots. You have always been too large for everyday use, the new one is more attractive in this respect, but like a good natured awkward person I like you and will often hunt you up for reference.*
>
> *To the New Year 1886 this book is respectfully dedicated. Whether my pen will fill its pages or not, God alone knows. Perhaps it may never be filled through neglect, but I do not believe it will and if it is only written in once in three months it will eventually be filled. That is if I live long enough, which I pray I may, to live and do my duty is what I wish and pray for. Should I however be taken away, it is my wish that one of my daughters, Annie or Lizzie, continue to note down the events which immediately concern the family.—Mary L. Heckmann, Hermann, Mo. Jan. 3rd, 1886.*

The weather was warm enough in January to permit the boats to run and to give the men some relief from worry. But the reprieve was short lived— once again a cold snap caught the boats out of winter harbor. On January 9 the temperature was 18 degrees below zero and the Vienna was aground. Mary sympathized and worried, too.

The Vienna aground, they almost froze themselves working at her. By about 1 o'clock they got her afloat. William went up to the other boats, found them aground too, came home with the "blues" awful bad. Mercury did not get above zero all day.

Keeping the boats safe from ice was brutal work, and the bitter cold hung on for weeks.

The men began to put in an ice break above the Vienna on Wednesday, the day it rained some and looked as though a thaw had begun, but the next two days, Thursday and Friday, so cold the men nearly froze, gave them enough at the ice break and yesterday they left it, still needing a day or more work. Today is slightly better but still 18 at noon, 4 at 8 o'clock and 22 at 5 p.m.

When a thaw finally came, Mary reported that Fred worked all one morning catching drops of water from the woodshed for wash water.

The ice drama finally ended on February 14, to the great relief of all concerned. The long-awaited breakup of the ice jam on the river was a momentous event that drew a large crowd to the wharf. Mary, like the rest of the town, kept a steady vigil.

The ice broke for good at 6 o'clock last evening. At first it looked as though all was over with the Vienna, but the ice break, although it broke with the first move on Wednesday night, still done good service. The logs were sunk there and as the ice came down on it, it began to pile up, so the boat lay behind an ice break of ice. For a time I thought it would keep piling up until it would fill the bow of the boat, yet it did not scratch a line on her. I am very thankful that she is saved; the other two must be safe as George Talbot tells me the Dora left Gasconade for Pin Oak, at 8 this morning.

The mental strain put on us the past week would soon make one prematurely old. Wednesday at about 8 o'clock P.M. the boat set up a whistling. In the slush and rain one after another lantern was seen moving for the river until there was a pretty large crowd out. But before the ledman got there the ice breaker had made a big crash and went down. The ice only moved about 10 yards and stopped. The river kept rising very slowly, it seemed as though the ice were hanging by a thread almost. The mercury kept falling and on Thursday morn there was 7 inches snow on the ground, the heaviest snow that we have had at one time this

The ice-gorged Missouri River at Hermann. The large building on the left is the White House Hotel.

winter. The flag was put up and the mercury kept falling, Friday it moderated some. Saturday still warmer and at noon the whistle brought another crowd to the river, to be again disappointed. But at six it was a sure enough move, and I believe every man and boy was at the river.

Improvement work on the Gasconade River was progressing, but more pressure was needed to keep the appropriated funds flowing. Fritz Lang, the business manager and bookkeeper, kept excellent books so that a year's summary was easily available. Capt. Heckmann supplied the information requested and the newspaper kept its subscribers posted.

Improvement of Gasconade River

Capt. Wm. L. Heckmann having been requested by Major A. W. Miller, U.S.A. in charge of the improvement of the Missouri and its tributaries, to furnish a statement of the Gasconade during the year ending June 1st, 1885, together with suggestions as he desired to offer as to the best means of improving said river, has forwarded the following report:

The Gasconade River business is only in its infancy and business is improving yearly. Six years ago there were only shipped about 25,000 bushels of wheat and this last season 226,750 bushels. This is due to former appropriations judiciously expended. The inhabitants along the river are a thrifty people and are only now beginning to realize the advantage of the river route, they are erecting ware-houses and are putting in twice the amount of wheat they did in former times and land is advancing steadily in valuation. What is needed now is a low water state of 30 inches, this can be secured by a system of low water dams, confining the water in a channel about 33 or 40 feet wide, (this is quite practicable as there is a gravel subsoil and cannot scour). Our worst places are where there are two or three chutes, these should be closed except one, by erecting dams at the fork of the chute, allowing the water to accumulate and then run off gradually through one channel. Other places wing dams could be put in to good advantage. I am convinced if commenced on this system from the first shoal to Indian Ford as far as surveyed, a distance of 76 miles, a channel of 30 inches could be secured. $50,000 would do this work as material is convenient, and would also be sufficient to remove obstructions in the river and cut what trees are liable to fall in the channel. This amount expended would double the business on the River in two years.

Boats engaged in the river are viz:

Str. Vienna	drawing 12 inches	Capacity 70 tons
Str. Royal	" 12 inches	65 tons
Str. Dora	" 6 inches	100 tons
Str. Fawn	" 16 inches	70 tons

Statement of Traffic from June 1st, 1884; to June 1st, 1885

Freight Down the River

Wheat	226,750 bushels	$181,400
Livestock, hogs, cattle	1150 head	$12,500
Eggs	300 cases	$1,125
Lumber, Walnut	100,000 feet	$4,000
Lumber, Pine	300,000 feet	$3,600
Shaved Hoops	100,000 feet	$600
Railroad Ties	175,000 feet	$56,000
Miscellaneous Produce		$1,200
	Total Value	$260,425

Freight Up the River

Self Binders (38) and farm machinery		$9,000

300 sacks flour, bran and shipstuff	$1,160
Lumber, 100,000 feet	$3,000
Salt, 660 barrels	$900
Mdse. (Miscellaneous)	$12,000
Total Value	$26,060

Any other information you may desire, I will cheerfully give you.

Respectfully,

Wm. L. Heckmann, Master Str. Vienna

On March 28, 1886, Mary posted a diary entry describing the Miller family's arrival at the Hermann landing 19 years previously and her first meeting with the man of her life as he boarded the steamer Post Boy. *Little did I think I would marry him and in this short time be the mother of 9 children.* Mary must have been tired of counting children by this time. When she wrote this passage she actually had 10, with another on the way.

The rivalry between the Wohlt and Heckmann interests ended in April of 1886. Talbot sold his interest in the Fawn, Vienna and Dora to the Wohlt brothers, who added their steamer Royal to the holdings. These four boats became the nucleus of the Hermann Ferry and Packet Company, and the golden shekels once again rolled into the company coffers. All the boats were spruced up. The Dora went to St. Louis to be remodeled, and the Vienna went to New Haven for repairs after a cabin fire.

Just before Easter Sunday another Heckmann baby arrived with little fanfare. *Wednesday morning April 21st at 1:30 a.m. a little bit of a boy came here to make his home.* This son, Mary's 11th child, was called George Talbot Heckmann. Later in the year a visit from Tina and her new baby, Elsie, was duly noted in the newspaper. *Capt. Heckmann last Saturday chartered several saloons, because, as he says, it is not everybody that can be a grandfather at age 41.*

During the summer of 1886, a once-only event took place with both Will Heckmann Sr. and his cub pilot Will Jr. at the wheel of the steamer Royal. Years later the Vienna newspaper carried a story about the trip, written by Steamboat Bill.

Royal Makes Only Gasconade Voyage

In the latter eighties my father made a trip up the Gasconade River with the Steamer Royal to Arlington, Mo., where the Frisco Railroad crosses the Gasconade River. It was my pleasure to be on this trip, the only one ever made by a steamboat above Vienna, Mo. Steamboats had been running to Vienna for some ten years, but no boat had ventured above this port and when we did get up in the upper reaches of this river, it seemed we were entering a new world, and we were naturally very excited.

To the good people ashore it meant more, for most of them had never seen a steamboat. We had a heavy load of wagon timber, the river bank was full, and progress was slow up this swift stream. We could see the people crossing the side bottom fields and taking short cuts through the woods to head off and get a look at this boat, and whoever was on watch, the Dutch Captain or his Cub Pilot, their feet were on the big whistle treadle at intervals of every half hour.

In lots of places we would see one hundred people viewing the old boat. She was not much of a boat among the floating palaces on the lower Mississippi at that time, but up this little stream, to these people, our staunch Royal seemed colossal. Some of these good folks would follow the boat for miles along the bank, and at one place a boy and a big fat girl followed us for three miles, shoving vines aside, knocking down brush piles and skipping through the underbrush, overcoming all obstacles until they came to a large stream where they could not wade and it was too cold to swim.

To me this picture is still in my mind. I often wonder what became of that boy and the big fat girl. Hope they are still living and can see their beautiful little river rolling along.

About 15 miles below Arlington we tied up for the night and found a very old gray bearded man sitting on the bank. Father went out to talk to him and naturally some of us went along.

It soon developed that this old gentleman did not welcome the coming of a steam boat. He tried every argument in his power to get us to turn back down the river. Among other things he said, "This river may fall 20 feet tonight and leave your boat stranded up here." After he found he could not scare us, he became more friendly and gave us some of his life's history.

His name was Willis Hensley, no doubt the same man that lived in a log hut below the mouth of Frene Creek, or in what we call Frenchtown, long before the first German settler came to Hermann more than a hundred years ago. Next we hear and know of him during the Civil War at Hensley Ford on the Gasconade

Capt. Heckmann oversees the loading of wheat sacks aboard the Steamer Royal.

River, the old Fritz Miller farm. He told us that he had moved up the Missouri and Gasconade River seven times to get away from civilization and the German farmers.

We quote his own words as the conversation wound up and we went to bed. Hensley said, "To be honest with you Captain Heckmann, I do not want your boats to come up here. I have moved up the Missouri and Gasconade rivers seven times to get away from the German farmers, as you call them. I call them Dutch, and if your d— boats keep coming up here I will have to move again and I am too old for that. One can still catch a few beaver, mink and coon here, so please take your old boat and stay away."

At that time my father was 41 years old. Mr. Hensley was over eighty. His story tallies and the writer believes he was one of the first men to live in and see the beautiful site of our beloved Hermann.

Father promised to never come back with his boat and he never did, which leaves to him the honor and historical fact that the steamer Royal, in charge of the Dutch Captain was the one and only steamboat that ever made a trip to this

50-mile stretch of river on the upper reaches of the picturesque Gasconade.

Mary tackled the work on the boats with gusto. She sometimes went along as cook and trained her daughters to do the same. Both Annie, not quite 14, and Lizzie, not quite 12, cooked on the Vienna. Business must have been a little slack in June because Capt. Will took two parties from St. Louis for a big hunt. But by July it was all hands on deck. *All boats have all they can do, wheat is coming in fast. There are today twelve boat loads waiting for them. River is low and ground hard and dry, everybody is praying for rain.*

The family was pleasantly surprised by a visit from George Husmann, the man who had brought the Miller family to Missouri in 1867. The newspaper reported, *Mr. George Husmann, formerly a resident of Hermann and widely known as a horticulturist, pomologist and wine grower, was here for several days last week. Mr. Husmann is a gifted talker and we should not at all be surprised if he had not induced some of our wine-growers to follow him to his home, in Napa, California.*

In October the Vienna sank right at the Hermann levee, but was raised the following day and was soon back in working order. According to Mary, *She had been idle for sometime and was dry, no one thought to look into the hull and there was no watchman on her so the outside at the engineer house was two feet under water.*

The F.F.F. Club still managed to make a little news. The revelers were caught in a bad storm, and their steamboat had to take refuge under the Gasconade railroad bridge. Another storm blew the Fawn high and dry on a sandbar at Bluffton. Nonetheless, the excursions remained popular.

Going Fishing with a Brass Band!

The steamer Fawn will excurt up the Gasconade river next Sunday and anyone who has thirty-five cents to pay for his passage and a few worms to do a little plain fishing is invited. The Apostle Band will furnish the music.

Mary had overcome her aversion to steamboats, but she still disliked Hermann's excessive drinking and found the citizenry's German ways just too much to tolerate at times. The town was celebrating the 50th anniversary of its founding. Ever the organizer, Louis Rincheval planned a moonlight excursion to Portland as part of the celebration. Mary's comments about the whole affair were less than complimentary.

Tonight is intended to be a great day for Hermann, but the first, middle and end of it all is the drinking of as much beer and wine as all can hold. ... Yesterday, because it was Friday, could not do for the day proper, so they fired a 50-gun salute. That is they were to, but the old cannon busted on the 48th shot, and that put an end to one more of my enemies, peace be to its pieces. ...Tonight they had a torch light procession, got up only tolerably good, like everything done here. ...I done nothing for I always do all I can and could not put in any extra work.

Mary's "enemy" cannon was stationed on the courthouse bluff just above Wharf Street, so the shots were fired right over the Heckmann home. *On every occasion they were firing the old thing, making one nervous as long as the shooting lasted.*

The Leimer/Heckmann property had been sold to Martin Olman for $3,500, and the Heckmanns had moved to the Jordan house, better known as the Pete Miller house, at the east end of Wharf Street next to the White House Hotel. The move was done piecemeal and for a time the family had shivered in a damp house that had only one stove. The new house proved a most dangerous place to be. Mary wrote:

GRAND
Fishing Excursion

ON SUNDAY JUNE 14, 1885
—UP THE—
Gasconade River
to Turnpike and return

The Celebrated APOSTLE BAND is engaged for this occasion. The Boat will leave Loutre Island at 7 o'clock, Hermann at 7:30 A.M. and stop at all landings. Passengers will be taken on board at any place if proper signals are given.

The trip will be extended as far as Turnpike, provided the stage of water will permit.

Refreshments and Eatables of all kinds will be served on the boat and the management will do everything in their power to make the trip an enjoyable one for everybody.

ROUND TRIP TICKETS from Hermann, 35 cents; from Gasconade 25 cents; proportionate sums will be charged from other landings. The fishing season is at hand and that sport will no doubt, be indulged in to a great extend. Have your your hooks and lines ready and bring plenty of bait.

Everybody is cordially invited.
LOUIS RINCHEVAL.

We heard a terrible thundering and clapping noise, as though there were a terrible explosion, not only once, but three times in succession. William was sitting reading, he jumped up and looked up and down, and started down. I ran out too and across to the butcher's, asked her what it was, she said a gasoline explosion, and just at that, she cried, "Oh, look at Gussie." The poor fellow was so badly burned, they carried him home and in much less time than I can write it the White House wash house was one blaze. It seemed to me ages until the fire company got the engine at work, then after starting it they had to take it to the river and pump water from there. With hard work, they succeeded in saving some of the White House, about one-third,

the third story is burned out, the second badly damaged and the first in toler-
able good shape. All things were taken out but so many things broken and
damaged. The whole corner, Ettmullers office and drug store, Monnigs where
it started and the White House are all gone, also the corners. They had leveled
all the walls of the Monnig property today, it was very shocking. There are
some hopes of little Pfautsch getting well. When Annie, Kate and Alice came
home they were dumb-founded at the looks of things.

The riverfront held many dangers, especially for children. The newspaper
reported:

While some boys were playing on a rack heap that had lodged near the U. S.
water gauge, Richard Storck happened to slip and fall into the river, and but for
the timely aid rendered him by some of the boys, would have found a watery
grave. We have often wondered how the urchins fooling around the river escape
drowning—they are so extremely reckless.

It may have been Heckmann boys who came to the victim's rescue. Their
father had taught them to swim by the very effective method of rowing them
out into the river a considerable distance, pitching them overboard and saying,
"Now swim you young pup!"

Settlement of the insurance claims from the big fire was protracted. But by
the end of September, 1886, the White House Hotel was again under roof. In the
meantime the newspaper was giving free publicity to the Concert Hall Garden,
located just behind the Heckmann house.

There is probably not a more delightful spot in all the town to while away a few
pleasant hours than the Concert Hall Garden. Summerhouses, beautiful flow-
ers, shrubbery, gravel walks, in fact all that can reasonably be expected, have
been provided for the convenience of the guests, and the refreshments served are
of the very best quality.

A grand party was staged in November for the reopening of the White House
Hotel, with music by the Apostle Band. But if the Heckmanns attended, Mary
made no mention of it. The newspaper reported, *The formal opening of the White*
House last Saturday eve was an event which will long be remembered by all present. The
proceeds of the sale of tickets was $200, which amount has been added to the fund for the
purchase of a town clock.

At about the same time, Capt. Henry Heckmann, who left the steamboat
business after the Washington burned while he was at the wheel, opened a res-

An 1885 outing on the Steamer Royal. Tree branches were taken along to provide shade for the excursionists.

taurant. The newspaper reported, *Heckmann's Lunch Room, on Schiller, next to Leisner's furniture store, is now in apple-pie order, and open to the public. The location as well as the management is admirable, and all those who want a good nice lunch on short notice will find this the right place.*

The year ended well for Mary. *We had a nice tree for Christmas, every one who sees it thinks it nice.* In January the Harmonie had a Masque Ball, declared by many to be one of the finest affairs ever "gotten up" in Hermann—better even than the White House Hotel party. Mary and Will stayed at the ball until after midnight, even though Will was leaving on the Fawn at 6 the next morning. Mary reported that the affair was *very good*. This, for her, was praise of the highest order.

CHAPTER 10

In Sickness and in Health

Did we but know when an accident is about to happen
there would not be many of them. —Mary L. Heckmann

*T*he young girl who had left Pennsylvania in tears was now a strong woman, devoted to her husband and children and reconciled to steamboating as a way of life. Mary's life was good in most respects—money was more plentiful, and she was making many friends.

Jan 1, 1887—Another new year at hand, as we grow older how short the years seem, the Seasons seem to chase one another. Today was a beautiful day, not a cloud to mar the beautiful sky, but so cold. How I pity the poor unfortunates who have no good bed to sleep in, neither fuel enough to keep them warm. This morning the mercury was at 4 degrees, at noon.

The intense cold made washing difficult, but now Mary could afford to hire some help.

I washed part of the wash and sent the rest to Mary P. ... It is so cold now, we changed beds with the four girls. They sleep in our bed and we sleep next to the stove, as the little pet has such a bad cold. We cannot keep half comfortable in the big room, we eat breakfast and supper in the little south room.

The Missouri River was even more treacherous in winter than in summer. The entire town was shaken by the drowning death of John Land. The "Advertiser-Courier" gave this account:

One of those sad accidents that sometimes occur and which arouse the whole community, happened Saturday afternoon on the river, resulting in the drowning of John Land and a narrow escape from a similar fate of Wm. Monnig. Saturday morning Land and Monnig started from here across the river to attend the auction sale at the late Hill Lee's place.

Soon afterwards it began to rain and the large volume of water which flowed into the river caused the ice along the shore to become rotten and covered with water.

About 2 o'clock, Land and Monnig on their way home endeavored to get on the ice on the opposite bank, but it was with great difficulty and after breaking in several times that they succeeded, Land remarking, "Never mind, Billy, the ice along shore is always bad, it is better further on."

Land, who carried a long pole or slat, led the way and Monnig, who had lost his pole in the first struggle, following about ten steps behind. After being about fifty yards from shore, Monnig looked up and saw Land in a swaying motion and disappearing. He at once turned to the shore but also broke in and it was only after a most desperate struggle that he regained the ice and shore and from there Steck's store, where he was immediately put to bed.

In the meantime, Henry Tekotte and Peter Hans, also were on their way homeward from the opposite shore, out on the ice but further below. They saw a cap and pole laying on the ice further up, but being ignorant of the sad calamity which befell Land, they paid no attention to the same. It was then when Mr. Steck and others came from the store and shouted to them to be careful, that Land was drowned. Tekotte and Hans safely reached this shore and imparted the sad intelligence which spread from one end of the town to the other like wild-fire and was the only topic of conversation for the day.

Boats, as well as people, fell victim to the ice. Unlucky as ever, the Dora was the subject of a report in the "Franklin County Times."

The steamer Dora, which was sunken in the mouth of Charette Creek in the recent break-up of ice, was raised this week, and on Thursday the steamer May Bryan towed her down to the wharf of this city. The Dora is a good deal of a wreck. Everything above the lower deck is gone except the boilers and engines and they seem to be in a pretty dilapidated condition.

There is a big hole in her hull, which appears to be twisted out of shape. We learn that the owners have saved and can use nearly all the material of which the boat was composed, so that the loss is probably not so heavy as the appearance of the wreck would indicate.

The Hermann paper reported that Capt. Heckmann had successfully raised the Dora and that the damage was estimated at $1,000. The rebuilt boat was ready for business by May 1. Mary's journals recorded not a word of the calamity. William had the good sense to sell the ill-fated Dora to the Washington Ferry Company. She was finally destroyed by a fire caused by a lamp explosion in her boiler room, but not before sinking one last time. The "Franklin County Times" reported:

Last Friday morning when the steamer Dora was nearly opposite Tuque Creek on the Warren county side of the Missouri River coming down, towing a barge having on board about 1,500 sacks of wheat belonging to various farmers in Warren county, the barge ran onto a concealed snag or log, careened over and almost immediately sank with its cargo. The wheat lost is of the value of over $2,000, and although it has nearly all been recovered in a damaged condition it will bring but very little. The injury to the barge, the loss of the use of it, and the expense of saving it and the damaged wheat will make the loss foot up about $4,000. There was no insurance. Divers from St. Louis are here trying to raise the barge, but so far without success.

A delegation of the owners of the wheat were here last Wednesday trying to induce the Washington Ferry Company to pay them for their loss. The company insists that under the terms of its bills of lading, it is not liable, while the shippers insist that the contract in the bills of lading does not by its terms cover shipments on barges. Whether the company and the shippers will finally succeed in making a compromise without litigation is uncertain.

The true ownership of the various boats operated by the Hermann Ferry and Packet Co. is not entirely clear. Capt. Heckmann had leased the Dora to Washington to serve as a ferry, and Capt. Wohlt had leased the Royal to other ferry interests. Both transactions probably were due to lack of sufficient freight to keep the boats busy locally.

The general structure of the business was casual. Certainly, both the Wohlt and Heckmann interests had stock in all the boats. It was common practice to keep loans on the boats—financial records note various amounts borrowed, paid and borrowed again. Mary never mentioned these transactions, but like all the wives she signed loan papers again and again.

Steamboat Bill later wrote about his father's business dealings. *The boats were making good money and the cash kept rolling in, despite the fact Father had a quarter of the capital stock of the old Hermann Savings Bank borrowed for some 15 years, besides what he borrowed from his kin and friends. He even could get a loan from his worst enemy, and he had lots of them.*

With spring and a full river the steamboat trade picked up. The Royal and the Vienna left for the upper Gasconade where the bulk of the previous year's crop of wheat was awaiting shipment. *Everything looks as if the steamboat business this Spring will eclipse everything else*, reported the newspaper. *The steamer Royal left for the upper Gasconade, having on board all the appliance necessary for the work of pulling snags, and making the river navigable. The work is done by the Government and under the immediate supervision of Civil Engineer Beemann and Capt. Heckmann. ... The steamers Royal and Vienna have, since navigation opened, brought into this port about 15,000 bushels of wheat and all from along the Gasconade river, sometimes 5,000 sacks per day.*

Massive quantities of ties and lumber also were being shipped out of the Gasconade. William contracted to take about 35,000 railroad ties down the Missouri River to St. Charles for use in the construction of the new Missouri Central Railroad.

Indeed, it was a time of plenty along the banks of the Gasconade. Three Williams—Will Sr., Will Jr. and Billy Wild—came home with 35 ducks, two squirrels and a turkey, and Mary and daughter Annie had an all-day job of cleaning them. Annie later claimed one of the reasons she married young was to get away from the eternal work of the Heckmann household.

This also may have been a factor in Tina's early marriage as well, but it certainly did not influence her family size—she produced 11 children of her own. A few days after the duck cleaning, Tina came down on the boat and *found us cleaning house, we got the best three rooms pretty nearly done*, with Tina's help no doubt. Afterward, the women went visiting. Mary later wrote in exasperation, *Georgie can run around like the rest of them, he began walking three days before he was eleven months old. He keeps us in a stew, every time a door is opened he slips out.*

The Heckmann family had its share of mishaps. *Will is at home with a cut foot. He was up the Gasconade river a week, gathering up ties and logs, and was pulling out the last ties when he struck his foot instead of the tie. It is doing as well as can be. In April*

Mary penned a detailed account of a fishing trip that nearly ended in disaster.

We all went on the Vienna for a fishing trip up the Gasconade. We took eatables, bedding and all the children. We got to the stopping place about noon. William had a bad spell, he keeps getting worse all day until evening he got relief and slept well all night, but in the morning he was still too weak to go fishing up to the head of Round Island.

We lay opposite Round Island, just a little below where the slough comes out. ... I went down stairs to wash out some clothes for the children. I took Georgie with me, as Annie and Lizzie were washing the breakfast dishes. Eddie, Lottie and Martha were down on the lower deck too. Greeley and Oscar came along with the empty skiff, and I said, take Georgie and I for a ride. When I was in Bob wanted to go too, so we pulled up to Greeley's line and were going to get Ed, he kept calling we were to take him. When we got to the Vienna, as Greeley stepped out he capsized the skiff.

All I could remember until I was pulled out, I seen the skiff full of water, next the water gurgling down my throat, only sense enough left to shut my mouth. Some one had me by the hair, and again at the arm, then I got my head above water and seen the skiff laying on its side and Oscar standing in it. I caught the upper side and nearly threw Oscar in again, he had got in the skiff with a little help from Greeley.

Annie says when she heard the children scream, she looked and I was just going under the water. By the time she got here Greeley had me by the hair. A second after William got down, he did not know how, but his knees were all skinned up awfully. He got a hold on me and had to reach as far as he could to get Georgie, as I had him in my left arm, all the time until Greeley got me by the hair. I think I let go my hold, Georgie was sinking slowly. Annie caught Bob by the arm as he came up, after William had pulled Georgie out and helped Annie pull Bob out they pulled me out. After several seconds I got up myself, and then I only realized that the children had gone in too. There stood my little innocent pet dripping wet, and Bob screaming for dear life because he was so wet. I felt very weak all day, but it did not hurt any of us.

There is no suffering while in the water, it seems as though all the senses were benumbed. I was very near half-drowned but I cannot say there is any suffering. The worst is when you strike the water.

The narrow escape made a profound impression on Mary and others—she was asked to repeat the "swimming story" time and again.

In the toe of the one slipper that went down and came up with me, will be found the same chronicle of our fishing trip. Together with some other articles, kept for a memento of the event. I thank God every moment that he saved us all, for had my children been lost I would not only have felt the loss, but self-reproach, for being so fool-hardy. I should have taken better care, about balancing the skiff. Did we but know when an accident is to happen there would not be many of them.

Mary's tale of the fishing trip wasn't the only fascinating story making the rounds in Hermann. Julia Heckmann, daughter of Henry Heckmann, had married Gustave Wohlt and was a highly respected matron in Hermann society. She found herself in a strange situation, which the newspaper took particular delight in reporting.

A somewhat interesting and, to the parties concerned, a very important trial took place in Squire Scharff's court at the Market House in this town last Saturday. The facts appear from the records as follows: Mrs. Christine Baer had publicly and in the presence of various persons charged Mrs. Julia Wohlt, wife of Gustave Wohlt, with having stolen some money from her residence.

When Mr. Wohlt heard that reports were being circulated about his wife he very naturally became indignant and immediately consulted attorneys, the result of which was that an information was filed by the prosecuting attorney charging Mrs. Baer with falsely and maliciously speaking these slanderous words concerning Mrs. Wohlt. When the case was called for trial Mr. and Mrs. Wohlt were there with their witnesses and attorneys prepared to protect the good name of that lady, but the proceedings were cut short by Mrs. Baer, upon hearing the charges, pleading guilty, thereby admitting in open court that the statements she had made concerning Mrs. Wohlt were false and malicious. Judge Scharff said that considering the severe and groundless nature of the language used by the defendant he would place the fine at twenty-five dollars and costs. We make special mention of this case hoping that it may be a warning to those who are disposed to recklessly slander the good name of their neighbors.

The Heckmann house on Wharf Street was full-to-overflowing with people.

Relatives came for extended visits. Mary's brothers, who had brought a raft of cedar logs downriver, stayed with their sister. Hunters came and remained overnight. Even steamboat crew members sometimes ate with the family.

The situation was remedied in February of 1887 when William paid $3,000 for the Langendoerfer place, a fine, two-story brick home on West Second Street. Finally, there was room for all. Located high on a bluff overlooking the Missouri River, the property covered an entire city block and included a large vineyard. Mary was ecstatic. A home of her own, and a large one at that, with room for the children to roam without being forever on the railroad tracks or at the river's edge was a dream come true.

April 1, Easter Sunday—*I find I have skipped one whole month, March. I will go back and try to catch up some of it. On March 1st we moved up here, and since I have been so busy at one thing and another. We are all as happy as can be and are so glad we bought the place. We were glad too that we picked the day we did, for two weeks after it was very bad weather. Today is a beautiful, clear, calm day. We all had great fun watching all the children hunting Easter Eggs, there were so many places to hide them. We bought the cow and chickens that were here. I have boiled soap that is, some, and partly smoked the meat.*

The newspaper said, *Capt. Bill will now sit under his own vine and fig tree and learn to smoke.*

Mary was still sewing a great deal, but no longer of necessity. For Easter she went to sister-in-law Caroline Silber's shop and bought the children hats and dresses. With room for a garden, her horticultural talents came into full bloom. By mid-April her vegetable garden was planted, and she was awaiting delivery of an additional $6.65 worth of flowers, roses and seeds. *We planted 24 dwarf pear, 8 standard, 6 apple, 1 cherry, 1 plum. The 4 first Dwarf are Louis bou de Jersey, 12 Duchess, 4 standard Vicker Wakefield, Cherry May Duke.*

The Evangelical church bordered the Heckmann property on the east, and the Catholic church was on the next hill to the south. The family gathered in the upper part of the vineyard to listen to the Evangelical's new organ, and from the same vantage point they could watch the Catholics march for Corpus Christi day.

About the same time that Capt. Will Heckmann sold the Dora, Capt. August Wohlt traveled to Paducah, Kentucky, to see about purchasing a large boat from the Memphis Packet Company. Nothing came of the trip, but plans were soon made to build another boat. Capt. Henry Wohlt was in failing health and taking

Perched high above the river and surrounded by vineyards, the Langendoerfer home was a dream come true for Mary.

less interest in the business, but his sons carried on the family tradition.

In early March of 1888, the Wohlt and Heckmann interests sold the steamer Vienna for $2,500 to Frank Blaske and Emilie Struttmann of New Haven to replace the Tilda-Clara, a four-horse ferry. The ferry, in turn, was sold to August Waibel of Glasgow. The steamer Vienna was under the control of E. B. Trail, father of the future Missouri River historian, "Doc" Trail.

The transaction provided sufficient excuse for an excursion. The Fawn left from the Hermann wharf, and the Vienna left from New Haven to rendezvous at a place known as the Berger Bottom. *Each brought a band so it is fair to presume that the occasion will be an enjoyable one,* reported the newspaper.

After selling the Vienna, the Wohlts and Heckmanns set to work in 1888 building the steamer Pin Oak at the Hermann wharf. According to the newspaper, The new *steamer Pin Oak ... has been purposely built to meet the wants of the Gasconade river trade and low water will be no impediment for the boat to reach the various shipping points along the river.*

While the men were giving birth to another steamboat, Mary was giving birth to another baby boy, John Henry, named for his paternal grandfather. The paper made the most of this event, as usual, mentioning only the father.

Capt Wm. L. Heckmann is the happy progenitor of another fine boy, making the total number of his offspring now clustering around the hearthstone twelve, seven boys and five girls. To have an even dozen of children who would acknowledge him as their pap, is an item the Capt. has longed for earnestly, and now that it is a fact his good-natured face beams with happiness as he accepts congratulations.

In contrast, Mary's account of the first baby born in the new house does not mention the father.

July 15—Nearly one month has passed since last writing. Today I write with a darling baby panting and squirming on my lap. He is big, pretty and good. Today, two weeks ago he was born, July 1, at 2:15 p.m. My life nearly paid the penalty, but I am growing nice and strong again, and I thank God for health and my fine boy, the seventh boy to be something great, if only he is good is all I ask.

Mary waited until the end of the year before clearing up the matter of her last birthing. *Our bright boy John was born and I nearly died, when he was ten days old. By mistake, I took linament and nearly strangled.*

Capt. Heckmann had acquired a reputation as a first-rate hunting and fishing guide. The newspaper reported, *The steamer Royal started out on a trip to Linn Creek, Camden Co. on the Osage river her crew are a number of jolly fishermen and hunters from Jefferson City, all intend to stay out a week or two and put in their time in hunting and fishing.*

In October the newspaper reported:

Capt. Wm. L. Heckmann, who a few days ago returned from a hunting and fishing trip laden down with delicious fish and game, bagged the first goose of

The steamers Pin Oak, Fawn and Royal

the season the other day and says he never enjoyed a more toothsome morsel
than the bird furnished. William is always ahead in everything that is good in
this world and knows how to enjoy the blessings showered upon him by a kind
providence.

Mary, meanwhile, was at home battling a diphtheria epidemic. The
Heckmann children came down with the disease in waves, and she lived an
endless nightmare of nursing and praying for their lives. Many people in Hermann lost children to the disease. Mary credited her children's survival to anti-
septic Listerine.

Just when it looked as though the children would all recover, William came
home ill.

William has Bilious fever and was just close on to Typhoid. He is very weak and
has been in bed 17 days. Had he taken typhoid he would not have gotten over it,
as he was too much brokendown in health long before he took sick. He has been
working too hard for his age, the boats have all been so busy the past four weeks,
the folks scarcely get any sleep. As for myself, I have been waiting on the sick so
long and all the worry, everyone wonders that I can keep up. Today I feel as
though my turn had come at last. My head aches, and I feel all broken up. God
should be merciful to a mother that cares for her children as she should and I am
sure I have more than my share.

With the money flowing freely, there were compensations. *I got a new wash machine, a new sewing machine and a new piano all in the past ten days.* And it was an exciting year for national politics.

> *Harrison has won according to yesterday's paper by 65 electoral votes majority.*
>
> *It has been an exciting campaign. The whole theme has been Free Trade and*
>
> *Protection. The understanding in the beginning of the campaign was that there*
>
> *was to be no slander or hard names, but the Democracy was so hard pushed,*
>
> *they first resorted to lies, and then cried "Liar, Thief, Raggle and Rascal."*

Mary happily reported her darning and mending were all done, quite a miracle, and a welcome end the for year.

> *Tonight we are all well. I hope we will be so fortunate in the new year than in*
>
> *this one just past. Still with all the trouble I bear the old year no ill will. In a*
>
> *business way it has been quite a good and indulgent year, so with many regrets,*
>
> *I once more say goodbye to old 1888.*

Young Bill Heckmann continued to have Gasconade River adventures with his father. The little steamer Pin Oak could operate on the upper reaches of the river, making trips to Paydown and beyond when water levels permitted. Shippers were ever on the alert for the sound of a steamboat whistle. Water departed the Ozark hills in a big hurry, and so did the boats. A boat with an unwary captain could easily be stranded.

On one occasion the Pin Oak answered a hale and found John Klebba, a good shipper, with a load of hogs to go. He asked Capt. Heckmann to stop at Hinchie's Shoal to pick up an old boar hog that was too mean and ornery to be driven with the rest. Years later, Steamboat Bill told the tale.

> *When the boat landed at that place we found tied to a big tree one of the worst*
>
> *looking four-footed creatures to be called a hog I ever saw. Picture to yourself a*
>
> *small-sized, lop-eared mule, with monstrous ivory tusks, some eight inches long,*
>
> *sticking up part each side of a big upper jaw, add a hump to his back; then*
>
> *imagine a long black tail the size of a large blacksnake, and you have a fair*
>
> *description of our hero, or what Mr. Klebba called a hog.*
>
> *The first thing dad had done to this so-called hog was to have its jaws tied*
>
> *shut so it could not bite; next he tied a rope around its neck and one to a hind*
>
> *leg. Things went well until they got the "big boy" to the end of the stage, and*
>
> *from here the animal decided not to go any further. Two men had hold of the*
>
> *line on its head, two others each had an ear, another was twisting its tail; and*

dad with Mr. Klebba were bringing up the rear with the tail line. They jerked and pulled, cussed and pleaded, but that old stag was an immovable object. So many husky humans around one poor innocent little hog naturally was a comical sight and the sightseers, the fireman, Erren Eberson and myself made the mistake of laughing. Both Old Rough Head and that old hog were getting warmed up now and when the former saw us grinning, he bellowed "Get out here Erren, you too, you darn little pup up there in the pilot house; we've got to get this doggone beast aboard that boat and down the river."

When Erren got out on the bank he said, "You'll have to weight him down. I'll ride him." So saying, he climbed on the old hog's back and got a hold of each ear. "Get up here young Bill," and I climbed aboard too and put my arms around his waist. Again they marshalled all their forces but that brute still stayed stationary. "Put that line on the steam capstan, we'll pull him on board or break his stubborn neck," bellowed Old Rough Head. They gave one good yank, which parted the main head line. The old hog saw his chance, and made a flying leap sideways, shook the men loose from his ears and flopped his tail.

Dad and Klebba could not hold the brute with the tail line and that hog started home with the two of us on his back. Up Buck Elk Hill we went, right through a paling fence, then up hill through the deer woods toward Paydown, Mo., 12 miles beyond. The boys in the Argonne Forest had nothing on us except that their fight lasted longer. Up through the post-oaks, the hazelnut bushes, grapevines, and briers we went, scratched, bloody and torn. Erren cried, "Bill, we've got to get off of here before this hawg starts down hill, we're going 60 miles an hour up this mountain; watch his smoke when he starts down the grade."

Steamboat Bill concluded the story by remembering that he and Erren did tumble off the hog. There they sat, bleeding but with no broken bones, contemplating the fact that "Old Rough Head" was back at the boat, waiting impatiently to get down the river. In the distance, they could hear the demanding *toot, toot, toot* of the Pin Oak's whistle.

"Hurry up! What did you do with that hog?" Capt. Heckmann shouted when the two injured fellows finally reappeared. "Do with him?" they replied. "Why not ask what he done to us?"

The first really ardent proponent for the temperance cause, a Dr. Brooks, showed up in Hermann, determined that Gasconade County was the darkest spot in Missouri and convinced that Hermann was hermetically sealed against any temperance advocate. Mary made no mention of this man, but the newspaper did—and he was hanged in effigy by the incensed townspeople. He later said, *They did not murder me, but it was not for the absence of willingness nor a desire to do so, but simply cowardice and the fear of consequences. They hung me in effigy and would have hung me in reality but for reasons indicated.*

George Pryor, proprietor of the Pryor Mill on the Gasconade River, was famous as a world-class litigator, once even showing up in Hermann on Christmas Day, complaining that court was not in session. According to the "Linn Liberalist," *The suit of Wm. Heckmann and August Wohlt, of Hermann, Mo., against G. W. Pryor, to recover $500 and interest on a promissory note was settled and dismissed this week.* This suit was in the Osage County Court at Linn, Mo. This was far from the last the Heckmanns were to hear of George Pryor.

Fritz Lang, the business manager of the Ferry Company, was a small man about whom a puckish reporter wrote, *When Capt. Heckmann & Fritz Lang walked up from the wharf to the White House some envious cuss alluded to the combine as the long and the short of the Hermann Ferry and Packet Company.* In July of 1888, the newspaper wrote:

This is confidential to a few of Fritz Lang's friends. He is to be married on the 12th of this month and we do not care to give the matter too much publicity. Never mind the lady's name, but we ask the gang, in the interest of harmony, to go slow. Forget, in your glad surprise, the horse-fiddle and deathdealing tin pan. Give it to him light. Don't fill him up with "barbed wire" that paralyses and afterwards deluge him with the sweet sounds of the charivari that annihilates. Remember that he is an orphan. P.S. It shouldn't cost him less than fifty bucks.

It was the custom of the black population from the north side of the river to celebrate Emancipation Day every year with a picnic at the city park. The Royal transported the crowd in several trips, both morning and evening. In August of 1888, the boat also went to Jefferson City to bring the celebrants from there to Hermann.

Just before Christmas the entire Heckmann family was marshaled together for a family portrait. With no electric lights there was a wait of several days until sunshine appeared one morning. The picture was taken, and the clouds rolled back in again. This was the round-dozen picture, counting Tina. Little did they suspect that three more Heckmann children would follow. Perhaps Mary expected it to be *the* picture of the family.

Mary welcomed the new year of 1889.

Beautiful clear day, slight wind, temperature about 40. Lizzie and I and some of the rest took a smoked glass and went up on the hill to look at the Eclipse of the sun. Watched it go down behind the hill, it was only 4/5th eclipsed, as the hill began to hide it from us it appeared like a horn of fire.

Having access to newspapers was a real luxury for Mary, and she often reported on the daily news. On May 31,1889, she told of one of the calamities of history.

The city of Johnstown, Pa. was almost wiped out of existence by the dam bursting above the city. It is claimed there were 12,000 people lost by drowning and burning. One of the stone bridges withstood the jam and there most of the wreck stopped. The water rushed over the bridge and more women and children were just poured over and under the bridge in a stream. Houses took fire and others were burned to death. One engine was carried some miles by the rush of water and set down as though it had not been touched. One passenger car was taken out of a train and everyone drowned. Some, yes many, families are entirely wiped out. There is a margin of thousands between the living and those found dead. The whole thing is almost beyond comprehension. Hence the 31st of May, 1889 will be known as "Black Friday."

A new boat was being built at Hermann, but not by the Wohlts or the Heckmanns. It was reported that the owners were Messrs. Feagen and Iven of Osage County, and the stockholders were farmers along the Gasconade River. It is unclear whether they were dissatisfied with the Hermann boats or just saw an opportunity to cash in on this lucrative business.

The wonder was that another group of novices again built a boat—and it ran. The machinery went in place in late December of 1889, but the boat did not pass inspection because of the hull being too frail. By January 15 of 1890 the matter had been remedied and the Annie Dell left for the Gasconade River with Capt. Wm. Towns in command.

Fishing excursions were still a source of interest to the local scribes.

The fishing excursions are getting ready for the upper Gasconade and members of the party are buying those standard works, Gulliver's Travels, Baron Munchhausen and Robinson Crusoe, and they hope to be so proficient in the

123

William and Mary Heckmann pose with their children for the "Round Dozen" photo. Older children are, from left, Samuel (seated), Fred, William Jr., Tina, Annie, Martha (seated), Lizzie (standing) and Lottie. The three little boys at their father's knee are George (in white), Edward and Robert (seated). John, the baby of the family, is on his mother's lap.

science of prevarication by the time they return that they will be able to make individual records. We shall hear how they slept in old log farmhouses, where they found the old fashioned fireplace, the old fashioned highposted and rope-corded bed, the old fashioned bedbug and the old fashioned hospitality of an honest God-fearing people. It is said that the Gasconade river has one grievous fault and some day it will have to grievously answer it. It graduates more fish liars than any stream its size in the United States.

The Heckmann brothers, William and Henry, were loyal members of the G.A.R. (Grand Army of the Republic) and both headed the Manwaring Post at Hermann at different times. In 1889 the state encampment arrangements were left to these two steamboat men, so naturally an excursion resulted.

The committee in charge of the arrangements for the Excursion arranged by the Manwaring Post G.A.R. of this place to be held on the 14th of this month, are working like beavers to get everything in first class shape and feel greatly encouraged in their work by the favor it meets on every hand. They have made arrangements with the Apostle Band, and Schaumberg's string band to furnish the music for this occasion. The Apostle Band will render their most favorite airs and we are told they will include in their selections many pieces which will awaken memories of ye olden times with the boys who wore the blue and those of their friends who remember the stirring days of '61 to '65. Schaumberg's string band so favorably known for their most excellent dancing music will keep up their end of the line and those desiring to enjoy good square or round dance will alike be pleased by the variety of melodies with which the gentlemen composing this band will favor them during the trip and in camp.

Mary went along and had a wonderful time, visiting the State House and seeing about plants. But she returned home to find cow trouble again. *Thursday our old cow was taken to the island —Wohlt's island, and I got a new milker from there. She killed her calf by lying on it and we had a great deal of trouble with her.*

William Sr. and William Jr. went to St. Louis to get young Will his first pilot's license. Mary reported, *He would have gotten them, but was found color blind.* The problem surfaced again later when Ed and Norman also turned out to be color blind. Ed claimed he could pass the yarn test and got by, and Norman stuck to the engine room where color did not matter.

Color blind or not, both Will Jr. and Ed were pilots all of their lives. Will Jr.

finally received his license in September, but nothing was said about how he managed this feat. Later, as a married man and father, young Will purchased an umbrella for his daughter Monica to match her new pink Easter dress. The umbrella was bright green.

In February the Heckmann children came down with influenza. Once again, Mary was nursing.

In all, nine of them have had it. Will and I are the only ones that escaped, so there were ten counting Tina that had it. All of Tina's family and all of the Millers at Bluffton were down with it. I hope we have seen the last of it and may never hear of it again. Last evening I was ready to go to the theater in town. Folks got one up for the Clock fund. At 7 o'clock both boats came in. I staid home, and the three girls and Sam went and they were well pleased. Brother John came down with the boat and went along to the theater too. Johnny and I had our photos taken about three weeks ago. They are good. Our flowers are doing excellent.

Competition from the Annie Dell may have been the reason the Ferry Company decided to expand its territory. The paper reported that Captain Heckmann purchased a small tract of land just above the ferry landing at Chamois and was talking of building a large warehouse on it. Rip-rapping to stop the ravages of the river at this point also was planned. Mary added her bit to this information. *Our folks are having a side track put in at Chamois and will establish a transfer there. The Portland folks are savage about it.*

The long-awaited Missouri Kansas and Texas Railroad (the "Katy") was going in on the north side of the river. The townspeople of Portland dreamed of finally getting their share of the river freight. A new railroad loading point just across the river was not a welcome thought.

Afternoon callers were becoming regular events for Mary. Usually she was pleased, especially when any of the Lessel family came. Grandma Lessel was a good and dear friend. One unexpected visitor, the wife of one of the original promoters of the Bluffton winery, did not fare so well with 18-year-old Annie and 10-year-old Lottie. *Mrs. Wesselhoeft paid us an unexpected visit. She did not make a very favorable impression on the girls, and I am afraid they did not on her either.*

The house was thoroughly cleaned, a new carpet was bought and installed and a bake oven and two kettles were walled in. Mary fussed that the brick layer *pottered at it in all about three weeks. And still there is some pavement to lay. Neither of the brick yards had brick until yesterday we got some again.* A well digger was called, and in September they finished the well. *Only went 103 feet and we have good water now.*

The summer was scorching hot, and the rains did not come. The garden dried up, and there was no water. The Gasconade River boats were in trouble, and even the ferry was in dire straits. The newspaper lamented:

On account of the low water stage in the Missouri the ferryboat will, for the time being, make but two trips daily to Loutre Island and return instead of four as heretofore. In order to reach Loutre Island landing from here the boat is compelled to make a circumnavigation of about the distance of three miles around the sandbars that have obstructed the channel of this place.

Before the end of the year, the ferry had shut down altogether. Several skiffs were offering means to communicate with the other side of the river.

The town of Hermann held a German Day celebration, but Mary was unimpressed.

Two weeks ago the Germans celebrated their, as they call it, German Day, but for the life of me I cannot see what these people born in Germany, have to make a fuss of what German immigration of two hundred years ago did for this country. It stands to reason that it was none of their forefathers done any of the pioneer work of America, and we who know that our ancestors were the first Germans here are too loyal to our country to give Germany any great honor. Never-the-less, Lizzie and George were Indians in the parade.

The St. Louis newspaper carried a bit of encouraging news.

The United States has today a smaller debt than any country except Germany. The regular interest bearing debt now amounts to only about $629,000,000. Of this sum $61,000,000 is in 4 1/2 per cent bonds, which mature on September 1, 1891, and $568,000,000 is in 4 per cent, which becomes payable at the option of the government on July 1, 1897. This is the whole of the national indebtedness which is any burden to the people, says an exchange, for the $346,000,000 greenbacks are virtually a debt in name only, and the $65,000,000 bonds of the Pacific railways are not, in the rigid sense an obligation of the nation.

Babies arrived at the Heckmann house so often that the event was barely noted. *Nov. 18, at 3 a.m. a little boy came to our house, we will call him Joseph Culver. He is just as good as can be.* To celebrate, William left for a long hunting trip.

Mary had always started a new journal on January 1, but the first entry of

1891 occurred on March 1.

Never before has my Journal been neglected so long. Perhaps it is because I have another baby to care for, and perhaps it is because William subscribed to the St. Louis Globe Democrat and because we have a horse and I have been out buggy riding when I could have written. But really I had not the slightest idea that three months had passed since I wrote a line. My baby is sweet and good, only he seems weak in his back. Last week he was quite sick, threatened with pneumonia. He still has a bad cough but he seems to be growing all the time.

Will brought brother John's horse Pete, and William got us a buggy. John left for the West, last we heard of him he was in Idaho.

The baby, whose name had been changed from Joseph Culver to Joseph Leising, continued to be the main topic of the journal entries, and the news was never good. *Our dear baby is still troubled with a cough, I scarcely know what to think of it. Sometimes I think he has whooping cough. I feel so badly too of losing so much sleep.*

March 22—Once more I have seen one of my children about to slip from my grasp. On Tuesday my dear little baby was taken with such a fever, that by 3 o'clock he had a slight spasm. The Dr. just happened to be here and we soon had the fever reduced, but all through the night the little lamb had spells of suffocation. Thank God, he is much better and I hope will soon be well.

April 12—Little Joe is often quite sick, he seems to have malaria besides the bad cough he has. I have made garden, have a patch up on Ruediger's lots and yesterday had all the flower beds made up. I only put out a few flowers, the trees are nearly in bloom. Easter fell on March 27th. It rained so the children did not have their usual fun, had to hunt eggs in the garret.

April 29—For the first time in my married life I have to chronicle the death of one of our children. Dear little Joe was real sick in all seven weeks. He did not seem to suffer much. Saturday 18th of April, he grew worse fast. About 9 o'clock he opened his dear eyes for the last time. William spoke to him and he looked up, after that he never looked at any of us. We gave him up at 8 o'clock but he lingered until the first stroke of 12 midnight.

I feel reconciled to my fate. I know I have a sweet little angel in Heaven, not dead but gone before. The Lord giveth, the Lord taketh away, blessed be the name of the Lord. Our angel was taken just when everything was in full bloom, all our trees were laden with blossoms. Everyone seemed very kind. Father, Mother, John, Gert and Tina were here from Bluffton for the funeral. We laid our darling in the cruel grave, Monday, April 20th.

Little Joe, In Heaven no larger will I grow,

But any kind Angel will know

When you call for your own little Joe at the Gate.

CHAPTER 11

For Richer or Poorer

*Everyone says they had a grand time and cannot get done
talking about the cakes.* —Mary L. Heckmann

*I*n 1892 the town of Hermann was in a promotional frenzy. A town clock finally had been installed in the bell tower of the German School, civic leaders
were promoting a pontoon bridge for the Missouri River, and Stone Hill Winery
was building a huge new cellar.

Across the river at the Loutre Island ferry landing, the Hermann Ferry and
Packet Company was building its largest boat yet. The steamer Gasconade was
107 feet long, 23 feet at the beam and 3.5 feet deep. According to the "Waterways
Journal," *she had white pine gunwales and her head, stern, bottom, knuckles and grub
streak were built out of three and four-inch selected hill white oak without a knot or sign
of sap to be found in same.*

Perrin Kay and Joe Shepperd were the main ship carpenters on the job.
Steamboat historian E. B. "Doc" Trail described Kay as *perhaps the most versatile
man ever connected with steamboats. He could build a boat complete, install all the
machinery and then capably man every position on the boat. No wonder the little steamer
Gasconade had class in her from stem to stern.*

The "Advertiser-Courier" waxed eloquent and thought the new boat would
be *as fine a craft as ever plied the waters of the Gasconade and the Missouri ... the
largest and finest running on our local waters.* The launching on May 4 was accompanied by more fanfare than usual. Mary, who by now was thoroughly

enjoying the steamboating life, invited several of her friends to go along to see the show. Mayor Leisner made what the newspaper called a short and appropriate speech, after which the guests and the Apostle Band boarded the Fawn and the Royal, which towed the new boat to the Hermann wharf.

By July 8, 1891, the steamer Gasconade had been duly inspected and accepted by the Custom House officers. The hoopla over the new boat continued.

She afterwards made a trial trip up and down the river, having on board such of our citizens as desired to take a pleasure ride. The inspectors and all other competent judges pronounce the Gasconade the best constructed boat ever built at this part of the state. The proprietors of the Ferry Co. deserve and have the appreciated thanks for their energy and enterprise in this matter.

The "Waterways Journal" would continue to sing the Gasconade's praises.

This boat came out of the Gasconade River loaded with 1,400 sacks of wheat and had the steamer Pin Oak, which had broken down, in tow. The Pin Oak had 900 sacks of wheat aboard. This was the largest trip on record down the Gasconade river. The piloting on this trip was done by Capt. William L. Heckmann, Sr. and no finer piece of work was ever accomplished on that creek they call a river.

While in charge of William L. Heckmann, Jr. this boat took 50,000 railroad ties, 200,000 feet of lumber and 1,000 cords of wood out of the Aux Vasse River, an even smaller stream than the Gasconade.

While in charge of Capt. Archie Bryan she boated lumber, some one-quarter million feet, from Sunshine Landing on the upper Missouri River to Jefferson City Penitentiary, 170 miles down stream. Capt. Bryan also did a lot of towing with this boat for the Missouri River Commission from Sioux City, Iowa, to the mouth of the Missouri. John Gilliam and Sam Heckmann were with Capt. Bryan as steersmen.

The Hermann Ferry and Packet Company kept the Gasconade for 11 years and then sold her for more than she cost to build. In the 11 years the Ferry Co. operated the Gasconade, they spent less than $700 on upkeep and repairs, and she never turned a wheel without bringing in some "bacon."

In 1896 the steamer Gasconade made history at the scene of yet another Gasconade River bridge disaster. A westbound freight was stopped for water at Gasconade City when its caboose, which was on the bridge, was struck from behind by another westbound train. The collision caused the bridge's second span to the east to give way and plummet into the river 35 feet below, taking with it six railroad cars.

The calamity was second only to the great bridge disaster of 1855. Miraculously, no lives were lost, but the railroad company estimated the damage at more than $150,000. Stranded passengers climbed down ladders to the steamer Gasconade, which transported them to the other side of the river where they climbed another ladder to board a waiting westbound train.

Another little boat, the gasoline steamer Jumbo, built at the Hermann wharf by Gustave Honnig and his brother, also made news. In May, the brand new Jumbo ran on a snag at Figler's ford above Powell's dam on the Gasconade and sank in five feet of water. She had 200 sacks of wheat on board, which were taken off by the other boats. *Heavy rains caused the river to rise rapidly and for several days the boat was "out of sight" as the boys put it,* reported the newspaper.

The Jumbo was raised and put back into commission, but a month later she was in trouble again. *Gustave Honnig of the gasoline engine boat Jumbo was arrested for violation of the revenue laws and taken to St Louis. Honnig was selling beer and whiskey from the boat to the people living along the river.*

August Wohlt, whom the court had appointed as receiver, advertised that the Jumbo would be sold at the Hermann wharf for cash to the highest bidder. *This is an excellent opportunity to get a good serviceable boat at a bargain,* stated the notice. *The boat is suitable for a small ferry or can be rigged for a short packet.*

In the same issue some wag voiced his opinion of the Missouri River.

Talk about filters! Just eat a quart of Missouri River water, and stand in the sun for five minutes and you will find the aforesaid water coming out of every pore, beautifully filtered, while your stomach becomes converted into a sand bag and you can hear the gravel rattle as you walk.

The Jumbo was not the first boat involved in peddling libations to settlers along the Gasconade River. Steamboat Bill told this tale about Hugo Kropp who, unlike Mr. Honnig, at least had a license to sell his golden lager.

Hugo Kropp owned a big brewery at Hermann. He was a dyed-in-the-wool river fan, and he heard about a fast and highly profitable trip of the big Exporter. He was building a little sternwheel pusher and decided to name her Exporter to deliver his beer and ice along the Gasconade and Osage rivers.

She was a natural high pressure sternwheeler and had a monstrously big upright boiler. When they had her out shoving a large barge after dark, she

The Steamer Gasconade helped with rescue efforts during the second Gasconade River bridge calamity.

An excursion party aboard the Steamer Peerless

The Steamer Annie Dell brings in a bumper crop from the Gasconade River.

looked like Halley's comet going up the river. When she made her first trip up the Gasconade River, wheat was about ready to cut and newly mown hay was lying on the ground. As she went up this picturesque little stream and you looked back it seemed the whole world was on fire. (And it was!)

The Exporter had a short furnace and they had to saw the cordwood in two. Young hickory, ash and hill white oak then cost $1.20 per cord. Oscar Staude was one of the firemen. He said, "Well, Cap'n, you will not believe me, but some of them sticks of wood would go up about 1,000 feet." Out of this boiler, wood and flame would go up in the air faster than a carp would go down through a blue heron. This boat only made three trips when she quit, or she would have "busted" the big brewery from lawsuits for ruined crops.

Oscar Staude also remarked, "That big boiler was the hottest thing ever put on a river craft and Old Duck Fritz was one of the hottest old-time river engineers that ever lived. When the Exporter was running hot and Duck Fritz was full of tanglefoot, it was one man's duty to pour water on the back of the pilothouse to keep the whole outfit from burning up.

The local newspaper wielded a great deal of influence. Then, as now, advertising was an important part of the newspaper's income—whatever affected local businessmen concerned the paper, too. The editor lobbied hard for one progressive cause after another.

Why do not some of our enterprising business men take hold and push through to final success a plan for supplying our town with Electric Lights? This could be easily and cheaply done and the result would be of vast benefit to property owners and great convenience to the citizens in general. There is certainly nothing to be lost by inquiring into the practicability of such an undertaking. … We are in dead earnest on the electric light question and we don't propose to let up until the streets are lighted. Take hold of the matter gentlemen, and let us keep up with the march of the times.

A vigorous campaign for a pontoon bridge was next.

Our business men are losing a great deal of valuable trade by the condition of the river. A few thousand dollars properly expended would soon restore the trade and the outlay be more than returned. Let a meeting be called to devise a means to either build a pontoon bridge or restore the channel to our side of the river. Who will take hold of this matter?

The subject generated a great deal of ink until wind and ice wrecked the pontoon bridges at both Lexington and St. Charles. These disasters were enough to cool the ardor of even the most vociferous proponent, and the newspaper quickly reversed its position. *A pontoon bridge is little better than no bridge at all.* Before long the editor had a new crusade.

The Gasconade should have a ferry crossing above the railroad bridge large enough to carry teams and loaded wagons. This would give us more trade and convenience to travelers. The old state road would again be connected and give our farmers a chance to do more business with those on the other side. We can have one here as well as at Stolpe. The conveniences would be many and the troubles few, why not have it?

Newspaper reporters must certainly have appreciated William Heckmann— he made good copy and lots of it. *Capt. Heckmann came into port last Monday, having rowed 50 miles down the Gasconade river in a skiff. The steamer Pin Oak had become disabled and the Capt. came down and took the Royal to the rescue.*

The death of General William Tecumseh Sherman, who had led Union troops to victory in the Civil War, dominated the news for a time. Carloads of dignitaries passed through Hermann en route to St. Louis for the funeral, which William attended as part of Hermann's G.A. R. delegation. A month later the grim news came that *the relic cranks are daily raiding the tomb of General Sherman and the guards have to keep a close watch to prevent them from literally digging the old man out of his grave. One man offered $2 for a pound of dirt from the grave.*

On a lighter note, the entire town was caught up in a flurry of preparation for a grand music festival. The Heckmann family housed some of the visiting guests, and the whole affair was such a success that it won even Mary's approval.

We have just passed over a great event for Hermann, a great occasion that was looked to with hopes and fears, no less than the Convention of the Southwestern Band Association of Missouri. The Governor was here, everything passed off very pleasantly.

The newspaper was rhapsodic.

The sunshine, the songs of the birds, the perfume of flowers and the sweet melodies of the Band Association, are surely influences from heaven, sent to scatter peace, happiness and contentment here on earth. … One of the little incidents of the Festival was Mrs. Nasse spontaneously rushing to the balcony of the Concert

Hall, and sprinkling an apron full of flowers over the heads of the incoming bands.

The big new cellar project at the Stone Hill Winery was duly reported. *The Stone Hill Wine Co., in making excavations for their new cellars are bringing forth and piling up rocks to make it a stony hill indeed. The cellars will be of mammoth proportions and eclipse anything in the west used for making and storing wines. ... The magnitude of the proposed new cellar may be inferred from the fact that 250,000 bricks will be used for arching the same.*

Machinery was arriving in town for the new Spery Pipe-Tong and Tool Mfg. Co. The steam hammer was immense, weighing more than 10,000 pounds and *looks formidable to hammer anything.* August Wohlt took an active interest in the new company. Boats were no longer his main priority, as the newspaper later reported. *August Wohlt who held a large block of stock in the Hermann Ferry and Packet Co., has sold the same to William L. Heckmann, Jr., George Schneider, Gustave Wohlt and others and will retire from active steamboating business.*

Hermann was booming, and the Heckmann family was comfortable and affluent. Mary was content—her husband at last had found his niche. Money was no longer a worry. A daughter would later recall that the usual practice was to pick up whatever was needed and say, "Charge it to Papa!" on the way out the door. Mary handled very little actual cash. Her inexperience in financial matters would later be the source of a great deal of pain and confusion.

Mary's grief for her lost child was diminishing, and she sympathized with others who had experienced loss—even the Eitzens. Charles Eitzen's daughter's family was nearly wiped out. *Father and husband and three children were called away within a year and nothing now remains but the widowed mother and one little son to whom we extend our sincere sympathy.* Eitzen's health was failing, and he and his wife were spending more time in California. His long feud with William Heckmann finally was laid to rest.

Flowers were always a joy to Mary. *Sam brought word home that Mrs. L.'s night-blooming cereus was in bloom. Annie and Martha went down first, and Lottie and I next. It was worth going a long distance to see, ten full bloom flowers at once, it was just majestic.*

The boats were busy, and the men were gone most of the time. As a result, the girls did not have so much to do and were, their mother said, *having lots of fun.* Mary was making pants and getting the little boys ready for school. *Theirs are all mended.* She made complete suits for the boys and knitted mittens for everyone.

It was a happy time in Mary's life. Too busy to hang around with his saloon friends, William was paying her more attention. The girls were old enough to help around the house, and she claimed her work was easier than at any other time of her marriage. The Heckmanns had raised a whole houseful of baby sitters, so the newest babies were not as confining as the earlier arrivals had been. The family was seldom without visitors. Tina often came from Bluffton on the boat and usually stayed for a week at a time. Other relatives came and went, as well.

Mary was pleased with how work on the house was progressing. An upstairs room was finished for the girls. The boys slept in the unfinished attic "dormitory." The cellar was white washed, and all the wine barrels were sold. Evidently, the Heckmanns did not plan any more home winemaking. The vineyard produced a bumper crop—more than 6,000 pounds of grapes—which was sold to Stone Hill Winery for three cents a pound.

In the midst of this beehive of domestic activity, the arrival of another baby was barely noted. A month after the fact, Mary wrote:

On March 5th, 1892 a nice little girl came here to stay. She is healthy and large, is growing every day. She did not see her Papa until she was two days old. She is so good, makes no trouble at all. And I am well too. William is determined she shall be called Mary, so we will call her Mary Isabell.

The newspaper had an announcement to make, too. *Capt Wm. L. Heckmann rejoices at the advent of the fourteenth child in his family. We congratulate him in the sentiment of the scripture: "Blessed are those who have the quiver full of them."*

Apparently William agreed. He loved having his children around and often took the smallest ones with him during slack times when he was running the ferry. Martha, now 14, quit school as was the custom for young ladies of the time. William had already taken the three older boys out of school at about age 13 so they could "learn" the river.

All the Heckmann babies had their pictures taken when they were a few months old. Mary, a pretty baby in her mother's estimation, was no exception. After attending a Knights of Pythias picnic with her seven youngest children, Mary wrote, *Mary was the best baby in the crowd, but today she is discontented, she wants to go again.*

In August the family went on a G.A.R. excursion and camp out. The newspaper was in fine form, as usual.

The boys in blue acquitted themselves nobly in their excursion last Sunday and our people as well as the citizens on the north side of the river turned out to give

them joyful welcome. Admiration for the true and the brave has always been a
trait of the human character and no doubt ever will be. It is not the love of
carnage and bloodshed that impels the public to pay homage to the heroes of
wars. On the contrary, it is only the love of home and freedom.

The steamer Fawn, towing a barge, left the levee about 8 a.m. Both boats
were loaded to their fullest capacity. Of course they were laden down with hu-
manity. The Apostle Band and Rebsamen's string band were on board; the former
to furnish music for general purposes and the latter for the dancing for young
people. Two or three landings were made for the purpose of taking on board all
who might wish to go along and eat bean soup and hard tack.

Things were peaceful and happy on the homefront, and the ferry company
was prospering. The Missouri Pacific Railroad purchased 800,000 ties at Osage
City and Gasconade City, and the ferry took 700 head of cattle across the river
for parties from Audrain County. But, as always, the boats were subject to the
vagaries of the weather. During a period of strong winds Mary reported, *August*
was on the steamer Gasconade with a load of movers, he says he never experienced such
a time in all his steamboating. At one point the boats had to unload at Gasconade
and Chamois because of low water. Sand had filled in against the switch.

More reshuffling occurred in the ferry company's fleet. The fine little
steamer Fawn was sold to Capt. Cliff B. Able of St. Charles to run as a ferryboat.

The Fawn has done duty here so long and so well that our people on both sides
of the river feel that they are losing an old friend. The Royal will take her place
as the ferry boat at this point. The Ferry Co. contemplates the building of a new
ferry boat after the newest and most approved pattern.

Steamboats were not the only business venture of interest to Will Heckmann.
He was buying farms and now owned three large Missouri River islands, including Graf Island which he purchased from Capt. Henry Wohlt. One published
report described Capt. Heckmann's extensive farm holdings.

He owns 1,600 acres of land, 700 in cultivation and has 13 tenants, 85 persons
altogether, living on his lands; he has threshed this season 1,867 sacks of wheat
or about 4,600 bushels and in addition has 300 acres of corn. He expects to have
1,000 acres of land in cultivation within three years when he will build a
steamboat and try to make money enough to keep his farms going.

Montgomery County was a constant source of difficulty to William concerning ownership of his lands in the Missouri River. Islands were exactly where

the capricious river chose to put them, and William waged an ongoing battle with authorities north of the river, who seemed to think all land so deposited should belong to Montgomery County.

William spent a fortune on his islands, clearing land, building houses and buying farm equipment. But his reasoning was a bit strange. Steamboat Bill quotes his father as saying, *They are clearing the land clean to the water's edge, they are using more water all the time for irrigation and we are having less rainfall. The time is coming when the Missouri River will almost go dry, and in dead low water it will stand in silent pools. Then these islands will be the finest land along the Missouri.*

If the river was drying up, it had a long way to go. In May of 1892, the paper carried this tongue-in-cheek item about Graf Island.

Capt. Heckmann had given up all hopes of raising any corn this year and has decided to cultivate water cress and pond lilies. The entire farm on the island will be used for this purpose, with the exception of a twenty-acre field which will be reserved as an artesian well. He has sent east for a number of trained mackerel to do the work of horses which have become useless by reason of their inability to swim.

Mary had planned a trip to Sedalia to see her sisters but had to call it off because of the high water.

All the islands were overflowing. The Mississippi also was high. The Gasconade valley suffered worse than ever, many not only lost their crops but the soil they were growing on. William saved everything but some of his corn stands in water. That is last year's corn in the crib and it was so rainy it could not be dried so he lost about three hundred bushel.

The Miller family in Bluffton had some interesting news. The railroad was nearing completion on the north side of the river, and the Miller's house—the one William had built from the wreck of the steamer Clara—was in the way. The MK&T Railroad moved the house 300 yards to the east, after which Mary reported, *Papas are all fixed in their new house.* The house still stands today, squarely on what is now the "Katy Trail," as one of the last relics of a once-booming winery town.

Mary's brothers George and Samuel had married sisters, Louisa and Ida Monnig. The Heckmann offspring, Annie, Lizzie, Will, Sam and Mary's brother, John Miller, went to Bluffton to the wedding and wedding supper at the Miller home. The wedding sermon took place at Monnig's at noon. *The girls say it was so very serious.*

The celebration of William and Mary's silver wedding anniversary was the social event of the season. Hundreds of people called to extend their congratulations, and the Apostle Band and Harmonie Singing Society serenaded the couple. Typically, Mary's comments were brief.

We celebrated our Silver Wedding on the 23rd of February, 1893. Had a grand time of it, everybody and his grandmother were here. Got a great many costly presents and everyone says they had a grand time and cannot get done talking about the cakes.

Tina gave birth to a son, and Mary's younger sister Alice married Everett Mosely. Charley Miller was paying a great deal of attention to Annie, and the family thought they were definitely a "couple." Mary wrote, *Charley Miller after looking for work all over St. Louis, he had less than a months work last time, he came up here, got a job at the government work.*

There was sad news from Bluffton, as well.

We laid our poor mother to rest. She died of bilious fever, being sick only six days. Martha was there when Mother died. I was up two days, mother did not seem to realize that she was very sick. I left at past six in the evening and she died at midnight. Sister Emma and Lizzie got down for the funeral, both spent a few days here.

In 1894 the Republicans of Montgomery County would nominate Samuel Miller for representative. The newspaper provided a hearty endorsement.

A better selection could not have been made if every Republican in the state resided in Montgomery county. Judge Miller is a man of fine attainments and has done much good to the farmers by his contributions to the agricultural press of this state. Judge Miller is well-known in Hermann, his daughter being the wife of Capt. Wm. L. Heckmann.

Back in Hermann, Sam Heckmann was plagued by a long streak of bad luck. He had accompanied his father on one of his big hunts, but the trip was disappointing—the hunters bagged only one deer. He returned home by train and, according to Mary, *was sleeping and run past Hermann, so while he was asleep in the depot at Chamois, his gun was stolen.*

A few months later he came down with typhoid again, and his mother thought he was at death's door. *At one time he was so low his heart had almost ceased to beat and his pulse was very weak. Brother John and I done all the nursing.*

After his recovery, Sam inadvertently made some local news.

Last Friday while the trainmen of the local freight were throwing empty beer kegs across the platform, Greeley Heckmann thinking that the freight had all been discharged attempted to pass the box car when an empty keg struck him along side of the head, felling him to the ground like a log. He was badly bruised and at the time it seemed as if he was seriously hurt, but we are happy to say is able to be around again.

On a happier note, young Will Heckmann was planning to marry Annie Buddemeyer. The groom-to-be bought furniture and took rooms at one of the Wohlt houses. *Everything nice*, his mother reported. A family wedding was held at the Heckmann home, which was decorated for Christmas—a beautiful tree gave a festive air to the ceremony.

The newspaper was duly appreciative. *Mrs. Wm. Heckmann is one of the fine old fashioned ladies of our town. When her son William was married last week she sent a big slice of wedding cake to this office. Thanks.* Hermann was having, Mary wrote, *an old fashioned winter—every ice house is filled.*

The ferry company continued to move ahead with the times, launching a new light draft, open-hull sternwheeler with geared machinery on Nov. 9, 1892. Weighing 41 tons and measuring 89.2 feet long by 18.8 feet wide by 2.8 feet deep, the Mill Boy was smaller than the Gasconade. She served two years as a packet on the Gasconade River, after which she was decked over and converted to a ferryboat.

The Mill Boy, in the charge of Will L. Heckmann Jr., would have a number of claims to fame. She made a 150-mile round trip from Hermann to Vienna in two and one-quarter days, loaded flat both ways—the fastest such trip ever recorded. With young Will at the wheel, the Mill Boy also was the only loaded boat that ever came down through Pryor's Bend at night. In her first year of operation, she paid for herself four times over.

While busy with the usual trade, the boats were always ready for fun. The newspaper never missed a chance to report on fishing expeditions, like this one chaperoned by Captain Bill. *The mere fact that only one diminutive, half-grown and half-witted sucker was hooked did not prevent the Captain from declaring the expedition a "success."* At one point the ferry made special trips so residents from north of the river could come to Hermann for a grand balloon ascension and to see Madame Crawford's daring parachute jump.

The steamer Peerless had been built at the Hermann wharf by Messrs. Fritz Lang, Henry Germann and William Greis, with Henry Germann as the head carpenter. In June of 1894, the newspaper reported:

The steamer Peerless went up the Gasconade river having on board as jolly a lot of fishermen as ever threw hook in water. Their motto: "Praised be all liars and all lies," was in keeping with the wonderful fish stories they told, and if Col. Annanis has been present he would have gracefully yielded his title as chief prevaricator.

The newspaper also made note of Louis "Jumbo" Rincheval's efforts to make sure everyone had a good time.

Louis Rincheval is making elaborate preparations for a fishing excursion up the Gasconade, the steamer Royal leaving this port at 8 o'clock next Sunday morning. The fishing party will undoubtedly be the greatest show on earth whose fame on brighter pages, penned by poets and by sages, shall go sounding down the ages. The fish have already been caught and are now on ice waiting the piscatorial excursionists. The weather and a kind providence permitting, we will be there, with a tin can full of worms and do our fishing in the old fashioned way.

Jumbo was always on the lookout for new amusements. *Louis Rincheval is entertaining our citizens with one of Edison's Phonography. The reproductions of music given by this wonderful machine are delightful and must be heard to be appreciated.* Hermann's jolliest citizen seldom passed up an opportunity to get in on something new. When the railroad was completed on the north side of the river, passengers could spend the night in Rhineland at the Jumbo Hotel, run by a most jovial host.

Gustave Wohlt, Constance Riek, Henry L. Heckmann and August Wohlt bought the old Schützenhouse property at the edge of town and formed the Hermann Distilling Co. Nepotism was encouraged. August Wohlt and Constance Riek had married two of Henry Heckmann's daughters. The newspaper wrote up an open house that was held in May of 1894.

Upon invitation of the management many of our business men and visitors within our gates repaired to the Hermann Distillery to view the working of an enterprise which has been in operation for the past twelve months. After being shown around and learning the difference between sweet mash and sour mash whiskies, the party partook of a splendid lunch and choice wines, and were again driven to town. The enterprise has been very successful in turning out an

excellent quality of rye and corn whiskies, and the unsold product for the past
twelve months now in the government warehouse, is about 7,000 gallons.

Capt. Heckmann was flexing his entrepreneurial muscles as well. Newspaper
stories foretold what lay in store for the Heckmann family.

Capt. Heckmann will, in the near future, erect a large flour mill, also a neat and
convenient club house on the site of the Old Pryor Mill on the Gasconade river.
... Gen. Tom Robinson, Col. Jeff Sway and Capt. Bill Heckmann held a meeting
in our town for the purpose of settling up the title on the George Pryor Mill and
farm property. It was settled by Capt. Bill getting it all.

Every newspaper within a 50-mile radius seemed fascinated by Capt.
Heckmann's plans for the mill. The smallest detail was reported, and when new
information was unavailable, they printed their own commentary. The Linn
"Unterrified Democrat" had this to say:

Capt. Heckmann, the steamboat man, is going to build a town at Pryor's Mill.
If the Captain will give each of his children a house and lot, he will have a town
and can be elected Mayor. ... Capt. William L. Heckmann is fixing to build a
roller mill on his Pryor's Mill farm, and after the completion of the railroad
across the river will retire from steamboat business and engage in milling and
farming.

The Hermann newspaper was keeping close tabs on progress at the mill.
Capt. Heckmann is boating building material up the Gasconade river for his new dwelling
on the Pryor Mill property. ... Capt. Heckmann went up to Pryor's Dam yesterday to
see how work on his new mill is progressing.

Mary, who by now was convinced that her husband was a genius at making
money, described an excursion to the mill on the steamer Royal. *Some 50 people*
left Saturday and came back Sunday. Just where everyone slept is a mystery. The
Heckmann family's new house was under roof, but still not finished. Later Mary
wrote, *Mill is running finely, we baked bread with our own flour.*

An earlier item in the "Unterrified Democrat" had described improvements
being made by the government on the Gasconade River, which held great significance for William's mill venture.

The Government employees at work on the Gasconade river have been doing
some important work. At Pryor's Mill, the slough which supplied the water to
turn the wheels of the famous water mill has been opened up and runs in the
main channel of the river. This will make navigation better at that point, the

The U.S. Government Boatyard at Gasconade

slough having so divided the waters that at certain times of the year it was almost impossible for boats to pass.

The late George W. Pryor built his mill on the Gasconade many years ago and this little mill stream was only four feet wide, but at last got to be over 100 feet wide. The new river improvements at the place mentioned will greatly facilitate the navigation of boats, but leaves the old-time water wheel as helpless as a fish on dry land.

The work of improving the Missouri River was expanding rapidly, and in 1892 the Gasconade Government Boat Yards became a reality. Located at the confluence of the Missouri and Gasconade rivers, the facility was an ideal spot for a marine way. A spur line from the Missouri Pacific Railroad allowed easy access to heavy supplies.

The boat yard began as a modest operation, with a two-story living quarters building, an engine and boiler room, a steam power saw and planing room, and a few other structures. One of the first boats constructed was the Margaret, an office boat. The Gasconade facility soon absorbed all other existing government boat yards—by 1894 there were 220 employees. Young Charley Miller found work there and promptly nearly tore off a finger.

Business may have been booming on the river, but William announced he was leaving the steamboat business to devote his full time and resources to the mill. Mary wrote, *William had sold his shares in the boats, so now he is out of boats.* The "Advertiser-Courier" carried the same information.

Capt. Wm. L. Heckmann has sold his stock in the Hermann Ferry and Packet Co. to Messrs. August Wohlt and Gustave Wohlt, and intends to devote all his time to the mill up the Gasconade river. Capt. Heckmann, retires from active service on the river of fully twenty-five years. During all this time he has never met with an accident, never sunk or injured a boat or lost a sack of freight. As a steamboat man he has been very successful and his untiring energy and strict application to business will no doubt help along in the milling business.

The newspaper story also included a prediction: *Capt. Heckmann will go back to steamboating the same as the Wohlts did.* Subsequent reports revealed that the mill was not doing as well as William had hoped.

Capt Heckmann of the Heckmann Milling Co. requests us to state that in consideration of the hard times he has instructed his Hermann agent to sell flour at $1.60 per 100 lbs. All who want a good grade of flour for family use can obtain same from Mrs. Caroline Silber.

Will's youngest sister had expanded her millinery business to a general store.

Wintertime was always hard on the boats. The Royal and Pin Oak were caught napping by a sudden drop in the temperature. Ice was floating so thick they could not make any headway. Apparently, William was not as uninvolved with the boats as earlier reports had indicated. Mary's journal tells of a hard winter's night on the river.

Will says he spent the worst night he ever had since he is steamboating. He says his cook kept up the cook stove fire all night and stood on a box before the stove to keep from freezing his feet. In the pilot house first a lantern fell and set fire to the floor. Billy Wild jumped out and broke down the bunk, they then made a bed on the floor, made up a big fire, and next their quilts were on fire.

Charley Miller took his first lesson in steamboating, he cannot say that he likes it. William put him off on the island to sack corn. He and the English man that is up there sacked seventy-five sacks and it got dark, so he came over in the Englishman's boat. Good thing he did for there were several days when it was impossible to cross. Since then they have not been on the island until today, if they get up, but he can get over to the other side, that is the Englishman, so I suppose he did not set down and starve.

In February Mary and William made a trip to the mill, perhaps making final plans before moving the family.

Before we got there we had to lay up for a snow storm. First we had a race for some distance with the Mill Boy, they got to the mill and laid up. There was six inches of snow, was pretty cold and still snowing. We waded about in the snow looking at the sheep, cattle and house, when we got to the mouth of the Gasconade river, found the Missouri full of ice and getting colder. The snow had delayed all the Coast bound trains. We stopped at the bridge and found that they would be along soon. Fred and I went to the depot and staid there two hours. I was sound asleep when the train arrived, got home and to bed by ten.

With the first hint of spring, the Heckmanns packed their belongings and moved to the mill.

March 5, 1894—*We left Hermann in a drenching rain, things got pretty wet, but not so badly damaged as one might expect. About 3 o'clock we left Hermann and went up to our island at Bluffton, loaded corn. I could not sleep for the bank caving in all night. Early in the morning we left the island and run until 3 o'clock when we arrived at the Mill. Now here we are safe and sound, nearly established in our new home. All are better satisfied than I expected. Have put a man to work fixing up the place. Our chickens are laying right along.*

Mary does not bother to say whether it was the Royal or the Gasconade that moved the Heckmanns and their belongings to the mill. Steamboats were, after all, an everyday commodity.

CHAPTER 12

The Heckmann Mill

The scenery is grand and the river as clear as it is possible for pure water to be.
And, in addition to everything else, the place is owned by one of the
most whole souled, hospitable and intelligent men one could
wish to meet. — "The Advertiser-Courier"

*S*ituated on the Gasconade River in the center of the great loop of Horseshoe
Bend, the Pryor Mill was a Lorelei, beckoning all passing steamboatmen. William
Griffee had obtained title to the site from the United States in 1835. When the
land was sold to Joseph Pryor, the transaction described a "tract of land ... on
which is situated a water grist mill." The impounded water of the Gasconade
River also was used to power a wool carding machine and a sawmill, which
produced fine walnut for commercial use.

The property became known as the Pryor Mill and eventually was inherited
by George Pryor, Joseph's son. Neighboring farmers from Gasconade and Osage
counties paid a toll to have their wheat and corn ground into flour and meal. In
its early days, the mill was so busy that farmers with their ox-drawn wagons
sometimes waited two or three days for their turn for service. Oral history recalls
the use of the mill by both Union and Confederate soldiers, with the two sides
declaring a truce in order to take turns using the mill.

Pryor's Mill flourished until about 1883 when steam mills, which produced
better flour with more modern machinery, were put into operation closer to
customers' homes. The temptation to see the mill in operation again was too

much for William Heckmann to resist. He envisioned a fine mill operation with a hunting and fishing resort nearby. A fleet of steamboats would arrive carrying grain—some of it from his own farms—and leave loaded with flour.

Capt. Heckmann believed he could compete with the steam mills by buying the most modern mill machinery available and then using his fleet of steamboats to take care of transportation problems. The citizens of central Missouri were kept fully informed of his plans. The Hermann, Vienna, Linn, Chamois and Jefferson City papers all joined in the fun—and then quoted each other! One paper printed the fanciful bit of information that *Capt. Heckmann plans to use his abundant power to generate electricity to run an electric train to Jefferson City.*

This item first ran in the "Jefferson City Tribune" and then was copied by the Hermann paper.

Seeking a Name

Capt. Wm. L. Heckmann, the well-known river man and miller, has had trouble in finding a name for the post office and shipping point at his mill, some thirty miles up the Gasconade river. Capt. Heckmann had lately expended over $35,000 on improving his mill, and he is very anxious to find a suitable name for the place.

It was first called Heckmann's Mill. There is a Hickman's Mill in the state, and it was soon discovered that the similarity of names would result in confusion. Several other names have been tried and rejected for the same reason. Capt. Heckmann says that he will give anyone a barrel of his best flour, delivered, who will suggest a suitable name and one that does not conflict with some other post office in the state.

True to the newspaper's prediction, it wasn't long before Capt. Heckmann was back into steamboating. He bought the Annie Dell to transport grain and other commodities and for pleasure trips. One group of grateful guests who had made a 90-mile trip on the Annie Dell composed a lengthy resolution, which was published in the Hermann newspapers.

Hunter's Paradise

Resolved, that the Gasconade river furnishes delightful sport for the fisherman, and the country through which it runs equally fine sport for the hunter, and

A festive crowd aboard the Steamer Peerless at the Heckmann Mill.

that we believe that anyone who makes a trip up this river for such purposes will have the desire to repeat his visits often.

Resolved, that to Capt. W. L. Heckmann, the worthy commander of the "Annie Dell," we are indebted for many courtesies and kind attentions. Whatever he could do to contribute to the pleasure of our party he did most cheerfully. He is not only an excellent commander but an enthusiastic sportsman. No efforts on his part were lacking to make all feel at home and desire to be longer in his company, and to repeat the trip up this beautiful river as often as business pursuits will allow.

Resolved, that the Club House which Capt. Heckmann has erected at his flouring mills about 30 miles from the mouth of the Gasconade for the accommodation of both ladies and gentlemen, with board, or the opportunity to board themselves, supplies a needed want, and that we can assure all that they will find this a healthy resort, with plenty of row-boats and good fishing and hunting.

The locality in question is one of the most beautiful spots to be found any-where in Missouri. The river forms an island, and on this island is a splendid club house designed for hunting and fishing parties. The scenery is grand and the river as clear as it is possible for pure water to be. And, in addition to everything else, the place is owned by one of the most whole souled, hospitable and intelligent men one could wish to meet.

When Mary stepped into this highly touted paradise, she found a house still under construction with no source of water other than the river. The setting, however, was gorgeous, and expectations were great.

According to plan, William had purchased and installed the most modern mill machinery available. He had hired a miller and built him a place to live. He also had built a fine clubhouse and was adding onto the house. They needed the extra rooms—relatives came in droves to see what the Heckmanns had bought. Every arriving boat seemed to bring more company.

Mary began life at the mill with a frenzy of gardening. She had one garden fenced and planted 200 asparagus roots, 500 strawberry plants, potatoes, corn and onions. As always, the house was full of children and relatives. Young Will was living in Hermann with his new bride, but the rest of the Heckmann offspring were usually in residence. The "big boys" were out on the river part of the time. The "little" boys—Robert, Edward, George and John—were enrolled in the local Horseshoe Bend School. The girls were usually at home, but sometimes went off to visit relatives. Accidents still happened. *Fred made the Vienna trip with Archie Bryan and shot a goose and got hurt in the face pretty badly.*

William spent much of his time trying to sell wheat and flour. This should have been easy, but it was not. Steamboat Bill recalled:

Just about the time this truly fine property got a good start ... we had a young depression on our hands. My father sent three carloads of flour to St. Louis, but never got any returns. He sent one of his sons, the engineer at the mill, down the river with two barges of flour and feed. The engineer did a fancy job of piloting but again my father got no returns for the flour, and his engineer never returned to the Heckmann Mill. The young man went on the Missouri River to seek his fortune.

Sam Heckmann is the son referred to in this story. He wanted to get married, and the mill was paying only room and board.

A bad drought didn't help matters. The boys were carrying water in buckets from the river, a good long walk, to fill a cistern which had been dug. The gardens dried up, but Mary's chickens flourished. The lack of rain and the heat brought forth more comments from Mary than in other years. *This has been the longest, hottest, dryest summer I ever endured in this state.*

Socially, life was different for Mary, but not really lonesome. Going to town now meant a five-mile trip to Mt. Sterling in the horse and buggy William had purchased for her before the move. The clubhouse was advertised "with board," which apparently meant that Mary fed the guests. In July she wrote, *a jolly crowd came from Fulton, thirteen women and girls and eight men. All were well pleased and say they will come again. ... Father came on last Monday and left Thursday, he likes the place. ... Yesterday they launched the ferry boat.* If the boat Mary refers to was really a ferry, it certainly would have made trips to the mill more convenient for many farmers. But it could be that she simply was accustomed to calling any boat a ferry.

Mary was pregnant again and not feeling well. The house, she said, was always grimy and the cooking was endless, as more boatloads of guests continued to arrive. Other chores also took time, too. *Boiled 13 kettles of soap the past month and have two to boil yet.* Help arrived in the form of a Mrs. Caspiri who came to live with the family until the end of the year.

A regular column by "Skipper" began appearing in the Hermann paper with news from the mill. The writer, presumably Capt. Heckmann, told of building new boats, including flatboats and the steamer Kingfisher. *The lumber used in the construction of these boats is called "Oregon Fir" and is especially well adapted for that purpose, combining strength with great buoyancy. Boat will be ready for business in ten days, and will ply principally on the Gasconade river.*

A boarder at the Heckmann home was featured in one column.

John Ingrum is here taking the Keely Cure, reason: beer boat has abandoned its regular trips on account of low state of the water. He started on some "medicine" today with a jug; but got lost in the woods and after wandering around aimlessly for several hours he turned up at the same place he started from, minus the "medicine." He has arrived at the state of the cure now, that makes him think that this country would be better off with free beer than with free silver.

Sometimes "Skipper" had a fishing report.

River is getting very low and the annual fall drive of the fish has commenced. The first to appear are the hickory shad and suckers, both of little value. Then come the buffalo and carp and perch, in October, the bass and cat fish and last but not least, in November, the Jack Salmon, the king of them all. As they try to pass over the dam they frequently get fouled amoungst the brush and rock and many a fine mess has been caught that way. Fish are now traveling to a warmer climate or deeper water.

Mary's last child was born at the mill in December of 1894.

My health has been just miserable for over a month, indigestion mostly. Mrs. Caspiri proved a good, kind and faithful friend. On the morning of the 18th of December at 2:20 a.m. a dear little boy came to stay with us. If the Lord permits, we propose to call him Norman J. Colman. Col. C. was with William on the hunt, down to Poplar Bluffs, they had a good time of it. William did not see our boy until he was two days old.

She could find little good to say about the old year.

It is very unkind to write words of rebuke after anyone is dead, but never-the-less, the truth must be told. The old year of 1894 was one of the hardest ever passed through in this country, in times of peace. For the first time in thirty years the Democratic party had full control of the running of the government and we Republicans are prone to say it is all on account of the tinkering with the tariff that the extra session of Congress done and yet with all they done nothing, have kept the country in a perpetual uncertainty.

Wheat has been down to thirty cents per bushel. In some parts of the country people are calling for aid. Crops have been a failure, in Nebraska and Dakota. In this state, first we had too much rain and then none. Have only had three soaking rains since the 3rd of July. No fruit of any kind, and few potatoes, vegetables too were scarce. So we have nothing to cook, but meat, canned goods and dried fruit. …We do have a lot of ice put up, very firm and five inches. We have no thermometer but they say it was 8 above zero the coldest day.

Considering the remoteness of the mill, the "grapevine" was most efficient. Even Capt. Will's theories about squirrels were found newsworthy.

Farmers and sportsmen all agree that there are practically no squirrels in the woods for the first time within the recollection of most of them. Some say the squirrels migrated, but this is not generally accepted. Capt. Wm. L. Heckmann, who is good authority on such subjects, says the squirrels were frozen to death

Steamboat Bill claimed the Kingfisher, which could run on nine inches of water, was the lightest draft boat ever built for western rivers.

during the long cold spell last winter. Timber cutters on the Gasconade have found a large number of dead squirrels in hollow trees and this certainly looks like a good proof of Capt. Heckmann's theory.

Readers of the "Vienna Gazette" learned:

Capt. Heckmann says that turtles and gars are the greatest enemies of food fish, and in order to destroy as many as possible he uses, for turtles, a box rigged something like a fish basket, which he places in a riffle with the top just out of the water. To dispose of gar he waits till ice forms in winter and cuts holes in some deep eddy, where they accumulate, so that they can be killed with a gig. Last winter Capt. Heckmann killed about 5,000 in this manner.

In the fall of 1895 the "Advertiser-Courier" reported:

Capt. Heckmann's new steamer, the Kingfisher, will unquestionably be the lightest draft boat that ever turned a wheel on our western rivers, drawing only three inches water with part of the machinery on board, and will draw when completed with everything on board, not to exceed 9 inches of water, will carry a capacity of 800 sacks of wheat. The boat with new barge now building, will be

The wrecked Annie Dell was rebuilt as the Steamer Jack Rabbit.

able to carry 300 sacks of wheat on the barge at the lowest stage of water.

A later report about a three-day hunting and trapping party said they *shot seventeen squirrels and caught ... their breath!* It also was noted that *Capt. Heckmann can come nearer running a boat on dry land then any other man in the state.*

The newspaper at Mt. Sterling noted that *the beer boat is making regular trips to Gasconade now, and a few who allow themselves to drink too much beer get filled up to the chin and raise no little disturbance and the good people who are far from being prohibitionists, but who can take a dram and go about their business, are getting tired of such.*

Boat traffic was heavy on the Gasconade River. The ferry company was running the Peerless, the Gasconade and the Mill Boy. Capt. Heckmann was running the Kingfisher and would soon have the Jack Rabbit in service, and the faithful "Jug Line" was still in operation.

Back in Hermann, a weekly river column kept readers informed about the waterfront activities.

The steamer Peerless went out Monday with a heavy list of up-freight, returned Wednesday with a fair cargo of grain. ... Joseph Meyer, our well-known school teacher, is at present engaged as clerk on the steamer Peerless. ... The river at this point is falling, but will rise again slightly in the next few days. ... The steamer Peerless, Capt. Hy. Germann, came in last Tuesday laden with 3 car loads of hogs and grain. … The steamer Kingfisher, Capt. Sam. Heckmann, came in with one car load of hogs, which she unloaded here. She went out the next day for Portland to unload some wheat. … The steamer Mill Boy, Capt. Wm. Heckmann, brought over two hundred cords of wood to Hermann in the last few weeks, which will be for sale anytime now. … The Hermann Ferry & Packet Co., will inaugurate a new time table for the Ferry boat, beginning June 15th, until further notice. The boat will hereafter make six trips, instead of four a day, to accommodate the farmers and traveling public. … The Gasoline Beer boat Hermann will make a trip to Loutre Island next Saturday evening to accommodate all those wishing to see the Theatre at the Concert Hall. … The steamer Peerless and barge Flora, Capt. Hy. German, will make an excursion to Brown's Shanty on the Gasconade river June 14th. This will be a delightful trip on the famous scenic Gasconade and ought to be well attended.

The ferryboat always doubled as a short trip boat between ferry trips.

The steamer Mill Boy, Capt. Will Heckmann, Jr. made the following extra night runs besides the regular ferry. Trip to Schick's Landing and Schwerkoetting's Island Chute, Tuesday night, brought in 310 sacks of wheat, trip to Gasconade Thursday evening in with 200 sacks of wheat, trip to the Becker's Landing Friday evening in with 60 sacks of corn, trip to Massie's Creek Saturday night in with barge Flora loaded with railroad ties, 830 in all; trip to Round Island Monday night took up barge Flora which is to be loaded with gravel. … The steamer Peerless, Capt. Hy. German, came in Wednesday night with 400 sacks of wheat and a lot of produce, which was transferred from the Cooper Hill Jugline of flatboats, owned by Langenberg Sons & Co. The flats are floated down the river until they meet the boat, which cannot go very far up the river on account of the low state of water and they are towed back by hand. Mr. Nixon, the foreman claims that the jug line left Cooper Hill 2 hours later than the steamer Kingfisher and came to Round Island, where they met the Peerless, 3 hours before the Kingfisher passed that point consequently they must have come over the shoals quicker than a steamboat can come down stream.

At the mill Mary was busy putting up food for the coming winter.

The leaves are turning. We have had a bountiful harvest of every description.

155

Wheat, corn, potatoes, apples, all kinds of vegetables. We have some 200 quarts of pickles, canned fruit and vegetables in the cellar.

The new boat has been making trips all along so she is sure enough a low water boat. Has never been aground yet. In October Eddie, John, Mary, Norman and I went to Bluffton on the boat. … Had quite a pleasant time of it, only Norman was strange. Wherever I went he would not go to anyone. The carpenters are still here, had expected them to go, but they will be here a while longer.

At about the same time as Mary's visit to Bluffton, a terrible murder occurred at Mt. Sterling, only five miles from the mill. The victim was Bill Lalk, the man who years earlier had helped Capt. Henry Wohlt build his first steamboat on the Gasconade River. Strangely, Mary never mentioned this news in her journals, but the crime was well-covered in all the area newspapers. This story appeared in the "Advertiser-Courier" on October 2, 1895.

Brutal Murder

The pride and boasted law abiding spirit in this county received a rude shock last Friday when it became known that a murder most brutal and foul had been committed that day at Mt. Sterling, a small hamlet situated about thirty miles southwest of Hermann, and that Bill Lalk had been shot through the heart by John Hartley, without any apparent provocation.

The story which led to the tragedy is a long one, and to those who were acquainted with troubles brewing in Mt. Sterling, the sequel is not altogether a surprise, although they now stand aghast that the terrible deed has been committed.

The causes leading to the killing of Lalk was the contention over the ferry right at Mt. Sterling. Lalk, had for many years been the ferry keeper at that place and during that time had got into a dispute with Frank Schwegler about some land on the river, claimed by both of these men. Ejectment suits, damage suits and actions for malicious trespass between Lalk's family and Schwegler have been pending, and are now pending, in court, until Schwegler became disgusted and sold out and moved away.

A short time before Lalk's license as ferry keeper expired, John Giek circulated a petition to be granted a ferry license, which was generally signed by the citizens in that neighborhood, and a license was by the county court granted to

156

John Giek when Lalk's license expired. Lalk, after the expiration of his license again became an applicant for the ferry privileges, but as the court had already granted a license to Giek for five years, it could find no authority to revoke the license unless a breach of conditions was shown.

Lalk refused to move his boats from the landing. He was convicted for obstructing the public highway and refusing to pay the fine, served his time in jail.

All this time, John Hartley had been running the ferry for Giek, and it seems that he and Lalk, who was living in a house at the edge of the river at the crossing, took a violent dislike to each other and an unfriendly feeling toward Lalk was generally manifested by those coming to town. Some time in July last, while Lalk was away with the threshing machine, his wife acting as cook, and no one but the children at the house, the house one evening caught fire and was burned to the ground. Criminations and recriminations followed, and the whole neighborhood was torn up about the affair. Thus matters stood last Friday.

The river for some time past being easily fordable at Mt. Sterling, John Hartley, the ferry hand, put in his time fishing and hunting. On Friday morning he came to Mt. Sterling on company with Jesse Woody, who is a cousin of Lalk's wife. Only Woody had a gun, and while sitting opposite Schaepperkoetter's store, Lalk sauntered up and engaging Woody in conversation, said to him that he had simply come here to make trouble and to kill him. While this talk was taking place Hartley stepped up and saying to Woody, "give me that gun" took it from Woody, stepped back two or three paces and holding the weapon to Lalk's body, pulled the trigger and Lalk fell to the ground mortally wounded, having been shot through the heart. The bystanders seemed horrified and not having presence of mind enough to apprehend the murderers, who very leisurely made their escape and are not yet arrested.

The brothers of Mr. Lalk have offered a reward of one hundred dollars for the arrest of the murderers and the county court, which will meet Friday, will also offer a reward. The Governor, no doubt, will also do something in this matter, and it is reasonably certain that the fugitives will soon be behind the bars.

No arrests were ever made, although rumors about sightings of John Hartley circulated for years. Also common were rumors that he was sheltered and provided with food while he "holed up" in the Horseshoe Bend Schoolhouse.

Two years later word was received that the sheriff of Stoddard County in southeast Missouri had arrested John Hartley. The newspaper reported:

Several messages were exchanged, and upon the positive assurance that the prisoner was John Hartley, and no other, sheriff Barbarick, accompanied by Lalk's brother, left last Sunday morning to get the man. When they got to Bloomfield, Stoddard county, and were confronted with the prisoner they at once saw that while he answered the description in many respects and answered to the name of John Hartley, he was not the John Hartley wanted for the murder of Bill Lalk. The sheriff got home yesterday busted and disgusted.

The Heckmann Mill was a popular destination for honeymooning couples. Annie Heckmann and Charley Miller were married on November 28, 1895, at Will Jr.'s home in Hermann. The newlyweds then drove to the mill in a wagon—a cold start to a honeymoon. Mary later wrote:

They intended going east to Pennsylvania to see Charley's family but had to postpone that because he had to fill in for a man at work. Ed and Emma Heckmann's daughter Kate was married on Christmas Day to Charley Johnson. They intended coming out here but the high water, or rather the deep mud prevented. As we have a barrel of molasses ... the girls kept saying Kate was coming out here to spend her molasses moon.

In Mary's view 1895 hadn't been much better than 1894. *I only said Happy New Year to one person, as it seemed like a farce to say it.* But she was cheered by a gift from the miller and his wife—a fine wire flower stand.

Something I have wished for years, but never felt I could afford it. Mr. and Mrs. Lehrack ordered it for me. Indeed, I am delighted with it. ... Yesterday I thought I would look at the flower pit, and when I opened it found about four inches of water around the pots, so the boys helped me get them all out and I distributed them here and in the girls room, and today the pit is even full of water and the river is worse than full, it reaches to the bluffs.

Caroline Silber was selling her brother's flour at her store in Hermann. After her husband's untimely death, Caroline raised five children by herself and turned her tiny millinery business into a fine general store. Then the shocking news came that her son, Adolph, had been found dead in the Missouri River at St.

Louis, an apparent suicide. The entire family was deeply distressed. The idea of suicide was unacceptable to them, but there were no clues providing any other explanation.

The August Wohlt family also had news of a very personal nature. Mrs. Wohlt's sister, the abused wife of a man dying of tuberculosis, was pregnant again and very despondent. She decided to remove herself from a hostile world and take her two little girls with her. While on a ferryboat at St. Louis, she suddenly threw one little girl in the river, then the other, and then followed herself. The girls were rescued, but the mother drowned. The Wohlts, who had no children of their own, took the little girls to raise, along with another little girl from an orphanage.

The death of Charles D. Eitzen and the reading of his will caused quite a stir. Will Heckmann was up the Gasconade River at the time, so his fine voice was absent from the funeral renditions by the Harmonie Singing Society. Eitzen made a number of generous civic bequests, including $50,000 for the building of a new courthouse, causing many to think more kindly of the deceased. The "Advertiser-Courier," which often had been critical of Eitzen, now did the noble thing and lauded him in fine style.

> *It is needless to say that his munificent gifts to the county, to the school, the churches, the town—was and is the sole topic of conversation everywhere in the county since the provisions of his last will became known. Everybody feels honored in living in a community which was the home of a man like Chas. D. Eitzen. Many who spoke disparagingly of his frugal habits and his great wealth, now freely acknowledge that he was "the noblest Roman of them all," and that they did not know what they were talking about.*

By March of 1897, work on the new courthouse was in full swing. No detail was too small for the newspaper to report. The bricks were counted—400,000—and it was noted that a beer bath was being brushed on the brick walls to give them a fine uniform color. *Good vinegar would produce the same results but as long as beer is cheaper, the latter is used. The workmen are not permitted to indulge in the beer.*

Mary's mood was grim. *It seems as though my work increased instead of diminishing. Now the boat is done, they get in sometimes twice a week, they want clean clothes, potatoes, apples and often meat and all this helps to make me more care and work. Norman too can walk and is into all kinds of mischief.* For reasons unknown, the "little boys" were now taking their lessons at home rather than at school, another chore for their mother.

Early in 1897 the Heckmann family abandoned life at the mill and moved back to their home in Hermann. Mary never stated the reasons for the move, but the decision must have come as a great relief to her. The family returned to Hermann in relays.

> *On February 7 Martha and all the school boys moved to our house in Hermann where Annie and Charley have been living since December. They, Martha and the boys, only took beds and used Annie's kitchen utensils and stove. On February 28, Norman, Mary, I, the chickens and most of the household goods came to Hermann. March 19th at 4:30 a.m. Annie had a little boy. On March 18th, Lottie, Lizzie, the horse Pete, and all the rest of our household goods came. We are all living at our old place and are all very glad of it except Norman, he will not go to see anyone; as soon as he gets to the end of the vineyard he wants to go back home, but he likes this place.*

The isolation of the mill had left the Heckmann girls without much of a social life. The move back to town changed all that. The girls were known for their lovely singing voices, and on Memorial Day, Martha and Lizzie sang with Mr. Ripstein and Mr. Thudium at the cemetery. Mary's social life picked up, too.

> *On June 13, a Sunday, we made a trip to the mill, a party of mostly women and teachers. Had quite a nice time of it, only on the way down, through Fred's carelessness William was thrown overboard with Norman in his arms. They were safely pulled aboard, the boat was slightly hurt.*
>
> *Mr. Terrel was with us, he is here from Texas to buy a boat, thinks he will take the Kingfisher. On June 13th our boat the Kingfisher was accepted by the Texas parties and the next day she started to St. Louis, before they were out of sight a wind storm struck and William says he would have sold out cheap just then, but they reached St. Louis in good shape. The same week, our folks began pulling the Annie Dell to pieces with the intention of making a new boat of the light weight barge. Are getting on with it, expect to have it done or inspected tomorrow.*
>
> *We had one of the most prolonged thunder storms we have ever known. There was such a terrible peal of thunder so near us we thought the lightening had struck us, and at 3 in the morning it did strike the house at the east end, it seemed to divide and come down both chimneys, knocked some plastering off in*

A careless pilot caused William Sr. and young Norman, who are between the smokestacks, to fall into the river shortly after this picture was taken.

the upstairs room where the boys were sleeping and the plaster burst a box that
was against the wall, no other damage was done but it was a close call. The
same week we had a small cyclone, done a great deal of damage about here,
mostly in the vineyards and orchards and grain. Our summer house was turned
a summer salt into the garden, plowing down half the sweet peas and making a
large hole in the onion bed.

The "Advertiser-Courier" stated the real cause of the Annie Dell's troubles.
*The Annie Dell was towed down from Heckmann's Mill Monday by the
Kingfisher. She is completely dismantled, pilot house, smoke stacks and cabin
all washed away while she was laying on blocks at the mill. The Gasconade
river rose suddenly and before the owners could get her on high ground the
river got over her and completely dismantled her on the upper deck. It is the
intention of the owners to repair her here.*

The ferry company was having a few problems of its own.

The boat excursion last Sunday was well attended, fully 200 persons being of the party. The boat reached Brown Shanty on the upper Gasconade about 3 o'clock p.m. where the excursionists spent about an hour with our Second Creek friends who had come to the landing to greet them. Everything passed off pleasantly until on the return trip a point above Fredericksburg was reached, where in trying to make a landing the rudder became unmanageable and the boat passed under an overhanging tree which tore down the sun roof erected over the barge and causing consternation among the passengers. Nobody was seriously hurt, with the exception of a young lady who fainted from fright and fell to the floor sustaining slight injuries.

At Spohrer's landing, Judge Wm. Toedtmann, upon leaving the boat, slipped on the muddy bank and fell into the river, but with the assistance of some of the passengers managed to scramble out again. These incidents very naturally cast a gloom over the entire excursion party and when the boat came into the harbor at Hermann at about 9:30 p.m. the music of the band was conspicuous by its absence.

Mary was an excellent chronicler of family news. She wrote of Sam's marriage to Gusta Bensing and of babies born to her brothers Sam and George. Tina had another baby, as did Mary's sister Gert, and Annie had a little boy named Ira. Lizzie Teubner moved back to Hermann with her family, and they buried Lawrence Rauss, a brother-in-law.

The Hermann River News column was always interesting, even when reporting routine events.

The river at this point rising slowly, caused by rise of 10 feet or more in the Gasconade river. ... The steamer Kingfisher, Capt. Wm. L. Heckmann Sr., came in with a mixed cargo, consisting of flour, hay, shipstuff, eggs, chickens and grain, unloaded and departed the same night. ... The steamer Gasconade, Capt. Archie Bryan, came in with a barge load of wheat and boat loaded with grain, unloaded and again went out. ... The steamer Mill Boy brought in 300 sacks of new wheat, the first wheat of the season. ... The steamer Gasconade was in with 2 car loads of wheat, unloaded and left with barge Flora, for Washington with the E.F.R. Base Ball Club. ... The steamer Kingfisher and barge loaded threshing engine and outfit here to go to Heckmann's Island. ... The "Hermann" Kropp's beer boat made her regular Mt. Sterling trip on Friday returning on Saturday.

The Heckmann men frequently made the 36-mile trip from Hermann to the mill.

They killed nine hogs at the mill. Fred came in on the wagon with all of the offal and William and Sam came down in the skiff with the meat and they can be thankful that they did, for it is now very cold and blustery, they would have suffered awfully from cold.

Mary made sausage, lard and pudding from the meat.

Hermann was finally getting its power plant and would soon have electricity, so the town would be alight. The steamer Jack Rabbit was finished, and by the end of 1897, Mary was convinced that all was right with her world. By now, the family included an enormous cast of characters.

We had a fine Christmas tree here Christmas eve, Lizzie and her children were here. Sam, Fred, Bob and Charley Miller went over the river for Minnie Teubner in the skiff. We were so uneasy about them, they were so late. The river is full of ice along shores, they crossed this chute in a skiff and dragged the skiff over the bar opposite the house, must be a quarter mile wide just here, they crossed the main channel, and walked and hunted to McKittrick just opposite here on the MKT Railroad two miles from the river. Minnie came down on the Local and it was late, so it was dark before they crossed the bar, and we were very uneasy about them. We did not light up the tree until they got here.

Annie, Charley and baby Ira were here. Will's had a tree for their children. Annie and Charley were here for Christmas dinner and Will's Annie and the little ones. Will had to go back to work, he is watchman of the government fleet all in the water at Gasconade. The river was so low they could not pull any of the boats out.

Christmas night there was a Christmas tree at the Sunday School. We all were there except Norman who did not seem well. He staid home with Papa. Just eight of our children took part in a Kantata gotten up by the Sunday School. Lizzie was one of the Community, Martha organist, Lottie, King's daughter, Bob, Santa Claus, Ed, Micky McGin, George one of the little boys, John, one of the little boys, Mary one of the little girls. I was quite well satisfied with it all, think they all done well. Sunday, Papa, Mary, Norman and I were at Will's

Annie's for dinner. In the afternoon we nearly all went to Sunday School.

The "Advertiser-Courier" was overjoyed by the return of Capt. Will to the Hermann fold.

When Captain Wm. L. Heckmann went away from Hermann to pitch his tent at Pryor's Mill, we said that he would come back. All good things come back; the sun comes back when the night is done; the flowers come back when the snow is melted; the crows come back when the long summer day is ended; the birds come back when the ethereal touch of spring has loosened the icy bands of winter; and Captain Heckmann comes back when the harbingers of spring are beginning to harb. We welcome the able Captain back to the hurley-burley of metropolitan life. We have had a sore struggle getting along without him, during the weary months since he went away, and his coming restores confidence and relieves the stringency of the money market, and makes everybody feel gay. All hail to the Captain who in triumph advances, the whole population to welcome him prances.

CHAPTER 13

The Curse of Debt

*Certainly we who trusted mostly for McKinley's administration
and protection to bring things out all right are still
patiently waiting.* —Mary L. Heckmann

*I*n the midst of all his grand plans for the Heckmann Mill, the one thing William Heckmann failed to do was study the markets. If he had, he would have realized there were 15 other mills operating within a 25-mile radius. Located far up the Gasconade River, the site was just too distant for many farmers, and the idea of transporting grain by steamboat instead of wagon never really caught on.

Financially, the mill was a disaster of the first order. It was written that Capt. Heckmann had invested $35,000 in the venture. That sum may be somewhat exaggerated, but even so there was little hope of returning a good profit on such a large investment. Steamboat Bill later wrote that for many years a large mill wheel lay on the bank at Hermann, a reminder of his father's first "bust" in business. He dubbed it the Heckmann's "Wheel of Misfortune."

The prosperous family that had moved to the mill with such great plans and expectations now returned home to Hermann in dire financial straits. William Heckmann had borrowed against everything he owned to finance the mill project, and now he was broke. He still had his farms and some income from the steamboats, but his creditors had begun to clamp down. The easy flow of credit at the stores came to an end, along with Mary's hope for the future.

Nonetheless, daily life had its pleasant moments. Mary had celebrated her 50th birthday in February of 1898—*got some nice presents and had quite a little crowd here.* The girls went to an entertainment at the Concert Hall and came home bubbling with news about the wondrous new grafophone.

Mary enjoyed having young eligible girls in the house. *Lottie and her crowd made up a picnic and got wet. It rained real hard, they all got wet. I drove out with their lunch, but came home before it rained so much, even if we did eat ice cream under umbrellas.* While social events claimed the attention of the girls, their mother was thoroughly digesting the daily St. Louis paper.

The sinking of our battle ship Main in Havana harbor from an explosion has roused the nation from center to circumference. I believe there has not been such an excitement since the firing of Sumpter. All are in suspense waiting the decision of the investigation to decide what caused the great calamity, everywhere there is suspicion of foul play on the part of the Spanish at Havana. There were 244 lives lost, many are wounded, and are cared for at Havana and Key West. ... The country is in an uproar, from all parts the War spirit is heard from, and Spain's people are anxious for the fray, but they do not know what they are bringing on themselves ... wish and hope that war may be averted.

Nostalgia was the order of the day when old soldiers met.

Capt. Wm. Heckmann, Louis Poeschel, Eugene Nasse and Chris Schlender are the only four now alive of sixteen soldiers who guarded the Merrimac bridge during the war. Their meeting here last Sunday was pathetic and they all blew their noses vigorously, which men always do when tears come into their eyes.

William and young Will exchanged the steamer Jack Rabbit for stock and returned to the good graces of the Hermann Ferry and Packet Co. The eternal entrepreneur, William was working every angle he could think of to make money. By the spring of 1898, the financial picture looked somewhat brighter. The "Advertiser-Courier" reported, *Capt. Heckmann this season will get the biggest wheat crop in years, exemplifying the old saw "that all things come to him who waits."*

Excursions now featured both steamboats and the railroad.

There are few families in town that did not have visitors last Sunday from abroad. The excursion train from St. Louis brought in 700 people, the steamboat Mill Boy brought in a big crowd and the west bound local passenger train also had many people ticketed for Hermann. It seemed as if everybody had a friend in town, and in the evening as train time drew near, groups could be seen

The Heckmann daughters: Seated, from left, Mary, Lottie and Lizzie. Standing are Martha, left, and Annie.

emerging from almost every house making their way to the depot. Wharf street was packed with people—the whole town having turned out to see their company off. Hermann had on tap her old fashioned hospitality, and the latch string with tassels on it was still hanging outside on the doors.

The three oldest Heckmann sons, who had been taken out of school at age 13 to "learn the river" on their father's boats, were all working now. Young Will, now 31, was married to "Will's Annie." He had two children and was in charge of the government steamer Arethusa. He and Annie had built a fine new home with steamboat gingerbread trim on the corner of Second and Mozart streets at the end of the Heckmann family's vineyard.

A crack river pilot, 29-year-old Sam Heckmann was married and the father

The Heckmann sons: From left, Ed, Robert, Fred, John, William Jr., Norman, George and Sam.

of one child. He was in charge of the steamer Jack Rabbit. Fred Heckmann, the sharpshooter of the family, was 26 and talking of joining the navy. The newspaper reported, *Fred (Hitz) Heckmann has enlisted in the naval reserve. He is a licensed pilot and river engineer and a young man of much intelligence.*

Fred was courting Philopena Morlock—Pena to the family—and had become very self-conscious about his nose, which was deformed from a childhood injury. Mary was most sympathetic to her son's worries about his appearance—his brothers were all handsome, making comparisons inevitable—and supportive when he went to St. Louis to have his nose fixed by a plastic surgeon. *The operation was performed but we have had one letter from him, are anxious to see how it will turn out.* Plastic surgery was in its infancy, so this was quite a daring undertaking.

Despite their mother's heartfelt pleas, the younger boys seemed destined to follow in the footsteps of their father and older brothers and take up life on the river. Ed, George and John all liked to hang around the boats, but since their father no longer ran a fleet of steamboats, berths were harder for them to find. Eighteen-year-old Bob, although never quite as fascinated by steamboats as his brothers, helped out as cook, deck hand, clerk and general roustabout whenever his father needed him.

George, the family daredevil, would go on to become one of the river's top marine engineers. Like his mother, George kept a journal, which included many stories about growing up around the boats.

In 1900 I was 14 years old. The Mill Boy was then the Ferry Boat at Hermann, Mo. At that time they were making four trips per day. On the last trip of each day the leaving time was 4 o'clock. The Public School was five blocks from the river and school let out at four. If I could be the first kid out and then run like Hell I could make it in time to make that last trip.

I reckon I had some help. I have an idea the Captain would delay a few minutes waiting for me. Ferdie Bohl was the Engineer. It was on this boat that I learned the bell signals and learned to handle the engines. Was I a proud kid when he referred to me as his assistant engineer. I also learned how to clean up grease and oil on that boat.

Norman, the baby of the family, was famous for his ability to howl loudly. Even he was encouraged to play around the boats. *Norman celebrated his sixth birthday by falling off the stage plank on one of the ribs of the barge, seemed to be hurt very badly, but got over it before night.* Norman somehow managed to hit Pena in the face with a baseball bat. Fred attempted to discipline his little brother, which his mother found most amusing.

Mary rejoiced that Robert had remained in high school and was acquitting himself in a scholarly way. The Adelphian Literary Society had a good local following for its intellectual programs. A report on the debate at one meeting included a few words about Robert Heckmann.

The question was resolved, that Washington deserves more honor for freeing America, than Lincoln for preserving it. Leander Graf and C. M. Danuser firmly stood up for Washington, while they were strongly opposed by Robert Heckmann and R. E. Breuer. The debate was decided in favor of the affirmative but the negative also deserves praise, for Robert Heckmann brought forth some thoughtful arguments, and Mr. Breuer, though it was his first attempt, also did exceedingly well.

Young Robert was up against some formidable brains. Graf was an attorney, Danuser was a teacher who later became superintendent of schools, and Breuer was a county judge. Robert would go on to graduate from the full four-year "Classical Course" at Hermann High School. Only one other student, Ida Walker, graduated with him, although several students completed a shorter course in stenography.

While the boys could almost always get jobs on the boats, paying work was harder for the girls to find. Daughter Lizzie went to keep house for Dr. Feldman who was ill and claimed it was the beginning of the end. *He told Lizzie: "Your mother shall have of everything I have in the garden," and sure enough, he sent me of all the shrubs he has and everything grew.* Lizzie, who never married, made a career of keeping house for others and even ran an orphanage for a time.

Mary, whose ideas about how her younger sons should be helping out did not include steamboats, took Bob, Ed, George and John and a hired hand to the lower island to plant corn, potatoes and horseradish, going up on the boat and coming down in the skiff. Later in the summer she packed up the six youngest children and went to the mill for two weeks.

> *I had to cook for all of us and two work houses for a week. Then Sister Lizzie came up and brought Mrs. Dans along, so she helped me some but it made the family larger and of course more work. But the little ones had a jolly time and the girls here in Hermann had a good rest. There were only four of them at times.*

Although Heckmanns no longer lived at the mill, the home there was seldom empty. *Annie, Charley, and Ira came home from the mill. Lottie, Ed, John and George Klinger are out there yet, they went out same time as Charley and Annie.* By this time Annie, the daughter, was often called Sister Annie to distinguish her from Will's Annie. Later, when John married Annie Kuhn, she became John's Annie. Sorting out the Williams—senior and junior—the Annies and the Marys was a confusing business. Adding to the difficulty was the matter of daughter Lizzie and sister Lizzie, along with son John and brother John Miller.

News from Judge Sam Miller, Mary's 76-year-old father, was always welcome in Hermann. He wrote in the "Rhineland Sunbeam" that at 500 feet, Montgomery Hill was the highest point within 20 miles of Bluffton.

> *I know from personal observation as I have been on the top of it when a fog closed in from the north and covered the whole landscape and hid it from view. The top of the cloud was as low as a lake and not a thing visible but the blue sky and sunshine. It is a rare sight but a grand one. The whole bottom is often enveloped in a dense fog for hours in the morning, while up there the sun is shining in all its glory.*

Samuel Miller was a prolific writer and not without a sense of humor. In "Colman's Rural World" he wrote:

> *Some years ago one of my sons was setting out some peach trees. There happened to be a dead dog on hand which was put in the bottom of the hole covered well with earth, and the tree set thereon. That tree had the lead of all the others in the lot. Last year it bore a splendid crop and this season it is full again. The most interesting part is that the tree is a Susquehana, and that the variety is usually a shy bearer. Of course the dog was absorbed by the tree and passed into the peaches, and the question arises: Who ate the dog?*

Judge Sam Miller

Mary's Aunt Eveline Evans died out in Pennsylvania. Mary, who had money worries on her mind, received $6.16 from the estate. *What became of the rest, Uncle Carp knows. I call this hush money.*

Two generations of family members kept Mary busy with an assortment of ailments. William underwent eye surgery. Mary doesn't say why, but does report, *They do not look quite right yet, but he exposes himself too much to the sun, cannot expect then to get well until cool weather sets in.* William's brother, Henry Heckmann, was declared fatally ill with congestive chills, but made a miraculous recovery. *I never seen anyone as sick as he was to get well again, but he is well again, about as well as can be.*

Son John came down with a severe inflammation of the bowels. Ed had diphtheria. An antitoxin from the doctor cleared up his throat overnight. Lizzie, Martha, Lottie and George all had the grip, a disease known as flu today. Mary had other worries about the safety of her offspring.

> *Yesterday I spent a miserable afternoon. Ed and John were over at their Aunt Lizzie's and I wanted Fred and Bob to go over and get them, the river is full of floating ice. William came home he said he believed the boys had gone up to Gasconade to get the little boat to get the hogs in. Between anxiety and not*

171

being well I had one of my very worst afternoons. At dark they got here, sure enough, they had come down in the little boat built for two for smooth water, and not for ice either.

Lizzie was across the river because *in November the hotel keeper at McKittrick came over in great haste and wanted my sister Lizzie to come over there and take charge of his house. So nothing daunted, she pulled up, and at 4 o'clock she went over, and on the 24th, Thanksgiving Day, I sent all her household goods over.*

By the end of the year, Mary's patience with family troubles had worn thin. *If this is a harbinger of what the new year brings for us, I feel sorry for US.* Indeed, the new 1899 did begin badly. As was her custom, Mary extended charity to a tramp one bitterly cold night. But the man later turned up on the Heckmann's doorstep nearly frozen to death. *This tramp was found by Greeley when he left the house to go home. Had he not come up that same evening the tramp would have been frozen before William got home at 8 o'clock.*

The "Advertiser-Courier" reported the story in detail.

A strange man was last Wednesday evening found at the doorstep of Capt. Heckmann's residence in an unconscious and frozen condition. He was taken into the house, and everything done to bring him to, but apparently without avail. He was taken to the court house where the doctor, who had been called in, ascertained that the whole left side of the man was frozen. The stranger is apparently 45 years of age, poorly clad, and a few hours before he was found, had asked for and received food at Capt. Heckmann's house. He started west, but it seems his strength gave out, and dragging himself back to ask for shelter in the hospitable house, fell exhausted at the door steps where he was found.

The newspaper must have kept a well-marked calendar. *Next Sunday will be the 30th Anniversary of the marriage of Capt. Wm. L. Heckmann and his estimable wife and many of our citizens will offer congratulations to as well mated a couple as live in this benighted portion of God's footstool.*

William accompanied Norman Colman's party on the annual hunt to Ripley County near the Arkansas border. While away from home, William wrote often with news about the success of the hunt. Mary always seemed pleased about these trips, which often lasted two or three weeks. She considered Norman Colman, who had been secretary of agriculture under Grover Cleveland, a fine man, and she was proud of William's close association with him. Colman would be instrumental in the 1903 founding of the University of Missouri School of Journalism, which was funded by a $2 million grant from the Pulitzer Foundation.

The town had a great shock when word came from Chicago that a terrible murder had been committed. A Hermann boy was dead, and two other Hermann boys were suspected of being the murderers. Mary wrote, *There were three poor mothers prostrated with grief.*

At about the same time George Starck and Ottmar Starck of Hermann were arrested for selling whiskey, or distilling and forgetting to pay the government revenue. Mary was skeptical about the wheels of justice.

We see nothing in the papers about the Starck trial, surely Uncle Sam will not stoop to accepting bribes. From the flitting to and fro of Mr. O. to Washington and back, such things might be feasible. That would be the only way they would attempt to settle things for they think it is the almighty dollar does it all.

She added later, *It seems the Great Western Wine & Liquor Co. of St. Louis has absorbed the Great Western Wine Co. The new company has been incorporated with a capital stock of $10,000 of 100 shares, is owned as follows: George Stark, 60, Ottmar G. Stark, 20 and Albert Thiele, 20.* Exactly how this related to the arrests is not explained.

The promised bountiful wheat harvest came to pass. *William keeps coming and going to the mill, he is filling his elevators for Harper and Talbot with wheat, for speculation.* Mary herself had been suffering with some sort of skin poison for weeks. *My arm and eyes are still not well, have tried about everything anyone ever told me, it gets better and then all at once it will be worse.*

The houseplants were always a source of extra concern in the fall.

The flower pit is finished at last and I am well pleased with it. The pit proper is of brick, then about eight inches of space between them is a frame of cotton wood boards, and they are banked up with earth. Everything in it looks nice and I think every rose cutting I put in will grow. The garden is spaded and everything is "ship-shape" for winter. I sold the little cow last week and got twenty-six dollars for her. Since Fred quit work on Dec. 2, we have only gone to the butcher once as he and papa and the other boys kept us in meat. We got a hog from the mill too.

At the close of 1899, Mary wrote:

I close the old year hoping in my heart that all may be well for us in the New Year. When the bitter cold winds blow we must be thankful for the blessing of plenty to eat and the good house and fuel to keep us warm, but, oh, how many things we wish and long for even when it comes to good warm clothing, it is *lacking. How I have prayed for only enough so that we might have some little enjoyment without first considering the cost there of. How often I have prayed for deliverance from the bondage of the <u>curse of debt</u> for the day that I could hold up my head and say I owe no man a dollar, but I have given up all such hope. That day will never come, and yet I cannot help but think that I am just as worthy as many another one. I have struggled and hoped and struggled and hoped again and what is my reward? A few more burdens placed upon me. And these I am to bear with a smiling face and appear to enjoy it all. But what is the use in repining, I was born to be a slave, I might just as well take up the poor wife's burden and go on through life to the end looking for my reward in the next life. But I sometimes think my trials drive me to such anger and rebellion against fate that my future reward will be withheld, like Moses and the promised land.*

The steamer Jack Rabbit was sold to G.H.C. Bodeker, and Fred went along to deliver the boat to Murphysboro, Illinois. A frightening telegram arrived with the message that Fred was very ill with inflammation of the bowels, bringing back memories of Julius Silber's death. Mary caught the night train and arrived at midnight in Murphysboro, where she stayed until Fred had recovered. On her way home she stopped at Shaw's Garden in St. Louis to pick up rose bushes for Will's Annie.

In spite of the economic uncertainties of the day, the year 1900 saw a flurry of activity at the Hermann wharf. The "Advertiser-Courier" reported:

A new steamboat company with a capital stock of $10,000 has been formed in Hermann, for the purpose of running a regular Missouri river packet from St. Louis to Rocheport. The company for the present will put two boats in commission: the one now building at our wharf to be used for the Gasconade river trade, and a much larger boat for the Missouri river. Capt. Wm. Heckmann, Jr. last Saturday left for the Ohio river to find such a boat, and it's likely that he will secure a boat suitable for the trade.

The gentlemen interested in the new enterprise are George Starck, Phillip Haeffner, John Haid, August Wohlt, John Ochsner, George Kraettly, Will Heckmann, Jr., Henry Sassmann, Capt. Wm. L. Heckmann, all of Hermann, and Dan Jackisch, of Gasconade. ... The company contemplates building a substantial and spacious warehouse at Gasconade, in which all freight from the

The Steamer W. H. Grapevine

Gasconade river will be stored, to be from there transferred to the St. Louis
Packet. The men interested in this enterprise have business experience and
success seems assured if hard work and good judgment can make it so.

The new boat built by the company was the steamer Buck Elk, which was
launched on the Fourth of July, just in time for wheat harvest. Mary said, *All were*
along except Mary, Norman and I. A few days after the boat went to work and has been
busy since. The newspaper described the new boat as *100 feet long with 18 foot beam,*
and will not draw more than eight inches of water.

As promised, the new company also purchased a big boat. The steamer
Grapevine really was big by Hermann standards, big in size and, with a purchase
price of $10,000, big in cost.

William went to Kansas City to buy or get the Grapevine, he was up last week
to get her elementions, contemplating the building of a boat like her. He found
the Grapevine could be bought, he came home, held a meeting of the stockhold-
ers and decided to buy her. Done the talking by long distance phone. They

The Steamer Buck Elk

intend putting her into the through trade to St. Louis from Rocheport.

Steamboat Bill often wrote about the final days of steamboating on the Missouri River.

In the old times almost every pilot wanted his own boat. Today they depend on large companies owning the boat and only look for a berth. Such old boatmen as Col. Hunter Ben Jenkins, George Keith, W. R. Massie, W. L. Heckmann, Sr., Hal Dodd and Joseph Kinney went broke fighting the railroads on unimproved rivers.

When steamboating was good and wages high in the mountain trade, many boatmen saved their money and built, owned and operated their own boats. One prominent pilot who could never save any of his money was famous along our rivers for his ability to cuss out any boat he happened to be working on and always winding up with a wistful: "If I just had a hundred thousand dollars I would build a boat that would run on this crazy river."

When our main boatmen began to fail in business, they used every method known to men in order to get capital to buy or build boats. They induced farmers, merchants, and shippers to invest in the river saying to themselves, "If these men furnish the capital and I furnish the experience, all will be well again." Sometimes all was well, but more often the ventures were complete failures. This was partly due to lack of business ability among pilots whose specialty "knowing the river" did not include "knowing how to squeeze out a profit."

An old joke that went the rounds of the St. Louis theaters during these years involved a comedian who came out on the stage telling the audience how much money he had—in fact, so much money that he didn't know what to do with it. The experienced audience was always convulsed when one of their number shouted out, "Buy an old steamboat."

In 1899 I financed (promoted) a stock company, taking in a number of

friends, shippers and boatmen. We built the Buck Elk at Hermann, Mo. for the
Gasconade river. She (a boat is always called "she"—some say because the
trimmings cost more than the hull) was a fine boat that naturally hunted deep
water.

Some boats hunt the deep water and some find all the shallow water in the
river. The difference in the hull and rudder construction accounts for some of
this. On the other hand, two boats built over the same model and given identi-
cal machinery and power may behave as exact opposites. I have seen this in a
dozen sets of boats, both stern and side-wheelers. One boat will act unruly and
her sister will do all the things she never could or would do.

The Buck Elk was so successful for several years that our hearts filled with
pride and we knew that our faith in the river was justified. The river "was
coming back" so we increased our capital stock and built or bought three more
boats, the W. H. Grapevine, the Kennedy and the steamer Columbia. Our opti-
mism was unjustified, or perhaps, our expansion was too rapid. At any rate,
our company failed soon after this.

It should be noted that the Grapevine was purchased just after the Buck Elk
went into service in 1900, not years later as indicated above. The purchase of the
steamer Columbia is unconfirmed. In 1905 William Heckmann Jr. formed another
company and bought the steamer Lora, which was renamed the Omaha.

The newspaper kept a close eye on all waterfront developments, even fire-
wood.

For the first time in many years, the Ferry Company this winter did not have
for sale any cord-wood, the boats last fall being unable to make landings in the
Gasconade river. It was a great inconvenience to people in town, but all right
for the farmer near by who had wood to sell.

An odd bit of steamboating news surfaced about the steamer Benton.

A charge from Saline county being telegraphed that its captain had stolen wood
from along the river bank. Capt. Boland, in defense, revived an old statute, a
relic of the days when boats plied on the river. This statute gives a captain of a
boat the right to help himself to fuel whenever and wherever he may find it
necessary to replenish his supply, and pay reasonable price for the same.

Stories abound about tricks played by steamboat captains to insure having
sufficient wood for their boats, but having a legal leg to stand on was news.

The old generation of Missouri River steamboat captains was disappearing. Capt. Henry Wohlt, who had been forced to leave the river because of eye problems and failing health, had died at age 66. For a time after leaving the river he became a miller, operating the Spring Creek Mill in Franklin County. His obituary lauded his pioneering efforts to build steamboats suitable for the Gasconade River.

Capt. Archie Bryan died at age 69 at his home in Washington, Missouri. His obituary told the story of a remarkable life.

> *In his young days he went overland to California where he was engaged in mining and mercantile pursuits. In 1853 returned to Warren county by way of Nicaragua. He engaged in steamboating and sailed the Missouri river from its source to its mouth, and up the Yellowstone, on the Cumberland, Ohio, Osage and Gasconade. He was the oldest captain on the Missouri who had been continuously in the same business. He was captain and had proprietary interest in more than a dozen steamboats and the last few years had been captain of the steamer Gasconade, doing work for the government.*

While the Buck Elk was under construction, the newspaper reported that the Hermann Ferry and Packet Co. also was building a boat. *The new steamboat built by the Hermann Ferry & Packet Co. has been named "Henry Wohlt" in honor of the late Capt. Henry Wohlt, who was the pioneer steamboatman on the Gasconade river.*

According to river historian Doc Trail, *the steamer Henry Wohlt was built by ship's carpenter John Bohlken, a master craftsman and his steamboat hulls were the very best. She was a very successful little boat and always in charge of Captain Gustave Wohlt.*

Norman, the youngest Heckmann son, began his river service on the steamer Henry Wohlt. Capt. Gustave Wohlt could only steamboat in German and would yell down to Norman, the deckhand, "Schieb Sie ab, Schieb Sie ab"— "Shove her off, shove her off!"

In 1901 the Henry Wohlt paid for herself twice over in the Gasconade River trade. She was a scow (meaning square) bow boat and a good carrier, but according to various Wohlt and Heckmann pilots she never handled as well as the steamer August Wohlt, which was built later.

The tie business was on the decline, but still an important source of income for the boats. The "Jefferson City Journal" reported that *railway tie timber in the trees in the woods will be worth ten to fifteen cents per tie in less than eighteen months. Railway tie buyers have nearly cleaned out the Osage Valley of the timber from Linn*

Creek to the Missouri river. Osage, Gasconade and Franklin counties are now being *ransacked for railroad ties.* There was bitter irony in the tie business for the steamboatmen. By hauling ties, they were literally helping to pave the way to their own demise.

Loading and unloading the boats was a dangerous business. *Capt. Wm. L. Heckmann narrowly escaped being crushed to death. While witnessing the unloading of a huge iron roller for Brachts mill, the slide on the skid broke, the roller falling towards Capt. Heckmann, crushing him sufficiently to bruise him severely, necessitating his removal home in a buggy.*

Capt. Gustave Wohlt had his own brush with death.

While crossing 5th and Olive street and trying to avoid a street car, he was struck by another car coming from an opposite direction and thrown between the cars, happily not under the wheels. He suffered a severe cut and bruise on the back of his neck, but was able to come home that night.

The eternal fight to get money appropriated for river improvement continued.

Capt. Wm. L. Heckmann received a letter from Congressman Champ Clark wherein the latter says that Judge Burton, chairman of the River and Harbor Committee was much impressed with the statement as to the volume of business done by boats at Hermann prepared by Capt. Heckmann. Mr. Clark is hopeful of good results and will use this utmost endeavors to get an appropriation for Hermann harbor. He thinks there will be no trouble to get something for the improvement of the Gasconade.

The year 1900 ended differently from most for the Heckmann family. The holidays had always meant more work for Mary, but now it was up to a new generation to carry on family traditions.

Christmas passed off more pleasant to us than for several years. We had no tree, left that to the married children, who each had a fine one. Papa, myself and the four smaller children called on all. First at Will's house, then at Annie's, and from there at Sam's, all had beautiful trees. Santa Claus was real kind to us.

CHAPTER 14

Disaster

*In the spring our credit had run so very low and I resolved
to only buy necessities, so we were all short of clothes. Some times even short
of what we needed on the table.* —Mary L. Heckmann

*T*imes were hard, credit was tight, and there was little money coming in. Nonetheless, early in the year 1901 William bought another tract of land across the river from his friend I. H. Talbot. *They fixed up the papers yesterday,* Mary wrote, so she no doubt signed again. Just where William found money for the purchase, she does not say; certainly, he had no ready cash.

During the freeze-up all the family were home, and the boats were snug in their winter quarters. Then the weather moderated. The boats were taken out and, of course, got caught in thick ice, with their owners heartily wishing they were back safe in the Gasconade winter harbor.

Sixteen-year-old Ed Heckmann, who was ready to quit school, went to St. Louis looking for work, but there was none to be had. Mary had given up on Ed as a preacher, but she was still working on him to go into teaching. When no other work showed up, he capitulated and applied for his certificate. He began teaching at the Mud Creek School near Hope on the Gasconade River—and he hated it.

After three days he heard the whistle of his father's steamboat, turned the school over to his oldest pupil, who was older than he was, and left. At the river bank he took off his shoes, tied his shoe laces together, hung the shoes about his neck and swam out to the boat. His father gave him a pat on the back and, at the first chance, a berth on a boat.

From that inauspicious beginning, Ed would go on acquire what may be the most extensive pilot's license ever issued. He always claimed the school district never paid him for his three days of teaching, and he had to pay for three days rent before his landlady would release his belongings. Mary's only comment was *Ed has given up his school, he says he just cannot teach.*

Mary's dream of having a professional man in the family was revived when Bob received his certificate and began teaching at Stolpe. With the boats in winter quarters, Bob returned home on weekends by skating down the Gasconade and Missouri rivers. One dark night he skated into an air hole in the Missouri River. After a lengthy struggle, he finally had the presence of mind to let one of his mittens freeze tight to the ice so he could pull himself out.

Walking down the railroad tracks in wet clothes, it soon occurred to Bob that he would probably freeze to death. He returned to the pitch-black river, clamped on his skates and skated the rest of the way home. Not wanting to alarm his mother, he climbed up to the porch roof and went in through a window. Ed Heckmann, the best storyteller in the family, later told the tale of the night he was awakened by an ice-cold brother who suddenly crawled in bed with him.

The next day Bob put on his skates once again and returned to Stolpe, towing a sled with stoves on it. His mother barely commented on the crawling in through the window incident, and she never mentioned his icy bath. Perhaps she never knew.

So large was the family by now that Mary fretted that if she missed a few days in her journal she had trouble remembering everything. In February of 1901, Mary and William celebrated their birthdays—she was 53 and he was 56—and their 33rd wedding anniversary. Brother Bob Miller bought an island at Bluffton. He and Tina were living there, still having a baby every odd-numbered year.

The grandchildren kept coming, with the sisters-in-law trying to top each other's baby stories. Will's Annie bragged that her baby girl was born with a cowl, a "veil" that was supposed to be a sign of good luck. Sam's wife Gusta, who had just given birth to a baby boy, thought up a topper. "Yours has a veil," replied Gusta, "but mine has a tail."

Telephone service and postal Rural Free Delivery had come to Hermann. *We used our new telephone for the first time* . And excitement was building over the approaching St. Louis World's Fair. A national holiday was declared in commemoration of the anniversary of the Louisiana Purchase.

Mary was eloquent about the spring weather. Clearly, her thoughts were beginning to take on a more religious bent.

The 16th of May was one of the most glorious days we ever have, the sky was clear and blue, every tree, the grasses, the grain fields, all shades of green. There was a slight breeze gently swaying the foliage. The temperature must have been about 70. The river was as calm and placid as could be, every object was clear and distinct. The birds are so plentiful they sing both day and night. This May day just described was a day such as we look for in the great and grand home prepared for the true and good in the great hereafter, where all is peace and joy.

The St. Louis and Hermann Packet Co. was again looking for another boat. *William was to Pittsburg to look at a boat, preparatory to buying it.* This boat was the Mayflower, to be renamed Kennedy.

In April of 1901, the "St. Louis Democrat" reported:

The St. Louis and Hermann Packet Company, of which Capt. Wm. Heckmann is president, has purchased the steamer Mayflower from Capt. Klein, of Pittsburg, Pa. for $10,000. Capt. Heckmann left last night for Pittsburg to bring the steamer to this city and expects to arrive in about two weeks. He will place the boat in the Missouri River trade, along with the steamer W. H. Grapevine, which the company is operating between this city and Rocheport. The company is making an effort to revive traffic on the Missouri, and has met with much encouragement having more business than it could attend to with the Grapevine. The steamer Mayflower is well known here. She was built for the excursion business at Pittsburg fourteen years ago, and after operating about the Smokey City a few years she was brought to St. Louis, and for several seasons she vibrated between the Tennessee and Lower Mississippi rivers. She was the property of the Tennessee River Packet Company, and was sold to Capt. Klein about two years ago.

With two steamboat companies operating out of Hermann, there was more river news than ever, with a constantly shifting cast of boats and owners. The newspapers reported that the ferry company *operates three boats, and if for any reason, one of them is sold a new one is built in its place at our wharf, it being a rule of the company to build all of its own boats. A new boat will be built this spring to take the place of the steamer Gasconade, which was sold to parties of Chattanooga, Tenn., last fall.*

Keen competition for river business kept the steamboatmen scrambling for new ways to serve shippers.

Capt. Gus Wohlt of the Hermann Ferry & Packet Co., left for Cooper Hill and other points along the Gasconade river with a view of selecting points at which warehouses may be erected for the accommodation of shippers. At present and here-to-fore shippers have been put to great inconvenience and risk in hauling wheat and merchandise to the riverbank and leaving the same without shelter and care until the boats would arrive.

The "New Haven Leader" reported that *Capt. Wm. L. Heckmann of Hermann was here and made arrangements to have a boat warehouse built on Henry Zibelin's property at the boat landing. The new warehouse will be built at once and will be 16 x 24 feet in size.*

Another form of competition appeared in the form of railroad transportation out of the upper reaches of the Gasconade River.

The Railroad is now completed through Gasconade County. Bland will be the terminus of the road for about 2 months. Trains will run regularly from St. Louis to Bland and all intermediate points. The period of construction will never be forgotten as long as the present generation lives. It took six thousand dollars worth of powder for the Neely cut alone. Men who have a long head and a wise look tell us, that this railroad will change this country in fifteen years more than anything else that ever happened.

By June, Capt. Heckmann was in Batesville, Arkansas, contracting for steamboat work on the White River. Steamboat Bill later wrote with bitter regret about his father's forays into Arkansas steamboating.

The St. Louis and Hermann Packet Company had plans made to build a brand-new and much larger boat for Steamboat Bill, in fact the stockholders were willing to put up any amount of money for any kind of boat he desired. Just then my father took a big railroad contract for freighting on the Upper White River in Arkansas. We bought the brand-new steamer Kennedy and took the steamer Buck Elk out of a very profitable trade on the Gasconade River. Both these outfits went to the upper White and Dad said for me to get along another season with the Grapevine and that "the two boats on the White River will make enough to buy any kind of a boat you want."

We lost $25,000 on the White River. ... Our stockholders became discour-

aged and sold the Grapevine, Kennedy, Buck Elk, Columbia and barges, ware-houses, all for a song. We even lost the little Napoleon, Andy Franz, as a clerk who would have saved us some of our loss. We left for the White River with the steamer Kennedy in January ice. George Keith took us out to Memphis and the king bee of the White River pilots, Ed Warner, took us to the upper reaches of that stream. Andy came aboard at St. Louis to ask for a clerkship but found four Heckmanns, Bill, Sam, Fred and Ed headed for Arkansas to see the Upper White. He said it looked too much like a family boat and he did not ask to be employed while, at the same time we were looking for a clerk.

We did not only lose our all but Steamboat Bill also lost his one ambition in life which was to build a suitable boat for the lower Missouri River trade. Thus my claim still stands, that if they had given me a proper boat at that time I would still be doing business at the old stand, despite railroads, trucks or aircraft.

The one piece of good news was a good wheat harvest that summer. *Capt. Wm. L. Heckmann informs us that from 3 acres of ground on his island in the Missouri river, near Bluffton, Henry Gerringer threshed 62 sacks of wheat, which is an average of 35 bushels per acre. This is not only a very large, but in fact, a most extraordinary yield per acre, and speaks volumes for the fertility of the soil on the captain's island.*

At last a partial settlement was reached in the ongoing battle with Montgomery County over property rights. Mary wrote, *William was at Montgomery City looking after his island property. Montgomery County wants to take advantage of a law passed in 1895 making unreclaimed lands subject to sale, the parcels to go to the school fund. They claim our island came under that head. This has cost us $25.00 all told, I think it a wrong ... The lower island is decided in our favor, the upper is under advisement in the Judge's hands.* William eventually obtained clear title to the second island by paying $2,000 to the county.

The "Advertiser-Courier" used somewhat stronger language to describe the case of Montgomery County vs. W. L. Heckmann. *It is an action to steal the islands from Capt. Heckmann, who with his grantors, has been in posession for more than fifty years.*

The law on islands also wreaked disaster on Bob Miller—this time Gasconade County wanted the land. The "Advertiser-Courier" reported, *Robert Miller for about five years occupied and improved an island in the Missouri river which in a suit in our circuit court was adjudged to be school land and given to Gasconade county. It was recently surveyed and found to contain 216 acres, which last Tuesday, by order of the*

county court sold at public sale and bid in by Messrs. R. A. Breuer and J. W. Hensley for
$517. The case is still in the supreme court.

Death once again touched the family, claiming the life of Judge Samuel Miller.
I think Father was asked to take a task at the Pan-American Exposition, he left
in a hurry. When I heard it I felt uneasy feeling sure that something would go
wrong with him. About the 12th of September he returned to Rhineland sick as
he could be, they were afraid at Gerts that he would not live over the night, but
the next day he went home to Bluffton, took to his bed, and remained there
almost continually until the 24th of October when he died. He lingered between
life and death for three weeks. I was at Bluffton for three weeks before he died,
got home the 26th of October. We buried him next to Fred Teubner. Mother's
grave first, brother David second, Fred third and Father fourth.

Mary was worried about her sister Emma, too, and surmised, *Am very much*
afraid she is sicker than she knows of. Mary left on the steamer Grapevine for the
first leg of a trip to Sedalia to see Emma. At Bluffton they stopped to pick up
sister Lizzie and her daughter, Isabell. *Lizzie got stuck in the mud before she got aboard,*
such a sight!

The Miller estate was settled with each of the 11 Miller children receiving
$27.50, and Ida Miller gets the *place from her father.* This statement is a mystery,
since Ida is not a daughter of Sam Miller.

While they were in Sedalia a telegram arrived with the news that Henry
Heckmann had died. Mary complained about the funeral arrangements. *It was*
fearfully hot. William wanted to have Henry's funeral in the morning, but of course, it
had to be done the old way, set it for four o'clock and many people were nearly overcome
with the heat.

The older generation was fast disappearing. Uncle Carpenter Evans died
out in Pennsylvania, the last of Martha Miller's family. Aunt Lizzie Miller also
died. *It is very sad, she died of fatty degeneration of the heart. Poor Uncle Abner will be*
almost lost without her. They were such close companions.

The Methodist church was claiming more and more of the attention of the
women of the Heckmann family and Bob.

The Methodists had an entertainment, A Panoramic View of the Life of Christ's
Life on Earth. It was good. … Had revival meetings in the Methodist Church, a
young stranger named William Brennecke was here also, Brother Koeller as-
sisting. Mrs. Koeller, Martha, Lottie and I went to the altar, besides many

others. ... Brother Brennecke came home with the girls, he is staying at Isenburgs.

Mary's efforts to steer her boys into the ministry had been in vain, but now a young preacher was interested in her family—particularly the girls. William Brennecke was nearly seven feet tall and a spellbinder in the pulpit. In Mary's eyes he was perfect, and she promptly invited him to supper. *Brother Brennecke missed the train, spent the evening here. Brother Brennecke and Martha take a great interest in one another.*

Just before Christmas George developed typhoid fever and was ill for several weeks. So once again, Mary's holiday was devoted to nursing a sick family member. But this did not prevent her from attending the Christmas entertainment at the Methodist Church. Nor did it prevent Rev. Brennecke from showing up again on Christmas night.

Martha was the belle of the Heckmann girls, and before long more suitors appeared.

A Prof. Path spent part of his vacation here in Hermann, at Backshies, his brother-in-law. He took a fancy to Martha, and soon after he left, sent Mr. Backshies to negotiate for Martha's hand. Since his death another Prof. Diehl has addressed her by letter.

But Rev. Brennecke definitely was first in the race for Martha's hand. His written request, addressed to Mr. and Mrs. William L. Heckmann, soon arrived.

My dear friends:

When visiting at your home recently, I had a mind to speak to you concerning that which actuates me to write this letter. But, since Mr. Heckmann was not at home, at the time, I neither spoke to Mrs. Heckmann.

You are both well aware of the fact that I am in love with your estimable and amiable daughter Martha. Martha won my admiration the first time I saw and met her. This admiration was soon associated with a sincere love, which found response in her noble heart. In fact, I can truthfully say, I have loved Martha ever since I have known her and my love and admiration increase as I learn to know her better.

After deliberately and candidly thinking and talking over such an important question as marriage, we have decided to become husband and wife. We believe that we will be extremely happy together. In consequence of our engagement, I take the liberty and pleasure to ask for your consent and blessing upon our engagement and subsequent marriage.

I informed Martha, from the beginning, that I am a poor young man. I have not made her any great promises outside of entire devotion and love to her; but expect to do more than I have promised her and not less. The only wealth I possess, is an immaculate character, a manly and Christian purpose in life,— i.e. an ardent desire to do good and help better the world and an education. The latter I am continuing by a correspondence course of study. In about two or three years I hope to be situated so that I can continue my work in a University for another year or two and thus equip myself for more usefulness.

I admire Martha as a noble womanly woman and she admires me as a manly man. Neither of us is looking for perfection in the other; but our love is sincere and our aspirations and ambitions are in harmony. We sincerely believe that the good Lord has guided us together and that we will be happy as husband and wife.

Soliciting an early and favorable reply, I am truly your,

W. T. Brennecke

He received an immediate reply in the affirmative.

The local newspaper had become an outlet for Mary's writing. She covered several social events, including the 92nd birthday of her friend, Grandma Lessel.

She has a large circle of old and young admiring friends, who fairly adore her, and each recurring birthday fills the Lessel mansion to its utmost capacity with people who have come to offer congratulations to the venerable woman who has lived such a long and useful life. Grandma Lessel, has always enjoyed splendid health, is a great lover of flowers, and while the "sere and yellow leaf rests upon her brow," her garden is a veritable paradise with its profusion of flowers, all of which have her constant and loving care. May she live to round out a hundred years of life.

Sadly, in only a few months Mary would write Grandma Lessel's obituary. The funeral was distressing. The new automatic apparatus for lowering the coffin broke, and it dropped from top to bottom with a thud.

Nothing, it seemed, could go right for the Heckmann family. Even the vineyard did poorly. The new year of 1902 had not dawned with great cheer. Mary had been discouraged and said so.

If anything we are worse off than ever, evening and morning I pray for a change, but oh, it does not come. God alone knows what the end will be. Lottie continues her stay in St. Louis. I do not blame her much, if I could shake off the continual curse of debt for a while I would gladly do it. One fears to eat sufficient, everything is so high and so scarce, and the head of our house has wrapped himself up in debt, until no one knows how he will ever extricate himself. Such a life is scarcely worth living, wherever one looks someone or something stares one in the face to remind one of debt and yet the people are very good and very lenient with us.

Mary sent off $40 to advertise the mill, but finding a buyer for an obsolete mill was going to be difficult. *I pray the good Father that all may come out well.* The steamer Kennedy was laid up for want of work, and the other boats were doing very little. William was traveling back and forth to Arkansas, looking for work without success.

Despite the Heckmann's troubles, the blooming of young love in the household had a salubrious effect on Mary and made her feel better about life. Her chicks were hatching in the new brooder house Bob bought, they were papering part of the house, and the fall weather was beautiful. A summer drought had made navigation difficult, but plentiful rains in October provided some relief. The newspaper complained, *Several days of drought should be encouraged. Not all of us are running steamboats.*

Apple butter time produced 25 gallons to put away for the winter.

We are having the most delightful weather. Mornings are pretty cool, mercury some 40 to 50. The sunsets are glorious, not a cloud to be seen. Along the horizon is the peculiar sunset glow, shades lighter until overhead the sky is a clear cream tinted white. … The year so far has been all we could ask for on earth. We have had an abundant harvest of wheat and corn promises to far exceed anything we have ever had.

The year ended with not one, but two weddings.

On Dec. 10th the wedding party drove to the church, Martha and William Brenneke were married at 7:30 p.m. We had a very nice wedding supper, everyone said they enjoyed themselves. The following day William Brenneke united our Fred and Pena Morlock in marriage. We had an early dinner and Martha and William left for Sedalia on their way to Billings, Mo. The next morning, Fred and Pena took the 4:30 a.m. train to go south to take charge of the Kennedy on the Mississippi and White River.

CHAPTER 14 ≈ DISASTER

The book 1902 is closed forever, what we have done and what we have left undone remains on record. It cannot be changed. I truly hope the good I have done will in fact counterbalance the mistakes I have made. May this New Year bring me and mine brighter days than we have had for many years.

Nationally, the Anti-Saloon League was making headlines, and locally, William Brennecke was preaching rousing temperance sermons, not the most popular topic in Hermann. Mary rejoiced when *a grand sermon touched Robert's heart and he expressed his desire to unite with the church, thanks be to God.*

The ice was perfect for skating, and the entire family, with the exception of Mary, went out on the ice. Norman claimed his skates were too sharp—the cause of his frequent falls.

There were a few things Mary could not fix with glue.

George loaded up one of the old rifles and it bursted when he shot, fortunately he only cut up his hand awful. He might have lost both hands, even his head if some of the pieces of the barrel had hit him as it was shattered into small pieces. Some going entirely over the house.

The aging captain certainly had not lost his rowing skills. William, who was up at the mill at the time of George's accident, came home wet and tired, having rowed a distance of nearly 50 miles in January cold and rain. A few days later he took the boat up to Bluffton and came home in the skiff.

An astounding number of people were coming and going at the Heckmann home—by Mary's count 553 from January 1 to May 19. This may have been what prompted her to leave for a long visit to Sedalia to see her sisters and to Billings to see Martha and her new husband.

While there, she became worried about the news of floods.

Pitiful stories of devastation along the rivers. Letters from home tell me all the people had to be moved off the islands. They fear too that the lumber will be washed off our farm at Loutre Island. On her return home she wrote that *high water has ruined all our crops on the islands, every person and all their stock is taken off, and all houses gone but one. The river lacked two feet here of being as high as 1844, the greatest flood the white people here know of.*

In his book "Sixty-five Years of Steamboating on the Missouri River," Steamboat Bill describes the devastation of the flood of 1903. Not all of his facts can be verified, but he tells the story as only one who was there could.

In the year of our Lord 1903, along about the middle of June, continued rain on the upper Kansas river swelled that stream until it went on a rampage such as had never before been seen. More rain and still more rain on down the river caused the Grand, the Chariton, the Lamine, the Osage, the Gasconade and every creek or branch to go clean out of their banks and come tumbling into the Missouri.

All this water pouring into the main stream with a liberal amount of snow water from the mountains sent the Missouri swelling until it went plumb crazy, causing untold misery, loss of life, and tremendous damage to property.

At this time seven different steamboats were running out of the port of Hermann, Mo. These boats saved many lives and millions of dollars worth of property while the M.K.& T. railroad on the north side of the river was someplace underneath the water.

Most of the lowland between St. Louis and Kansas City is on the north side of the Missouri river and here was the greatest misery. The crest of the flood came at the time that the large and abundant wheat crops in the river bottom land were ready to cut. To see these vast fields of waving grain disappearing under water was a sad sight, especially for the few steamboats left on the river. Wheat was their main item of freight in this last ditch fight against the railroads. But even sadder sights were to come as the Big Muddy continued to swell and go roaring toward the sea.

My father owned three large islands on the river, two just above and one just below the mouth of the Gasconade river. The largest of these islands was below the Gasconade and as different owners came in possession of it, it was called variously McGirk's, Graf's and Heckmann's island.

Father had nine substantial houses on the lower island and seven hundred acres in wheat and corn in addition to his own threshing outfit, farm machinery, horses, and mules to be used by his tenants in cultivating the land. The river went clean over this island. While father was out with the steamer Kennedy moving other people's property, his own island was washed away.

After working night and day for about three weeks in rescue work, father came back to inspect his own island. He found thirty acres of the island left with one house on it, turned over and leaning crazily against a big cottonwood tree.

The steamer Kennedy was a two hundred ton boat, stern wheel, roomy,

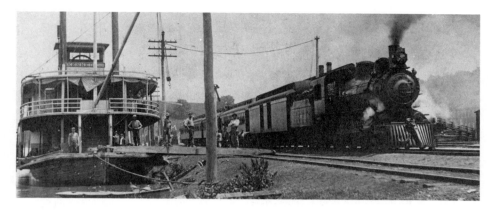

The Steamer Kennedy during the flood of 1903

light and fast—in fact, the fastest boat that ever was operated on the Missouri river. Father was in charge of this boat all through the flood and it was his last big steamboating. It was typical of this great-hearted man that he should be rendering a last tribute of help to his many friends along the river even while he himself was suffering a property loss so great that recovery was impossible to a man of his age.

When the river was nearing its crest an urgent telegram for help came from St. Charles, Mo. The big body of land between the Mississippi and the Missouri known as "Missouri Point" and the home of St. Charles White Corn was under water and crying for help. Things above and below Hermann were pretty well in hand and the fast Kennedy lost no time in getting under way "far down Ole Man River."

The steamer W. H. Grapevine, in my charge, had been above New Haven, Mo., for two days and nights moving people and their property out of Pinckney Bottom. Just about dark the Kennedy came alongside and father asked for a pilot as he had been without sleep for several days and needed help very badly. I loaned him Capt. Roy Coulter, a famous river pilot.

It was dark when they backed away from the Grapevine, 8:30 p.m. to be exact, and at 10:30 p.m. they landed at St. Charles, sixty-one miles down the river, having made one landing to pick up Jim Murdock. The Kennedy was burning coal and cordwood. The old Dutch engineer had thrown the cutoffs on *the engine away and they were working her to the last ditch as the old boat went down the river that night. When they passed Pinckney Point that boat was flying and big sparks with pieces of wood were soaring high out of her smoke-stacks. When she passed Washington, Mo., lots of people thought that a comet was sailing by the town. This downstream trip of sixty-one miles in less than two hours was the fastest time ever made by a steamboat on any river in America. At and below St. Charles, the Kennedy worked for three days and three nights taking people off housetops, out of trees and moving livestock up to dry land. They cut telegraph wires and ran boats over the M.K.& T. tracks that were miles from the main river, so wide had the flood spread.*

On the trip down to St. Charles, I mentioned that there had been one stop to pick up Jim Murdock. In steamboating days the Murdocks were prominent men and river shippers and boosters. They lived across the river from St. Albans in the big river bottom out from Matson's.

In 1903 Jim Murdock owned a fine, big farm on the banks of the river he loved so well. On the way down on this eventful trip the steamer Kennedy landed alongside Murdock's house and father found his old friend sitting up in the second story of his big house. The water was already half-way up to the second story and it was hard to make Murdock believe that it would come any higher, or that it was time to move. When invitations and coaxing did not convince him, they shanghied him and went on down the river.

When they came back up the river, near old Howell's Landing in St. Louis County, they saw a big white house lodged against some willows and cotton-woods. Dad said: "Look, Jim, there's your house." Murdock merely snorted at so preposterous a statement, but when they ran the Kennedy close this proved to be the case. They landed, went inside, picked up the things of most value and went on up the river where the house was supposed to be anchored. Not only was the house gone, but most of the land was washed away. And what seemed to hurt Murdock most, two beautiful black stallions were lost some place in the swirling waters.

My charge, the steamer W. H. Grapevine, had been running as a passenger and freight boat between St. Louis and Rocheport, Mo., a weekly packet with a two hundred ten mile run. The river commenced to swell ... and when we reached the mouth of the Missouri, seventeen miles above St. Louis, just before dark, the saddest sight ever to stir my eyes on our rivers was before us.

It was impossible to run this stretch after dark on account of the "drift" and everything imaginable coming out of the Big Muddy. We could see houses, whole trees—roots and all, tumbling into the Mississippi. Hogs, horses and cows were swimming for their lives. Chickens, rabbits and such small stock were riding along on anything afloat. What a gamble of death for these innocent creatures!

All the way up to New Haven we moved people and whatever they could salvage onto higher ground. Just above New Haven, we were hailed into Pinkney Bottom where we worked three days and three nights doing real rescue work in this vicinity. The Grapevine was the largest boat operating out of the port of Hermann, Mo., and my crew were mostly young men and I could still act young in those days. We waded, swam, pulled and tugged with men and beasts, bringing scared, helpless humans and their belongings out of the swollen river for some two weeks. We knew our business on the river was ruined for the year but we fought a young man's fight in the faith that the river would one day come back to its own.

The six other boats, besides the Kennedy and the Grapevine, that operated out of Hermann, in charge of Captain August Wohlt, Gustave Wohlt, Samuel M. Heckmann, Henry German, Roy Coulter and O. J. Heckmann deserve their share of the credit too. They landed at Rhineland, Morrison and Berger, Mo., in places one would never believe a boat had been unless he had watched a real Missouri river flood.

It is doubtful that Mary ever comprehended the true enormity of the flood disaster. *Papa, Ed and Norman went up to look at the islands. Found things in very bad shape, all the houses will have to be repaired more or less, some are gone, and about 100 acres of land gone. 200 acres covered with sand making it useless.* With no crops to transport, the St. Louis and Hermann Packet Co. tied up its boats. Mary sadly reported, *Papa took the Grapevine down the river to St. Louis sold it to parties on the Ohio River.*

Steamboat Bill later wrote about the last days of the Grapevine in the "Waterways Journal."

It should be easy for me to write about the <u>last</u> days of this "old lugger" on our *rivers. As you will see, she was the <u>last</u> boat to come in to St. Louis with her spars and rigging hung for use on short notice. She was the <u>last</u> spoonbill packet and she was the <u>last</u> real steamboat on the once famous and profitable St. Louis and Rocheport packet trade. She was also about the <u>last</u> in any steamboat race. … During the season of 1901 she was the most regular boat that ever ran on the Missouri. In making 39 round trips in this trade, loaded flat both ways, she never wet a spar, and never failed to leave St. Louis every Saturday night. When early Friday morning fellow boatmen came down over the levee, or the watchmen on the old wharfboats looked up above the Eads Bridge, they were disappointed if they did not see the Grapevine lying at the foot of Franklin Avenue.*

In the wake of the flood, the Heckmann men continued their struggle to make a living on the river. Ed, who was nearly 19 by now, was on the Buck Elk building up hours on the river to qualify to take the examination for a pilot's license. Fred, who had been out of work for several months, finally got a berth on the steamer Atalanta—and promptly sank her near the mouth of the Gasconade.

William was working hard to get logs off the Talbot land, virtually the only things he owned that had not been destroyed by the flood. No longer a young man, he went to Bluffton and returned completely tired out—he had walked the entire distance along the Katy railroad tracks on the north side of the river, some 12 miles and then another four miles to the river. Occasionally, he found a berth as pilot—in October he left on the U. S. steamer McPherson. An excursion was tried successfully, but the excursion business was not the solution to expensive boats lying idle. The Buck Elk secured a contract with the government to work on the Gasconade River. The "Chamois Enterprise" reported:

At present the government fleet is at Catfish Rock, or Brown's Shanty. Everybody is happy over the expiration of law protected turkey season ending Nov. 1st. What a pleasure it will be for the boys to bring in a big gobbler for the cook who is quite a menagerial man. He has a Jersey hog, game rooster, maltese cat, crow, hawk, mink, coon, opossum, three musk rats, skunk, trapped by the water and brought to camp. The skunk was trapped within 20 feet of the fleet and for some reason we had to move the river. We had a coon supper recently. The snag boat Buck Elk is at present at Deer Slough working down the river. … Fishing is no good at present. Some of our gang say this is on account of the moon.

Ever the proud mother, Mary would write in her end-of-the-year summary, *Our children, one and all, have done nobly. Lizzie worked two months to help along, Lottie went to school at Springfield to improve herself, and now is doing good work for good pay. Robert worked on the Buck Elk, Ed on the Kennedy, earned about $130, half of which he gave to his father, and some to me. John at home here worked well besides attending school. George is nearly self-supporting while he works at the machinists trade in Springfield.*

Even the little boys were growing up. Fifteen-year-old John shot his first wild goose, and he plucked it too, his mother said. Norman, the baby of the family, was nine now. A luncheon for his friends and lots of cookies made his birthday a happy one.

As for Mary, she was finding solace in her church and devoting herself to temperance work. Perhaps she harbored memories of all those lonely nights at home when William was at the saloon—an old sore had festered long enough, and now she saw a way to do something about it. Or perhaps she wanted something to blame for her family's predicament.

She later wrote,*The past year has been a trying one to me especially. William can sleep off his cares and worries. In the spring our credit had run so very low and I resolved to only buy necessities, so we were all short of clothes. Some times even short of what we needed on the table.* As times became more difficult, she turned to God for answers.

> *I must admit I have often felt downcast, but He never allowed me to grow despondent. He has given me hope, faith, determination. I have enjoyed sweet communion with Him and also with the sisters and brothers of His church. May God bless our little church, our few earnest people. May He, in His mercy, increase it exceedingly. May all my children strive for the attainment of salvation, so that we may all meet at the Great White Throne where Our Father sits with Our Savior at His feet. Father in Heaven, Bless us all.*

The local minister came to talk to Lizzie and Robert about being baptized at church the next day. They were, and their mother's heart swelled with joy. One Saturday evening Mary and little Mary went calling. *When we got to Ellis, Isenburgs were there and Wallace Kessler, who has been wrestling with the Lord for some time. We had a blessed prayer meeting. I am so thankful that we just happened to meet in that way. Praise the Lord.*

Mary's fire for the temperance cause was sparked by a Mrs. Woods, the Missouri president of the WCTU (Women's Christian Temperance Union), who lectured in Hermann. *The unexpected has happened. Mrs. Woods had quite a nice meeting, she spoke very nicely. Ten (5 men and 5 women) signed the total abstinence pledge.* Mrs. Woods came back to lecture as often as possible, staying with the Heckmanns when in town. On one trip she organized a Band of Mercy.

WCTU meetings were being held at the Heckmann home, and temperance tracts were arriving in the mail. Sunday blue laws were discussed at one WCTU meeting, a dangerous and unpopular subject in Hermann where the old German custom of making the most of the Sabbath was observed. People from the surrounding countryside liked to come to town on Sundays to go to church, do their shopping and, finally, stop by a saloon for a nice cool drink or two and a visit with friends.

Mary beseeched her sons to take the pledge and reguarly made the rounds of Hermann's saloons to make sure none of her boys was in them. The Heckmann offspring were not overly thrilled with this strange turn of events and began referring to their mother as "Carry Nation."

It did not take the WCTU long to recognize the talents of such an ardent and literate convert as Mary Heckmann. She began writing news releases and brochures, and at a meeting in Chamois she was elected district president. *I read a paper on "The Danger of Treating, or the Foolish Habit Among Men of Treating."* This was a subject on which Mary was especially well-versed. Her husband had been one of the best "Set 'em up, boys" in town.

CHAPTER 15

The Aftermath

We are having a number of red letter days of late.
—Mary L. Heckmann

*F*or William Heckmann, who was already deeply in debt, the flood of 1903 meant total ruin. Entire crops were wiped out on several hundred acres of his land, homes and outbuildings were destroyed, and the steamboat business was non-existent for the remainder of the year. None of his farm holdings could produce anything without a heavy investment of both money and labor, and he had neither.

The timber on the last tract of land he had purchased from Talbot was one of the few assets he had left. This is where he turned, taking out logs for the market. The work was physically staggering, and Will Heckmann was no longer a young man.

Even the Hermann Ferry and Packet Co. had problems. The year 1904 had hardly begun when the steamboat Peerless, which was ferrying at St. Charles, was damaged by ice and sank in six feet of water. But at least Will Heckmann was no longer an owner of the boat. The steamer Mill Boy was sent to St. Charles as a replacement until the bridge across the Missouri River there was completed.

By May 1, 1904, the Peerless was repaired and scheduled for service on the Gasconade River, and the ferry company was building another steamboat. The Mill Boy would be sold to parties in Washington, Mo., for use as a ferryboat. Although Capt. Will was no longer part of the Hermann Ferry and Packet Co., they were still on good terms.

> *Capt. Henry Wohlt, now dead, has a boat named after him, now Capt. Heckmann,*
> *who is still with us, has a boat named for him. The company intends that all the*
> *old river men shall be honored by having boats named for them, and the next*
> *boats built will be named August Wohlt, Gustave Wohlt and Fred Lang. ...*
> *The new ferryboat now building at our wharf is 90 feet long and 20 feet in the*
> *beam and will be a light running boat. The work is all done by home help under*
> *direction of John Bohlken and if the boiler can be procured in time, which, on*
> *account of the strike of the ironworkers in St. Louis is now doubtful, the boat*
> *will be ready for business in four weeks.*

The Wohlt family was doing well. Gustave Wohlt continued with the Hermann Ferry and Packet Co, and August Wohlt was getting the hang of having fun. After being elected the first mayor of Hermann, he built himself a little steam pleasure boat, the Ideal. After the voting, he took the elected aldermen up the Gasconade River for a week-long hunt. Another time the paper reported that August and his friends had gone for a day's outing, *catching enough fish for a square meal, which means something.*

But the St. Louis and Hermann Packet Co. was discouraged with the river business and sold first the steamer Grapevine, then the Buck Elk and finally the Kennedy. The Buck Elk went to yet another new Hermann steamboat company, the Buck Elk Steamboat Co. The new company ran a notice informing farmers and shippers along the Gasconade that *the Buck Elk will continue in trade there and will not be taken away again to some other point as heretofore.* This was a slap at Capt. Heckmann, who had sent local boats to Arkansas—a disastrous move.

William was at work rip-rapping the river bank at Chamois. *Capt. Heckmann is a man of large experience in the matter of river improvements.* Landowners on the north side of the river were raising money to make the Missouri River more navigable. The "Advertiser-Courier" reported, *The Missouri River Commission has agreed, we understand, to construct six dykes, each one hundred feet long, if the property owners will raise $4800, the estimated cost of same. It is thought that the construction of dykes will divert the channel and flow of water to the middle of the river bed, now mostly sand bars, and that the valuable land now crumbling into the river can be saved to the owners.*

Work for the Heckmann men was sporadic at best. Bill was on the Kennedy, Ed and his father were running the Buck Elk, and Sam and Fred picked up whatever boat work was available. When needed, Bob and John cooked on the Buck Elk.

The Steamer William L. Heckmann, left, with the Steamer Henry Wohlt.

It takes considerable diligence to sort out the various steamboat interests doing business in Hermann during this period. After a falling out with his partners, Will Heckmann Jr. found financial backing to buy another boat.

Capt. Wm. L. Heckmann, Jr. with two other parties of St. Louis has bought the steamboat Lora from the upper Mississippi, and will put her in the Missouri river trade this week. The steamer Kennedy, of which Capt. Heckmann is part owner, is still at this wharf and may be sold if a buyer can be found. Capt. Heckmann made an endeavor to buy out the other interests, but could not do so at a satisfactory figure, and now has secured the Lora, which is said to be a bigger and even faster boat than the Kennedy.

So now the Hermann Ferry and Packet Company, the St. Louis and Hermann Packet Company, the Buck Elk Steamboat Company and a fourth company running the Lora all were operating out of Hermann.

Aware at last of her family's precarious financial condition, Mary put in an enormous garden. The boys and Papa Will hunted to keep meat on the table, and there were hogs from the farm at the mill. Mary went into the chicken business in a big way and spent a lot of time keeping her little chicks dry and comfortable, catching a cold one time after chasing chicks in a thunderstorm.

One December evening William arrived with five hogs from the mill, and Mary prepared a late supper.

Ed had killed a rabbit so that had to be fried for supper. Papa, George and the man from the mill with five hogs. After they had their supper they carried in the hogs, we laid them out in the kitchen. The next morning Papa and Ed cut up the hogs, we made the sausage by 10 o'clock. … I put on the heads to cook, Papa and Ed ground up the meat and after dinner we made the pudding and pan hus. I rendered lard until 10 o'clock. P.M. Took my bath and went to bed, saying to myself, "Well done, thou good and faithful servant."

A few days later Bob provided a fine surprise for his mother—chickens. *He sent for a trio of White Wyondotts, unknown to me, they came Thursday.*

Mary was known for her home doctoring skills, but when Ed came home from the boat with a bad leg, she was perplexed. *Do not know what it is that ails him.* Fever and severe pain kept Ed in bed for nearly a month before a doctor was called and the leg was lanced. Osteomyelitus was not a common ailment, and the cure was not simple, as Ed would discover.

Bob also came home late one night needing treatment. *I had to fix up a great carbuncle on his cheek. He feels sick from it.* Sometimes neighbors sought Mary's advice.

I was to see what could be done for Laura's hand. I gave them some balsom in whiskey to use on it and have not heard since how it is. She had stuck a fork deep in the inside of the fleshy part of the hand. This afternoon one of the Langenburg girls called me up to know how to treat their Cyclamen. I began to think my calling or callings were rather changeable.

After raising 13 children, the 14th should have been easy. But Norman was capable of trying his mother's patience.

Norman complained of a sick stomach, so he remained out of school. He done some raking and then went to Mr. Fleisch and asked for tobacco, he gave him some. He had fixed up a pipe and Will's Annie seen him puffing away in the vineyard. Pretty soon he came into the house in a hurry, he laid down on the cot in the girl's room and in a few moments he was a sick boy. I smelled tobacco, so I asked, "Did you smoke?" Between paroxysms he nodded his head, "Yes." Slept all afternoon after the agony was over. We are having a number of red letter days of late.

Ten-year-old Norman was fast outgrowing all his clothes. Mary sent the children to the store to sell eggs and chickens, then she used the money to buy a hat, shoes and goods for clothes for Norman.

Poor child is first out of clothes. … Norman also made his first application for a job. He asked Greeley for the job of cooking. As Greeley had John he let Norman help load coal and he made the trip with the boat. George is playing gentleman at present. Bob is on the Buck Elk too. … Greeley came to get the boys to go along up to unload Buck Elk, cannot get through under the bridge on account of high water. They intend loading the sacks on barge and having the Kennedy bring it down.

When Ed was home he cooked and helped with the dishes, especially when his mother had other things to do. She prepared food for an outing on the Buck Elk by the Methodist Sunday School and *anyone else who chooses to go with us.* Pena also helped with chores, and she and Fred often ate with the senior Heckmanns. Between trips, the boys made turtle traps. It was Fred who helped John dress some turtles for Mary's turtle recipe, a family favorite.

To Cook a Turtle

Cut off the head and put on to boil (with the shell on) in a pot with plenty of water. Let boil an hour; remove the under shell, and pick the meat to pieces. Clean the top shell; add broken crackers, butter, onion minced and parsley chopped fine; a stalk of celery cut in inch pieces; also black pepper, a dash of cayenne, a very little alspice, and salt to taste. Put all into the shell, well-mixed and bake it. Serve with a sauce made of a pint of soup stock, half a pint of cream, two tablespoonfuls of flour, and three tablespoonfuls of butter.

Mary was adept at getting work out of tramps and other strangers. A couple was living aboard a flatboat that was anchored below the house at the foot of the bluff. Both were willing to work, probably on a barter basis. Mary even got the grass cut—*Mrs. Flat-boat Cole done it.* Flowers were plentiful. *Sent a large box of cut flowers to St. Louis for tomorrow is Flower Mission Day.*

With the opening of the river in the spring, there had been more work on the boats, but by the end of May Fred was out of work, Pena was pregnant, and Ed's leg still was not well.

It seems as if everything in the world were coming to me to worry me and cause despondency. No money. Papa not doing anything. Ed's leg worse. Papa has always been careless about his clothes, but now he goes like a tramp. For a man who has handled as much money as he has, it is an awful shame, a disgrace to see him in the condition he is.

Mary, too, was beginning to feel her age.

Had a bad night. I was to wake Papa for the early train, and was up three times to look at the clock. Papa returned on night train, when he awoke me, I was lost, it took me the longest time to find the door. Have been having these spells often of late.

When there was no boat work to be had, William kept busy with the logs across the river.

Papa, Fred and George were across the river working on logs today and came home wet as drowned rats. … Papa and nearly all the boys were over at his log pile. Had the Buck Elk to pull out the heaviest ones with the steam capstan.

There was still some money to be made salvaging ties.

Papa had me to fix a basket for himself and boys to go gather up ties. They did not know that the Kennedy was in, so they missed the boat, and instead of going up the Missouri they went up the Gasconade on the Buck Elk … Papa and the boys all came in time for supper, brought a lot of frogs and had them for supper. … As soon as all is quiet I fall asleep and cannot read.

Times were bad, but Mary never failed to rejoice in the wonders of nature.

We enjoyed a peculiar phenomena about 4 o'clock. A rain cloud over head was showering down rain, and the sun was shining from the west. The rain drops looked like pearls, a shower of pearls one might say.

Like his father before him, Ed was going courting in a rowboat. He often rowed eight miles upriver to call on Alice Bock, a Hermann girl who was teaching school at Gasconade. *Ed left at 4 o'clock this morning to pull up to Gasconade.*

Daughter Martha came home for a visit with her new husband. Anxious to be at her best when entertaining a minister of the gospel, Mary told her daughter, *I will quick clean the chicken house so William does not see me at the dirty job. Before I was done Martha called me and said "William is here."* Martha and William left Hermann to go to Madison, N.J., to Drew University. *Dear children, may our Good Father watch over them.*

Brother Bob Miller and Tina came down from Bluffton.

Bob and Tina started out in skiff for home, before they left we had been at the river once and came back because of rain, were scarcely in the house when we had the first hard shower. We ate our supper when someone knocked and here were Bob and Tina back all wet and dilapidated.

The whole family traveled to St. Louis to see the wonders of the 1904 World's Fair. The first place Mary headed was the chicken display.

It was St. Louis Day and there was such a mob as I never expect to see the like. We were to the Baby Incubators and seen Jim Key, the wonderful horse performer, he spells, does sums in arithmetic, takes letters from boxes marked and puts them into other marked boxes, just as anyone in the audience tells him. He is a wonderful horse. We were through the Agricultural building pretty thoroughly and then went over to the Horticultural building. Soon met Mrs. Cody of the Rural World, *pretty soon Col. Colman appeared with two of his girls from the office, so by and by, we found a room and had a good time. ... We called it the* Rural World *reunion. We remained for the illumination, it was just grand and then struck out for home. The Pike was one solid mass of people.*

October was harvest time, and the Heckmann vineyards were producing well. Mr. Fleisch, who worked in the vineyard, was usually somewhat "under the influence" and sometimes more than somewhat. The picking began on October 10, with Mary reporting that *Fleisch, as usual, got drunk and done more harm than good.* The next day, she said, *Fleisch never showed his face.*

Mary, John and Norman were out of school to help pick grapes. *The pickers finished the grapes at noon, had in all 10,117 lbs. The vineyard looks so pitiful shorn of all the fruit. ... Papa intends going up to Chamois on the night train, it is my duty to sit up until near the time so I can wake him.*

Son Fred called his mother on Nov. 27 to be the midwife for Pena, who gave birth to a fine baby boy. For the next week, Mary was running two households. The Heckmann children, who all had inherited their father's ability to entertain an audience, provided a diversion. *The folks are so funny I can scarcely write.*

The Christmas program at the church was about the only notice Mary took of the holiday. She was growing weary; the work was becoming too much for her. On Dec. 27 she woke John and Lottie at 3 a.m.

It was getting colder and pretty strong wind blowing, by the time I got up to start the fire for washing, the flame and smoke came out in the front of the stove

worse than it went up the chimney. I had quite a time putting it out and we
gave up the idea of washing, and had to do our cooking on the heating stove in
the dining room. ... Paper says we are getting a Nebraska blizzard. The next
day she reported, *No washing again, we are still cooking on the dining room*
stove, and all huddle together like sheep. ... George had to go to Rocheport to
the Buck Elk, they are in trouble, burned the boiler.

Mary closed the year with these words:

What has happened to our own family and those closely connected with us is
here written down. But the heartaches, the disappointments, the anxiety I have
had are not written down. Today especially has been one of trial. I am not at all
well, baking and cleaning and boys in and out, a turkey to roast for supper, all
the time I am so tired, so near ready to give up. ... I know I have not seen the
worst, it is coming, sure as fate. How will I be able to bear it? Oh, God, have
pity on me. Forgive me if I have annoyed anyone by these lines.

The Heckmann boys all tried to emulate their father, especially his popularity
and sense of humor. But not all their wives were impressed with their father-in-
law's ways. Mary had never really concerned herself with her husband's financial affairs. But Young Will's wife had a different point of view.

Will's Annie was determined to have good educations for her four children,
and to do that she needed to put a stop to her husband's constant financial in-
volvement in steamboats. She took charge of the family finances, and when her
father-in-law came to borrow money, she asked for collateral. On January 3,
1905, Mary recorded, *We sold this place to Will's wife today. Papa and I were at Breuers*
to sign the deed. Papa Will received no money in the transaction, only the cancel-
lation of notes for money already owed. In return, Will's Annie got the deed to
the house. For the time being, however, life went on as usual.

I was up at 3 o'clock to get breakfast for our Bob and Brother Bob. They left at 4
a.m. to walk to Gasconade. ... When I fed the chickens I found one missing.
Norman had hit it with his air rifle, and then thrown it into the gutter, and at
last confessed to his crime and brought the chicken to light. ... I had quite a time
getting in the wash, it was frozen and covered with sleet, had to take it through
warm water and hang it up in dining room. ... The sun came out and such a
grand sight as the vineyard and all the trees made was enchanting. The crust
on ice is strong enough for a light person to skate on. Walking is very hard

work. … George and a friend were skating below town and found the piece of ice they were on had left go and they were floating down the river, had moved about ten feet. They hurried toward the bar and had to run over mush ice that had piled up along the bar … Papa still not well.

Mary continued to write for the WCTU. *Sent my essay to Mrs. Smith. Miss Booker copied it in type for me.* She also fired off a letter to the editor of the "Advertiser-Courier."

In your several attacks on what you choose to call "Reform Women," and your insinuations that men are not strong as they should be in controlling their wives, it looks to me as if you were sadly retrograding. The time is past that woman must tremble at the sound of the foot steps or words of the man who had promised to love and protect her. Some men may think they are Lord and master, but they are very scarce at this date. This is not taking into consideration the half-brute who beats his wife. Please read what Lucy Stone says, and contradict it if you can. "The woman who sits by her baby's cradle, having learned no lesson of responsibility and self reliance, whose mind is narrow, whose arm is weak, and whose heart is timid, can impart to that child only what she herself possesses. What is so important to the public good as that women, who are the mothers, should have the benefit of that self respect and self reliance which comes with the possession of equal rights."

The weather was cold, the ice was good, and skating was the preferred mode of transportation on the river. The Heckmann boys skated back and forth to Gasconade, and the girls and Norman skated for fun. It was good news when two strangers arrived wanting to buy land. *Papa seen the man who wants part of the Loutre Island farm, said he will take it.*

But February 3, 1905, was *another black day for Hermann.*

About 10 o'clock Mrs. H. came over and asked where the fire was, she thought it must be the Courthouse, sure enough it was only too true. Tonight our grand Courthouse is in ruins, no one knows how the fire started. The firemen have been busy all afternoon, and this evening it took a fresh start, owing to some trouble with the engine.

Mary had her usual gathering of friends for her birthday. She enjoyed her gifts. *All were exceptional and received with thanks. I have every reason to be very thankful for the kind remembrance than even the gifts.* She also was pleased with her youngest daughter.

Mary done very nicely while I entertained the folks in the parlor. She waited on the table for Papa and the boys and Elmer Kuhn and Albert Wohlt were here. After they were done, she cleared off the table and washed up the dishes.

The townspeople were not as excited about the social aspects of the boats as they once had been. Capt. Will Heckmann was no longer the genial host, and "Jumbo" Rincheval was no longer planning the events. The steamer Wm. L. Heckmann did take out the usual Gasconade River fishing party. *They were amply provided with refreshments and well filled lunch baskets, all bent upon having a good social time and we suppose they had it. Eugene Rippstein brought home a catfish weighing thirty-five pounds.*

But the boats also could bring tragedy.

The steamer Lora came in about 8:30 and just as they landed, Annie Kuhn, Berdie and Hattie Parrott were going to step from the Buck Elk onto the Lora, Hattie Parrott stumbled and dropped into the river, no one was at hand to try to rescue her, and now we fear she is gone forever. Norman had gone to get ice cream and brought the sad news home. "Hattie Parrott is drownded." ... Robert is so worried, he worked until 2 o'clock in the morning diving and dragging in hopes of finding the body of poor little Hattie. He left again at 5 and worked until dinner time without eating. I was down to see Parrott's, they all take it so hard and yet bear up bravely. Robert left again after supper to go to the island below Franks to watch for the poor little girl, has been hunting all afternoon.

Mary stayed overnight with the distraught family, returning home at dawn to tend the chickens and milk the cow.

Slept half an hour when Robert called, "Mama, you are to come to Parrotts, they have found the body." We left everything and hurried down. The body came up not over a hundred feet from where it fell into the water. Poor Mr. and Mrs. Parrott, were not prepared for the shock, until Mrs. Haasenritter told them they could not see the remains. They have never lived on the water, therefore did not know what a sad condition a poor mortal is in after lying in the water 57 hours.

Even Bob Heckmann, the most organized and sedate of the Heckmann boys, managed to get into difficulty on the river.

Papa went out on Peerless to Gasconade for a raft of ties. Passed down at noon and got home about 4 o'clock. Bob put his skiff on the boat, he came down the Gasconade on a small raft and jumped off leaving his valise. The raft left the bank and he tried to catch it but it went into the current and he borrowed a skiff to overhaul it, as it was growing dark he did not see the raft again after he had a skiff. ... We only found it all out when Papa took the skiff back to Gasconade ... This morning he had to jump the train he fooled around so long and was late.

The break up of the ice was always thrilling and fraught with danger.

This day just as we had dinner on the table, John called to us that the ice was moving. We were all excited and scarcely ate any dinner. I telephoned to Gusta as I promised to let her know when the ice began breaking. Telegram from Sam saying the Buck Elk and barges had torn loose at Rocheport. George came home this evening from Gasconade says so far all is safe up there.

Mary had long been aware that George was the most foolhardy of her children and the most intractable. Her efforts to change these tendencies had been fruitless. But the mother of eight river-rat sons apparently develops a certain degree of immunity from worry. So she was quite calm in reporting that *One of the Buck Elk barges passed about 10 o'clock. George took the afternoon train and went to catch her. Mrs. K. telegraphed that the barge and boys passed Washington at 6 this evening. The barge "Norman" is safe and the open barge is at the Osage river, now will still have to hear of the Buck Elk.*

The fellow who was on that runaway barge, son George Heckmann, wrote a far more vivid account of the adventure.

The winter of 1905 was a time to remember for the rest of my life. They took me out of High School to go to Boonville, Mo. to move the Buck Elk and two barges down to the winter harbor at Gasconade, Mo. Greeley Heckmann was captain, and Frank Ingram was the engineer. The river was free of ice. We made up the tow and started down the river. The engineer started out without testing his boiler feed pump and before he got his pump started the water got so low that it cracked a seam in the top of the main flue of the Scotch Marine boiler.

We went to the bank below Rocheport, called boiler makers from St. Louis. In order to get at the leak in the main flue, they had to remove the two top layers of boiler tubes, which were rolled out on the deck of the smaller of the two barges. I was the only man on board that could crawl into the main head opening so I spent Christmas day inside the boiler bucking up rivets. By the time the boiler

*work was completed the heavy ice started to the extent that we could not con-
tinue the trip to Gasconade. I went back to school at Hermann, Mo.*

*Sometime later they had open water again so they moved the boat and the
two barges up into the mouth of the creek at Rocheport in what looked like a
safer harbor than where they were laying below Rocheport. However, in the
spring they had one of those flash floods out of the hills into the creek and the
force of the ice coming out of the creek took the entire mess and set them out on
the ice in the Missouri River. When the river ice went out the entire mess
started down the river.*

*Brother Greeley and his engineer Tim Easter started following the floatation
in a row boat, but spent too much time hunting ducks and lost track or sight of
the Buck Elk. They later reported her sunk. The facts will show differently. The
larger of the two barges floated into an eddy and was tied to the bank by some
fishermen. The Buck Elk went to Providence Chute, stopped in an eddy and
some farmers made her fast to a tree. The smaller of the two barges kept moving
on down the river.*

*The High School at Hermann at that time was right on the river bank. It
happened to be recess when that barge came floating past Hermann. On board
was a real good row boat. I asked the owner: "If I get that row boat off of that
barge will you give it to me?" He said, "Sure, but how are you going to do it?"*

*A Missouri Pacific train was just about due headed for St. Louis. My cousin
Allie Wohlt and I boarded that train. At Washington, Mo., we were far enough
ahead of the barge to make our attempt to get on board. We hired another row
boat from Capt. Blaske and took two more kids with us. Calculating that two of
us would bring one of the row boats back to shore and the other two in the other
row boat.*

*The wind was blowing off the Washington shore and we had open water to
row up stream about a mile before we met the barge. When we boarded the barge
there was a hauser (or line) hanging over board, so I suggested that we hawl it
aboard. So all four of us concentrated on hauling the line aboard. There was
more line out than we imagined and by the time we had the line on board things
started popping.*

We were down in the narrow part of the river passing the City of Wash-

ington and the ice was jamming the row boat we left in the river. Had to pull it on board to save it from being mashed. I knew enough about that part of the river to realize that it would be dark before we reached the wide river below South Point, Mo. I knew it would be sudden death to try to leave the barge in the black of night so the only thing we could do was to settle down for the night.

We rolled the boiler tubes which I mentioned before together, and as luck would have it there was lots of wood on board with which we built a fire. For wind breaks we stood the row boats on their side. One thing that made it rather safe from sinking when we hit grounded ice on the head of sand bars was the fact that the barge was protected by about two feet of ice frozen to the side of the hull. (During the winter lay-up it was a habit to keep open water between the hulls and the main ice by sawing out each morning a strip about two feet wide all around the hulls. Otherwise as the river would raise or lower it would have the tendency to pull the caulking out of the seams of the wooden hulls.)

Imagine, if you can, the sound when hitting so called icebergs on the head of a bar at about six or seven miles per hour which was about the current at that time. It was pitch dark and several times during the night we would get into an eddy and know that we were floating around in one spot and could do nothing about it.

The two kids that we picked up at Washington didn't seem much concerned and fell asleep at the side of the fire. Sparks would fly off the fire and set their clothes on fire and either I or Allie would put out the fire with a splash of water.

About four o'clock in the morning we came in sight of the only bridge at St. Charles at that time. The outline of the bridge could be seen by the full moon which was just coming up. We could hear the ice piling up on the bridge peers. (Nice sound) We left the fire die and decided that if it looked like the barge was going to hit a peer we would take our chances with one of the row boats to get to shore. However, we made it through the channel span, same as if we had rudder power.

After going under the St. Charles bridge, we took a new lease on life. We knew that it would be day light before we reached the next down stream bridge at Bellefountain. Just above the bridge we floated broad side on a large snag. That is where I made one of the biggest mistakes of my life. I slipped a regulation *bowline over a couple small branches. Took the line to the hand capstan on the head of the barge and we started to pull. We had the barge stopped and just started to pull her up beneath the branches of the tree when the line slipped off the limbs and on down the river we went.*

It would have been an easy matter to leave the barge at that point. Nice wide river and free of ice to shore I asked Allie how much money he had with him so we decided we had enough for rail road fare from St. Louis to Hermann. We decided to ride her on in to St. Louis.

After clearing the bridge at Bellefountain the barge took a sudden notion to leave the channel and headed into a narrow chute behind an island on the left side of the river where no boat had ever been. A farmer came out to watch us go past. We threw him a rope which he tried to wrap around a tree but after about three attempts he ran out of trees and on down the river we went. At the mouth of the Missouri river we wound up in the big eddy. Round and round we went and to this day I will never tell you why we got out of that one. I think the ice piled up so high under the barge that she slid out on the ice.

At that time the Upper Mississippi river ice was coming out quite heavy. The wind was blowing toward the Illinois side of the river. All the upper river ice and the Missouri river ice crowded together and we were right in the middle of the flow. I still think we could have walked to shore without getting our feet wet.

From there down the trip was quite normal until we approached the Water Intake Tower at the Chain of Rocks above St. Louis. As we approached, it looked like we were going down to the left of the Tower, but contrary again, the barge missed the right hand side by about ten feet. The attendant was on watch. I let out a loud yell. "Are the Tugs running in the St. Louis harbor?" The answer was "Yes." I said, "For Christ Sake, have one of them to come out and pick us up before we reach the Eads Bridge."

He done that and more. He called every newspaper in town and by the time we hit the harbor the papers were out on the street with extras. It was a big day in St. Louis. Everybody that was able to get to the river bank on both sides of the river was lined up on shore.

The Tug Robert E. Kerr picked us up just above the Eads Bridge, tied the barge off at one of the Elevators and then took us on board the Harbor Boat. On the Harbor Boat we were fed and cleaned up. The Wharf Boat where the Harbor Boat tied off was crowded with people wanting to get a look at the Damn Fools that made the run-away trip in the ice. Mistake #2 of the trip. If I had given our two friends an empty hat and sent them out on the Wharf boat they could have collected enough money to pay us a big profit. I never got the row boat but the owners of the barge paid us enough salvage money to make it worth while.

After we landed at St. Louis on our barge trip we decided to go home. At Union Station I bought a ticket to the first stop which was Tower Grove. At that point I left the coach and boarded the Engine Tender to beat my way the rest of the way to Hermann. (I always hated to pay rail road fare.) At Pacific, Mo. where they stop to take on coal, the damn fireman threw coal at me, I had to get off the head end and get back into the coach.

When the conductor came around to pick up my fare he said "Where are you headed?" I said, "Hermann." He says: "I have been reading about those four kids that came down the river in the ice on a runaway barge." I said, "I happened to be one of those kids." He said, "How in the Hell did you get from St. Louis to Pacific?" I said, "On the head of your train." He said, "Here is your money, you can ride free with me if you will tell me the story." Which I did.

It took awhile for Mary to grasp the full impact of just what George had done. *This has been one of the days to shorten one's life.* But apparently her joy over her son's safe return overcame her aggravation at his daredevil stunt.

George later wrote that when he returned home his mother seemed *real glad* to see him. He could see the river from the house on the bluff and asked her why the boat was taking on wood.

They are getting ready to go up the river and pick up the Barge Norman and the Buck Elk," she said. I said, "Good Bye." She said, "Aren't you going to stop long enough to tell me about your trip." I said, "Allie Wohlt will tell you all about it."

CHAPTER 16

The Lid Is On

Hermann which is famous for having the largest wine cellars in the country, no municipal government and an entire absence of the use of the English language, has also an enviable reputation for the magnitude of its thirst.
—St. Louis "Post-Dispatch"

$\mathcal{T}$he long-awaited "lid" on Hermann's saloons finally slammed shut. Bowing to intense pressure from the WCTU, Missouri Gov. Folk ordered enforcement of the state's Sunday blue laws. Needless to say, Hermann did not take the news well.

The Governor last week notified the sheriff that complaint had been made to him that the provisions of the dramshop law requiring saloons to be closed on a Sunday, were disregarded in this county, and that he, the sheriff see to it that the law is properly enforced. All the store and saloon men were at once notified that the "lid" was on for Sunday and every Sunday thereafter, and to govern themselves accordingly. Gov. Folk came in for much unfriendly criticism in resurrecting an obsolete statute and depriving a city of home-rule, and as the days passed by and Saturday evening arrived there was a suppressed, but intense feeling, and all kinds of things were predicted for Sunday, closing of the drug store, the bakery, butcher shop, electric light plant, etc. To prepare for the visitor who came from St. Louis on the excursion train, many families laid in a supply of wine and beer on Saturday, and the brewery did a land office business.

Sunday morning found all the saloons and stores with the exception of the bakery, butcher shop and drug store closed, and closed they remained during the entire day, excepting one saloon, we are informed, which opened to the St. Louis excursionists. Naturally the sole topic of conversation was the novel experience which the town was going through the first time in its history, and everybody was wondering what the outcome of this harsh proceedure would finally be.

The "Advertiser-Courier" found itself having to take a peculiar stand regarding enforcement of the law.

The communication sent to this office signed "A Voice from Hermann," wherein the writer upbrades Gov. Folk for enforcing the law closing saloons on Sunday cannot be printed because in language it is disrespectful to the Governor personally as well as to the office he occupies. We will here say that the discussion of the action of the Governor will not be swayed in one way or the other in the stand he has taken in this matter, and relief must come from the legislature.

Then, as now, the St. Louis press was smacking its lips over the prospect of some juicy news from a little town. The St. Louis "Post-Dispatch" subtitled the headline "Lid Threatens to Break Up Church" with "Unable to Get Beer 'On the Side' with Religion, People Give Up the Latter." The article went on to explain:

The thirsty St. Louis howl against the "Lid" is a mild murmur compared to the growl of disapproval sent up from this throat-parched community which, in its hour of distress, has suddenly discovered that the presence of the obnoxious "covering" is about to wreck the town's place of worship.

Hermann which is famous for having the largest wine cellars in the country, no municipal government and an entire absence of the use of the English language, has also an enviable reputation for the magnitude of its thirst.

A native son, in discussing the situation, said today: "You know, before the lid was put on, Sunday was a great day at Hermann. The farmers all came in on that day to attend church, to trade and to get a little beer. Now they don't get beer and they have stopped coming in to go to church. We are afraid that the lid is going to break up the place of worship.

This piece of idiocy in reporting outraged Mary Heckmann to the point of a rebuttal.

In Defense of Hermann

I wish to make a few comments on your article of July 7, from this place and your comments on the same. Hermann is famous for its beautiful surroundings, scenery and the cleanliness of its streets and alleys. We have many beautiful gardens and the culture of flowers is always noticed by every stranger who comes here. In the winter almost every home has plants and flowers in the windows.

There are also a great many good people in this town. Some little while ago, a Western daily published some remarks on Hermann to the effect that there is "an entire absence of the use of the English language." That article was too absurd to call for an answer, but this comes a little nearer home than that. There are very few people who cannot speak English and they are the old settlers. Those speaking the English use it more correctly than many so-called "Americans" in other towns of the State.

As to the Sunday closing, one farmer from the country nearby said, "If they close the saloons on Sunday, I will not go to church in Hermann." One man is not the whole community, and there is one church here whose people meet whenever the bell calls to worship. They need neither beer, wine or rum to attract them. Beer gardens Sunday excursions, even the children's May Picnic, do not deter them from doing their duty as Christians.

By this time Mary was seeding her temperance and women's rights writings liberally throughout the WCTU district—her articles were being printed in all the area newspapers. She also traveled a good bit lecturing for the WCTU. Presumably offerings taken at the meetings helped cover her expenses, for she always carefully noted the amount of the collection. Certainly, the Heckmanns had no spare money with which to subsidize her travels.

The Hermann paper lost patience and printed some scathing comments, including a dig about gray-haired ladies shouting the temperance pledge. Since the meeting in question was attended mostly by boys and girls of the Loyal Temperance Legion, Mary wrote another lengthy rebuttal, imploring the newspaper to say nothing rather than publish erroneous information. *You are afraid to publish any good about the temperance people so please leave them alone altogether.*

Mary's true feelings about the furor sparked by the Sunday saloon closings are revealed in her journal.

> *Hermann is on the warpath, all because the* Post Dispatch *has several items about Hermann and the closing enforcement. It is something like the homely old woman and a batch of photos that were very good likeness of her. She pitched them into the fire. The Hermannites see themselves as others see them and they do not like it one bit. I answered it, even if I did feel as if it served them right. We do not want the outside community to fully realize what a benighted, clannish, ignorant people we are.*

> *Yesterday our Robert visited two saloons, at Gauss' he found Mr. Begemann, Sr., Mr. Phillip Haeffner, the two Strahleys, and Fritz Ochsner. Mr. B. and Mr. P. were very indignant, called him names, and several told him to get out. … While Papa and Lizzie were still at the table, Fleisch came in and told Papa a lot of gossip he thought Papa ought to know, he and Papa worked themselves up into a towering rage. As F. put it, I am to blame for it all, because I helped about the Sunday law enforcement. He says Starck will not take the grapes because he says I am doing all I can against his business. Very fortunately, I was outside during all the Fleish confab and now think it was best that it was so, as I might have said something that would only have made things worse.*

> *The following day Fleisch was here, three quarters gone, he tried to patch things up by telling me how much he thinks of me, but he still thinks I done wrong by trying to enforce the law.*

As predicted, Mary's staunch stand for the WCTU did have consequences. The grapes were ripening, but sales were not forthcoming—the winery boycotted Heckmann grapes. The only sales were to a handful of townspeople. *Grapes weighed 8,744 lbs. We used about 1,000 lbs, altogether we sold and used 2,200 lbs.*

Young Bob Heckmann seemed to bear the brunt of the abuse.

> *Robert lost his job at the mill because Mr. Eggers is an old coward. He had promised Robert a job all the year, but he feared Begemann would make good his threat of withholding wheat, so to pacify all, he thought it best for Robert to quit. … Buck Elk came up with a mover to go up the Gasconade and Robert went along to Stolpe to see whether he can get his school back, he had given it up after being promised this job in the mill.*

Bob also received a letter that his mother said *for bigotry, audacity and foolishness, cannot be beaten.*

This has been a terrible day. As the saloons promised they all opened up except Wally, he has not once broken the law. The Fair Grounds had a bar open, and drunken men were plentiful everywhere. If defiance can bring on disaster, something will happen soon. ... the people going and coming, and the brass band and singing at the Fair Grounds was disgusting to look at. ... The agitation is still on about Robert's going to the two saloons last Sunday, but we find all the people worth our esteem look at his actions with approval. God grant that some good may come of it all. ... The latest we hear about the saloon business is Leander Graf told Bob he has not a friend in town. Bob told him all who had been his friends were still the same, and those who do not approve of what he done, he does not care if he has lost them. Fred and Pena have figured it out that we are to blame that they have to pay more rent

It seemed the entire family was besieged by problems.

Will is home, he has had a misunderstanding with his partners. Last night George came home, he too has quit his job. ... It seems to me I have lived six weeks since Sunday, all the vexation, talk, and abuse heaped on us the last few days is enough to made the stoutest heart grow weary. When, Oh God, will things take a change for the better? Thank God, peace has been declared between the two nations, Russia and Japan, our President done a great deal toward helping it all along.

Next William could not get men to unload the boat. The river was at flood stage again, and the steamboats were once again trying to save the lowlanders and their stock.

Trains are not running, there are several very bad slides on the track and the bridge is somewhat undermined, no news of any kind from outside. Water is coming up over on Loutre and the Missouri is wild, looks like more rain tonight. Our folks walked up the track this morning and say it is terrible what damage has been done to the R.R. in some places. Great large trees have come down and remained on the track, in other places the track is undermined. The bridge at the Frene Creek is unsafe, no trains at all. The rain that fell last night was 6 3/4 inches.

The following day *about 6 o'clock a train came into town with about two hundred people half starved, have been at Etlah since Tuesday, had eaten up all that could be found around the village, they reported a slide ahead of them and one below them so they*

216

could not go either way.

Even the hapless Norman was in trouble, accused by a railroad detective of throwing a rock through a train window.

Norman came home this afternoon crying. He said a stranger and old Lambs had halted him at the schoolhouse, and the stranger said he would have him arrested for throwing a rock through the car window yesterday afternoon. Soon after, the man came to the house, and said he was positive that Norman was the boy. We were surprised as Norman denied it altogether. We told him Norman had been with Milton Wohlt after school, but he made his threats all the same. Neither Norman nor I could eat any supper.

Mary, who believed her son was telling the truth, did some investigating of her own.

I went to Mr. Heinkie and asked him about it, and he said the man is a detective, and spoke to him about it, he says the man was not on the train when the window was broken, but came from Sedalia today. The man told us he had seen Norman throw the rock, which was a lie, another thing Mr. Heinkie says the train was through here by 4:06 p.m., while the man claimed it went through at 4:43 p.m.

The Heckmann house was on a high bluff. Just west of the house the terrain was such that the boys could play there and scramble down to the tracks and the river. Any rock thrown down the steep hill could easily have hit a passing train. The matter was finally resolved with a reprimand.

But a few days later a neighbor told Mary that Norman was slapping her girls. Then a little girl at school complained about Norman. His reply was, "But Teacher, I only kissed her." Norman later married that little girl, Irene Kuhn, and they lived to celebrate more than 60 years of wedded bliss. His brother John married her sister, Annie Kuhn, who would be known to the family as John's Annie.

The courthouse fire had done tremendous damage, but repairs went ahead with utmost speed. The newspaper commented:

When we look at the amount of work that is done for $10,500—the contract price for repairing the court house—it would seem to us that contractors for ordinary buildings make a whole lot of money or the contractor at the courthouse is losing on his job. The latter is hardly likely because Mr. Stumpe is smiling all the time and will occasionally beer up the men on Saturday evening.

Mary wrote about yet another Gasconade River bridge disaster.

The fast mail cars took fire and two cars full of papers burned up as they were on the bridge. It was impossible to do anything with them. The bridge was damaged so all trains were delayed. ... George was on the boat at Gasconade when the people woke him. He was busy afterwards crossing people in a skiff.

In June of 1905, the "Advertiser-Courier" reported that a new steamboat, the Julius Silber, was being built at the Hermann wharf. *It is massively built with a view of heavy wear, yet combining lightness and speed. When completed, the craft will be a desireable piece of property and a valuable asset of the Buck Elk Steamboat Co.* In July the paper said the new boat was *busily engaged in bringing the stream of golden grain in our town and contributing its share to the business activity of our wharf.*

According to George and Ed Heckmann, their brother Capt. Sam Heckmann designed the Julius Silber, and she was built by John Bohlken. George was 19 when he went to work on the Julius Silber.

My job at first was keeping steam on a traction engine to furnish steam to the steam box to heat the planking for bending to the various curves of her hull. She had one Scotch Marine Boiler with Gillette and Eaton engines. When she went into service the latter part of 1905 she was by far the most powerful boat for her power that ever drew breath on the Missouri river. To finish her I did most of the pipe fitting in her engine room, and believe it or not it held up good.

With my brother Greeley as captain and pilot and Kendrick as engineer, I was fireman and striker. That winter we laid up at the mouth of the Gasconade river. I spent the winter as watchman with my Water Spaniel dog Sandy. Nice and lonely winter.

The next spring with another brother, Capt. Bill in charge and Ed Roehrig as chief engineer, we left Gasconade for St. Louis to enter the packet trade from St. Louis to Lupus on the Missouri river. I was listed as striker. We towed the barge Norman to give us more freight capacity. She operated that year from March 12, 1906 to Nov. 1, 1906 when her boiler tubes started to leak so bad that we had to lay her up for repairs and finish the season with the Steamer India Givens. On that run we carried quite a few horses and cattle. When they got a real mean horse on board they would put him close to the engine room so the engineer on watch could quiet him, accomplished by various means. I was in the engine room when we had one such on board. I had a long handled brush on

The Steamer Julius Silber

the work bench and when he tried to paw a hole through the deck, I would start pounding on his rear end which was headed toward me. He must not have liked my treatment. He let loose with both hind feet, kicked the gate, the top board hit me in the chin and knocked me ass over appetite into the engine room. The chief almost fainted when he found me on the floor. I could not talk for about three days.

Meanwhile, the steamer Buck Elk spent the summer on the Osage River, boating lumber from the Osage Iron Works to Bagnell, a distance of 53 miles. That fall the Buck Elk advertised an excursion.

The Military Band at Fredericksburg will have its picnic and ball next Saturday, August 19. The steamboat Buck Elk will take passengers from Hermann and way landings and leave here Saturday morning at 8 o'clock, returning after the ball at night. It will be a fine trip by moonlight on the Gasconade. Fare for round trip from Hermann 35 cents, all other landings, 25 cents.

Mary reported that the Knights of Pythias held a Gasconade River steamboat excursion on the Wm. L. Heckmann. *They must have had a "high old time" from the way they shouted when they came in, and from the reports of the quantity of beer drunk. Papa and Norman went along on the excursion boat.*

The newspaper later reported, *The Hermann Ferry and Packet Co. has absorbed the Buck Elk Steamboat Co., and put the steamboat Julius F. Silber in commission. We trust the fool business of organizing rival steamboat companies have come to an end—It is on par with starting an opposition newspaper just because some one has been piqued and wants to get even.*

From 1905, when the steamer Julius Silber was built, until 1909, when the steamer August Wohlt was built, was the longest hiatus for boatbuilding in the history of the Hermann Ferry and Packet Company. The steamers Buck Elk, Julius Silber, Wm. L. Heckmann and Henry Wohlt were still running out of Hermann, while St. Louis was home port for the steamer Lora. News of the boats was mostly routine, with the exception of the Julius Silber, which seemed prone to multiple breakdowns.

Local boats kept the Hermann wharf busy, but there was other traffic, as well.

An excursion on the steamer Mill Boy and barge came up from New Haven last Sunday arriving here at 3 o'clock in the afternoon and leaving again about two hours later. There were over one hundred people, and when afterwards the big Kansas City boat Tennessee landed for the purpose of coaling, and her passengers walked about town, the streets looked pretty lively for a while. Six steamboats, a number of barges and the Anna Dell were at the landing all at one time and Hermann looked like some big port. In the morning the Steamer J. R. Wells was at the wharf, making eight boats for the day.

River improvement work now originated out of the Government Ship Yards at Gasconade.

New life has been infused by the order given that the Gasconade fleet at once go up to Heckmann's Mill and build a dam there. But the newspaper complained, *Every summer and fall we hear about making the Missouri river navigable and putting in a regular packet line of boats from Kansas City to St. Louis, but the enterprise never gets any further than in the Kansas City papers.* The "Linn Democrat" was advocating more Gasconade River improvements. *In addition to the $10,000 appropriated for the Gasconade, Congressman Shackelford secured an order for the survey of that stream from its mouth to the crossing of the Rock Island at Gascony, with the view of making a channel with a permanent depth of 3 feet. ... A boat line would then follow as a logical consequence, a really important matter to residents contiguous to the stream and in the vicinity thereof.*

But the agitation for a steamboat line was largely an exercise in futility. By this time not even the Missouri River could support any sort of regular service. In fact, the Hermann boats depended in large measure on work provided by the

The Steamer August Wohlt

river improvement projects.

>The much heralded steamboat line between St. Louis and Kansas City has already
>fizzled out. Capt. Sims of the City of Memphis has withdrawn the boat from the
>Missouri river trade, saying that merchants will not ship by boat because the
>insurance companies refuse to insure goods because of the great danger of snags
>and general insecurity of the river. The steamer Julius F. Silber is now the only
>regular Missouri river packet, but does not extend her trips beyond Jefferson
>City.

To the relief of her owners, the steamer Kennedy was sold to St. Louis parties. She left the Hermann wharf for the last time on March 30, 1906. Ever resourceful, Mary sent along flowers for Lottie, who was working as a secretary in St. Louis.

On one of her visits home from St. Louis, Lottie developed a strange problem that vexed the women of the household for two days. Handling long hair was quite a chore in the days when lye soap was the only shampoo available. One day after Lottie washed her hair, it tangled into two enormous mats about six inches from her head.

>We tried everything we could think of, nothing done any good. At last Annie,
>visiting from Springfield began on it, pulled it out strand by strand, now this
>evening we have one side untangled and have hopes of getting it out all together.

... Annie worked most of the day on Lotties hair, Lizzie and I helped at times. ... I worked at Lottie's hair until dinner, after dinner Lizzie worked all afternoon. ... After supper I worked at Lottie's hair until 9 o'clock, we at last got all the tangle out, we combed out a great deal, but still one does not notice it much. It was the strangest affair I or everyone else who seen it ever experienced.

Norman came down with a bad case of the mumps, and just when recovery seemed near, he suffered a relapse. Mary was up every hour to give him medicine for high fever and delirium. To make matters worse, young Will brought all four of his children to stay with his mother, since Will's Annie had the mumps, too.

All of the Heckmann children learned to play the piano by ear, some better than others. Fred had bought a piano and found a new gadget called the Apollo to help his playing. Mary was thrilled. *Heard the new Apollo play the piano, it is fine, anyone can play the most difficult pieces.*

Bob, the studious son, was a teacher and a salesman. *Robert is almost wild, he has the agency of the State for selling a compound to make coal oil and gasoline nonexplosive. It is a great invention. ... Robert burned his hand through carelessness. ... Robert started out on the road to sell his nonexplosive. ... Robert is doing real well with his work.*

Ed was the family's main financial contributor. *Ed bought us a new washing machine. ... I bought myself quite a quantity of dry goods. Ed gave me money to pay for it.* When it became apparent that the Bob Millers at Bluffton were having financial problems, *we packed a box for the folks at Bluffton. Ed furnished the cash. ... Bob also sent me three dollars, he is making extra pay now in the evening. I am glad he likes his work. Bookkeeping in the Republic office.* At Christmas Lottie played the lady bountiful with gifts for everyone.

By January of 1906, the Missouri River was still open to navigation.

The boys, John and Ed packed their belongings, traps, provisions, etc., and started out with two skiffs to go trapping on the Gasconade. Boys will go from there on the boat. ... Lizzie and I were thinking now it will be only the four of us to be left here at home. ... Mary, Norman, Lizzie and I when here came George, took a bath, hurried about supper, turned the house upside-down, was at the dancing school until 11 o'clock, came home and changed clothes and started to walk to Gasconade. ... Ed writes that they are comfortably fixed in the club house at the mill, and can withstand a pretty severe blizzard. I think tonight or tomor-

row will give them a fair test.

Norman was spending more time on the boats, even missing school on occasion. *Norman was along with Papa, took Buck Elk up to Gasconade winter quarters, returned in afternoon on train. Papa says Norman made a pretty fair cook on the boat.*

Nonetheless, the baby of the family could still howl like a child at every disappointment. *Norman had a hard cry about a pair of shoes. He thought he must have a pair, poor fellow. I pitied him, but that is all I could do, times are very hard with us indeed.* Mary later wrote that *Norman did not go to S.S. because his shoes are too badly worn out.*

At age 61 Papa Will was in failing health and often unable to work. Mary, who was 58, seldom took to her bed, but one day she had a dizzy spell on the same day Papa came down with chills. *Lizzie had her hands full taking care of me and ironing and then Papa came down too.* William was ill enough that Mary sent for her children. *Near 6 o'clock Ed and John returned from the mill. I thought it best that at least Ed come home.* Many people called to wish the captain well and to offer their services.

Illness in the family did not prevent Mary from observing the beauties of nature. *This night is beautiful, the sky is a silver white, the moon about a week old, the ground almost covered with snow, calm and cold. It is awe inspiring. One feels so small, so infinite.* As soon as William had recovered, she went calling. *I was about the neighborhood, having a sort of gossipy feeling.*

Nor did illness keep the captain at home. Papa Will and a Mr. Porter went out to the mill with a team and wagon and returned the next day.

> *Mr. P. did not seem so cold as Papa, I never seen anyone shiver like he did, it was pitiful to see him, if he does not get sick again it will be surprising. They were all covered with soft snow, Papa's gloves were soaking wet, inside and out. They had the snow in their faces most of the way. ... Papa went to Bluffton, crossed on ferry, to go up on the M.K.&T. ... Papa returned about dusk, all played out, his heart was wild and continued that way all evening. He came in skiff and was so cold. ... Papa's heart some better, but not behaving right yet, he has a fearful appetite.*

Jobs were still scarce. *I wrote my mouse story for the Globe Democrat tonight. ... Ed left again to go in search of work and Papa went to St. Louis for the same reason. Papa returned about 2 this morning, train was late, he is thoroughly disgusted with St. L., he has the promise of some good work, if all goes well.* Bob gave up on selling his non-explosive and went back to teaching school.

By March the boats were running again. Papa went to the mill with the steamer Henry Wohlt and fell into the river while he was there. In late March the weather suddenly turned cold, and the river filled with ice. The steamer Julius Silber was stranded at St. Louis, and the Buck Elk was trapped at Bonnots Mill.

Mary wrote that Ed, who had no luck in finding work in St. Louis, *is preparing to leave us for sometime, he wants to go to the Yukon river in Alaska.* Papa Will's good friend Capt. William Hoelscher of Washington, Mo., worked for the North American Transportation and Trading Company, which plied the coastal waters of the Bering Sea and the Yukon River and its tributaries. With an introduction to Capt. Hoelscher in his pocket, Ed left home to seek his fortune.

His mother packed him a "chip" basket of food and rode the train with him as far as Jefferson City, where she kissed him good-bye. The food lasted until he crossed the bridge over the Snake River in Idaho. He pitched the empty basket into the river and went hungry into Seattle. Tourist fare to Seattle was $30, and Ed had saved up $35 for the trip. But he landed the job and soon was on his way to Alaska, courtesy of the NAT&T.

One Sunday morning Mary was unable to go to either Sunday school or church because *Papa brought home four dressed fish heads, and I had to fix them up. It was rather hard for me to be kept home, just to fix up those heads. I was angry.* At the same time, she could enjoy a good joke on herself.

> *Mrs. Neidhart found a basket of what she and I believed to be petunias. She gave me a few and I brought them home, planted them carefully. The joke is, they are tobacco plants. Fleisch had given the plants to her, and now since he found out the mistake we made he said he will have it put in the paper.*

Papa's oldest sister, Louisa Schnell, was on her deathbed, and Papa himself was having more trouble with his heart.

> *Dr. W. came to see Papa, he says unless he takes his medicine he may drop dead any hour. He has grown melancholy and indifferent, seems as though he does not care to get well.*

The day before the July 4 celebration, the family was aroused by a terrible explosion.

> *Papa ran out, and shortly brought Norman in all powder burned, his overalls had been burning in several places, his face and arms were all burned and black of powder. I fixed him up in vaseline and rags, and pretty soon the racket began, he howled for two hours, he had a shirt and skirt on, by and by he said, "Now it does not hurt anymore" and soon he was gone. He was down at Will's house*

performing on the bicycle, had them all laughing like they were crazy. His face
and arm are quite brown.

No buyer could be found for the mill, the house had been sold, the islands
had loans on them, and money was non-existent. *A Mr. Edwards had to look over*
the islands, concerning the loan on them, and Papa had to go with him. A neighbor later
bought the Heckmann lots on top of the bluff. *Paid us $40.00 for them.*

The dam at the mill was the cause of some dissatisfaction.

Mr. Walker and another man here to see Papa about letting out the dam at the
mill. The land owners on opposite side of the mill think by letting the water
down the mill slough it will improve their land. We signed the papers to give
them permission to remove it.

Weather was the bane of women with their chores. One cloudy day Mary
visited her friend Mrs. Neidhart, who was cooking apple butter outdoors.

I knew she was all alone and went down to see how she was getting along.
When I got there I said, "What will you do if it rains?" "Oh, I'll just keep on
stirring." So she said while I was there she would cook herself a little dinner
and before she went into the house, it began to sprinkle. She got me a parasol, in
a few moments it poured down, lasted for about 15 minutes, but she kept on at
the butter and that was all the rain we had.

The grapes were again ready for market, and Fleisch had a lot of grape pickers
at work. But rainy weather made it difficult to pack and load the grape barrels.
The winery must have relented and bought Heckmann grapes again; at least
Mary mentions nothing to the contrary.

One evening the Heckmanns had an unexpected visitor.

About dark someone came striding into the yard, full tilt, and who should it be
but Bill Hensley, escaped from the insane asylum at Fulton. He is quite crazy
and told us how he had gotten out. We gave him his supper and Papa sent him
or took him to Reif's Hotel to remain over night.

This was none other than the famous "Tombstone Bill" Hensley, the man
who stole tombstones and smuggled them aboard the Gasconade River steamboats. He was certain that his old friend Captain Bill would reinstate him on the
boats.

At the end of October Papa left to meet Col. Colman's annual hunting party.
A letter from Ed arrived saying the season had ended on the Yukon and that he

was starting for home. Caroline Silber died on November 5. Papa was still on the hunting trip, so Mary handled the funeral arrangements.

Caroline's son, Victor Silber, who had worked in his mother's general store, had launched a career in sales. He started out selling stock in the Buck Elk Steamboat Company. Next he tried his hand at real estate, selling a "North Texas Paradise" with big ads and promises of trips to see the land. *Running a Special Pullman Sleeper out to Texas every first and third Tuesdays in the month on the M.K.&T. R.R. and by joining our party sleeping car accommodations are free to you.* Victor must have been a good salesman—he managed to sell land to some of the penniless Heckmanns.

With seven boys on the river, disaster stories abounded. The wonder is that the Heckmann sons all survived. They kept the local newspaper in copy.

Greeley Heckmann, while out in a duck boat on the river hunting, had a narrow escape from being drowned. One of the air chambers of the boat sprung a leak and began sinking, leaving Greeley no other alternative but to strike for the sand bar above Heckmann Island. He had on a heavy ammunition belt, cumbersome rubber felt-top boots, and when he touched the bottom of the river he felt like a lump of lead, and it was the almost certainty of death which steeled his muscles to perform the extraordinary feat of reaching shore. All this time a terrific gale was blowing, the rain came down in torrents, and when he reached shore bareheaded, a gloomy prospect was ahead for it looked as if he would have to spend the night on the bar without shelter. Fortunately, the steamer Henry Wohlt went up to rescue cattle from one of the islands, and noticing Mr. Heckmann, landed and took him on board. He lost his gun, boat and hat. After returning to Hermann Greeley headed for the Concert Hall Saloon to "warm up" and after sufficient warming declared, "Well, I've still got Gussie!"

Ed's leg was operated on January 19 at the St. Louis Marine Hospital. For once, his mother was maddeningly silent, giving no word whatsoever as to the success of the surgery. When Ed arrived home on February 5, she wrote, *he can walk without crutches, but walks lame, he looks well.*

Perhaps distance does make the heart grow fonder. Mary had never lost her nostalgia for the days in Pennsylvania. When a letter arrived with the news that both Henry Strickler, her one-time suitor, and her friend Sarah Hershey had died, it caused her to reflect on her life with some sadness.

Henry died on the 4th of April. The paper commenting on his character is very touching and to the point, he was a man among men, since my childhood I have known him, and he was ever highly esteemed. How changed my life would have been had he loved me as I loved him. I would now be the widow of a Mennonite bishop and am instead the mother of a family scattered from one end of this great country to the other. God knows what is best, I trust it was for the better work I might do in this field that I have influence I know, without boasting at all about it. It is given to us to know one another in the Betterland, then perhaps by this time Henry and Sarah have found our little Joe. I can imagine them saying, "You are Mary Miller's child" and taking him each by the hand.

CHAPTER 17

'Til Death Do Us Part

It is a relief to tell all to my books. —Mary L. Heckmann

*W*hen the Heckmann family numbered 12 children, Mary arranged to have a family picture taken, the round-dozen picture. Presumably, she thought her family was complete. But when not one, not two, but three more children arrived she had to reassess her thinking.

From early womanhood, Mary had believed that the Lord gave every woman a certain number of children. She was the oldest child in a family of 11, so her assumption that 12 should be enough is easy to understand. But after the birth of her 14th child, Mary changed her thinking about her role as a woman and as a wife, and she stopped giving the Lord credit for her pregnancies. Finally, when Norman was 11 and she was quite sure there would be no more babies, she arranged to have another family picture taken.

This picture was published in the "Union Signal" on January 17, 1907, with the following caption:

That the oft-repeated truism, "a woman's place is in the home," is an argument against woman's place in public work, has been amply disproved by Mary Miller Heckmann whose "credentials" are offered in the above illustration. Mrs. Heckmann is president of her local Methodist Missionary Society, local, county and district W.C.T.U. president, active and efficient W.C.T.U. press superintendent for her district, a successful homemaker, and the mother of fourteen children, worthy young men and women and promising boys and girls.

The story that accompanied the picture went into greater detail.

It is not at all likely that Mrs. Heckmann occupied all or any of these positions when her children were all small, but in managing her realm successfully and guiding all these boys and girls into helpful ways, she has developed just the qualities which make her efficient in work for the larger home now that her own children no longer need all her time. As Margaret Fuller said: "The wisdom that can maintain serenity, cheerfulness and order, in a little world of ten or twelve persons, and keep ready the resources that are needed for their sustenance and recovery in sickness and sorrow, is the same that holds the stars in their places and patiently prepares the precious metals in the most secret chambers of the earth."

The woman's suffrage movement is not inimical to the home nor does it hold in less regard than President Roosevelt the exalted services of women to whom motherhood comes in conditions that make it the crowning joy of life. But it does insist that the mother shall have equal rights with the father over the children for whom she has suffered and toiled, and this in Missouri, Mrs. Heckmann has not. It does insist that women who devote themselves to the duties of home and children during the best money-making time of life shall be recognized by law as entitled to an equal share in the family property. It maintains that women whose altruism, executive ability, and wise motherhood have been developed and trained by a life experience such as Mrs. Heckmann's, are in a position to render public service such as it would never enter into the heart of man to conceive of. And it seeks to remove from the mother, and from potential motherhood in all women the stigma of disfranchisement and from ranking before the law in the political category of idiots, lunatics and felons.

The poetic justice of this publicity must have been sweet, indeed, for Mary. After years of reading newspaper accounts of her husband's exploits, including birth announcements in which she was not mentioned, she had at last received credit for something in her own right.

The birthday month of February rolled around again, and Mary enjoyed her usual group of friends and relatives and a wonderful array of gifts. *Lottie sent a nice fine white blanket and from Lottie, Bob and George a dozen silver teaspoons and Ed a 20 dollar gold piece. Cups and saucers from John, Apron, cake, flowers and plate from*

The Heckmann family: Seated, from left, are John, Tina, William Sr., Norman, Mary, Sam and Mary. Standing are Robert, Lizzie, Edward, Lottie, William Jr., Annie, Fred, Martha and George.

Kuhns, Plate from Mrs. Begemann, plate from Mrs. Well, Cake from Miss Bek, two aprons from Mrs. Lessel, calico dress from Mrs. Steel, waist goods from Annie.

But on the first of March, the family received tragic news.

At 3:30 p.m. we received the most shocking news, a telegram announcing the death of our son-in-law, William Brennecke. We did not know of his being sick. In the evening Robert talked to us over long distance, wants someone to meet Martha, but we concluded to not do so. They at St. Louis received a telegram saying they would bring the remains to Hermann. ... Many people called during the day. By evening we received another telegram telling us the internment will be at Gordonville.

Ed and Lizzie went to St. Louis to meet Martha, but the train was three hours late. Lottie took charge of Martha's baby, Harriet, and the group finally arrived in Hermann. Martha returned to Gordonville for her husband's funeral, accompanied by her sister, Lizzie. *The school William was attending was just as kind to Martha as could be. Harriet slept since last evening until this morning. I never seen a sweeter child. ... Ed left for Seattle at midnight last night.*

William Brennecke had died without a penny of insurance, leaving Martha destitute. Her piano and household goods arrived in Hermann by train, and two more people, Martha and her baby, moved into the Heckmann home.

Dr. Sneed's name was in the diaries with increasing frequency. He was the family eye doctor, but his visits usually were mentioned in relation to Lizzie. Whatever the romantic interest may have been, nothing came of it. Lizzie never married.

Papa Will's health was growing worse—he was not sleeping well and sometimes suffered from choking spells. He had been sleeping upstairs with the boys, but now Mary moved his bed downstairs so she could attend to him. Nonetheless, on April 9 he insisted on rowing home from Bluffton. *Papa came back in skiff and says he had a tough time of it, he was about played out. I told him not to go, but he would not heed me.*

The end came on April 24, 1907.

Papa had a bad night again. In afternoon he walked out to the Linden trees, and was so much exhausted so when he tried to get up he fell, no one seen him fall, but when we got him into the house, we thought he would pant himself to death right there. The Dr. says he had a stroke of apoplexy, he cannot talk. We sent telegrams to all the folks. Lottie telephoned that she and Bob would be home tonight. What I have expected for two years has fallen upon me, may God give me strength to bear the trial.

... William is growing worse, there are no hopes for his recovery. We ex-pect the end to come by midnight. ... William lingered until 8:35 this morning, had a hard struggle for an hour before his soul took its upward flight. All the children are here except Annie and Ed, who is in Dawson, Yukon Territory just at present. ... This morning we received a telegram from Charley Miller an-nouncing the birth of a girl baby at their home, one soul comes to earth and one leaves it. ... People have been so kind, and so many have come to offer sympa-thy, I cannot number them all. The G.A.R.'s and K.P.'s vie with each other who can do the most for this departed comrade.

After 39 years and one month and 30 days of wedded life we are parted. May we meet in that Land where sorrow is no more.

In death, as in life, the "Advertiser-Courier" had only the highest praise for the captain. A lengthy obituary said *with him disappears, so to say, a part of the history of our town.* Capt. Will was described as *a most energetic and enterprising business man. In this connection he was one of the main factors in developing the river traffic and the steamboat interest of our town, having devoted perhaps the greatest part of his life to that business.*

Writing in the "Rural World," Norman Colman paid tribute to his old friend as an esteemed hunter, angler and companion.

He was untiring in his efforts to please his companions, and he did all he could both by song and story, to make the time pass pleasantly when on our hunting and fishing trips. No one enjoyed these trips more than he, and his untiring efforts for the success of the club and the associates to feel a tender affection for him which was cherished by all up to his death, and each and every one will feel a sense of personal and irreparable loss since he has passed away. ... Adieu, dear old friend, and may we meet in the happy hunting grounds over yonder.

It fell to Lottie to write the news of their father's death to Ed in Alaska. The letter took weeks to reach the absent brother.

Hermann, Mo. 4/25/07
My dear Brother,

It is with a sad heart I write to tell you of papa's death yesterday, April 24th, at a quarter to nine in the morning. While this was not unexpected, we

William and Mary Heckmann in their vineyard

did not think it would come so soon and it is hard to realize that he is gone forever.

Papa had been lying down most of the time since last Friday, just getting up for his meals, and Monday afternoon he went out under the linden tree and as he passed the window Martha spoke to him, but he did not answer. He sat there about a half hour and when he got up to come in the house, he fell, and Mama, Martha and Mary carried or helped him in, but he never spoke a word

233

after Monday noon. His right side was paralyzed soon after they got him to bed, but he was so restless. His left hand moved and pulled at the cover constantly. He seemed to recognize Mama Tuesday morning and pressed her hand when she went to his side, but Wednesday morning about 3 o'clock his left hand lay quiet and he never moved except to struggle for breath. We looked for the end at any moment after 3 o'clock, but he lingered until almost nine.

Ed, we were glad when he was out of his pain for he surely must have been in pain, altho he could not speak, but after all it is hard to give him up. I don't know whether you remember him so well as we older children do, but I can never forget how good he was to us always, and if trouble hadn't come to him in double measure, none of us could ever say that he didn't do what he thought was right. He was good as he could be.

We have not looked at papa since he died, but Uncle Ed says he looks very nice. They had to order a coffin for him. My dear boy, how I wish you were here too, but we can only pray that you will keep well and come back to us safe and well.

Mama says she has written since receiving your check and that she never ceases to pray for you, for it was surely needed, and Ed, I am so thankful that you arranged about the place before going, for awful as it must seem to you, Annie said to Gusta yesterday, "The place is mine."

Well, my dear boy, I hope my next letter can contain more cheerful news, but just now everything is sad. More of us will write later.

With dearest love from all who are here, I am,

Your loving sister, Lottie.

Ed was not heard from until June 11. *Had two letters from Ed, one addressed to Papa, the other to me, he at last has heard of Papa's death.*

Mary's lack of experience in handling money now became an important factor. The insurance check, promptly paid, seemed huge to her. The newspaper was impressed, too.

The late Capt. Wm. L. Heckmann was a member of the Endowment Rank Knights of Pythias and carried $3000 insurance. One week after proof of death had been made the widow got her money, a very prompt settlement indeed. Insurance in the K. Of P. is giltedge and so is everything else connected with the Order.

CHAPTER 17 ˜ TIL DEATH DO US PART

The insurance money had a different effect on Will's Annie, the business-woman of the family to whom Mary and William Heckmann had deeded their house. Ever-practical, Annie expected someday to be paid the money or take possession of the house. Although her timing was not the most diplomatic, Annie saw that money was available and made her demand. Mary was shocked and felt terribly wronged. Annie, on the other hand, felt she was legally within her rights and said so.

Had Annie come up to talk to her over this property business. Two years ago Will came up here with notes amounting to five thousand dollars as he said, we had often talked of giving him some security for what his Father had borrowed. This was his proposal, if we deed this home property over to him, he would call the deal off, provided we paid off the over eleven hundred dollar mortgage on the property. Papa talked to Mr. Breuer about it, and he said it was all right, at the same time Will said "Any time Papa has two thousand cash to hand over, I will deed the property back to either one of you." Not a word was said about time or date. Will and Mr. Breuer drew up a paper, as I believed to that effect. Papa and I signed it, and had some of the boys sign it. I have told all the children that this was the understanding about it. At any rate, she said she could prove by the paper she held that she could put us off this place at thirty days notice. I told her I never signed such a paper, she went down to the house and got the paper and proved it to me. Now the property is in her name, another thing Will did not mention and she does not want to give this up.

Mary's years of signing anything her husband put before her finally had brought on a reckoning beyond her comprehension. She herself had recorded in her diary, *Sold this place to Annie today.* Faced with the prospect of giving up her home or giving up the money, she sacrificed the house.

I know this worry is what makes me sick. I thought I was a pretty fair Christian, until Annie got through with me and then I concluded I was a liar and sneak and almost a thief. There is One over all, who can judge.

The real problem was Mary's naiveté—for too many years she had blindly signed papers without understanding that they represented money. She had been a happy lady when her husband owned three big island farms, a mill and his own fleet of steamboats. She had no idea that all were heavily mortgaged. Had conditions been optimal, the farms would have paid handsomely, but the 1903 flood changed that. The mill was always a dubious undertaking that turned out to be a disaster. Unknowing, or at least uncomprehending, Mary never realized the true enormity of the debt her husband had amassed.

Now she was a widow faced with the prospect of losing her home and the inevitable gossip produced by such a situation. She had no income, she was heavily in debt, and every asset was mortgaged to the hilt. Her own financial naiveté may have been her greatest blessing—she never fully comprehended the seriousness of her situation.

Throughout her life, Mary had sought the counsel of her sisters when troubled. Now she went to Sedalia to visit Emma and Lizzie and then to Blackwater to see Alice. Upon her return, she was ready to tackle the problem of where to live. *Talk of going to St. Louis to live.*

In late July Mary departed for St. Louis to house hunt, but her first stop was Shaw's Garden. *We enjoyed the beautiful flowers to our hearts content.* Thus fortified, she went to the real estate office. *Got prices etc. on houses, and looked at several, were disappointed and felt blue when we got home.* Later a friend of Lottie's told her *we could buy Allen's house, which we decided to do.*

There were still several of the children at home—Martha with little Harriet, Lizzie, Lottie, Mary and Norman. George and John came and went according to their work schedules on the boats, and Bob lived at home when he was not teaching school. Ed was steamboating in Alaska, but returned home during freeze-up.

On August 5 Mary placed an auction ad in the paper. *We will sell out here, all goods we do not need and move to St. Louis.* Later that month she wrote, *We are still in suspense, no papers from Mr. Allen, we begin to think he is not going to let us have the house.* But the matter was eventually settled, and the packing—a tale in itself—began in earnest. A new renter came to see the Hermann house, and the Heckmann family's belongings were crated and shipped by rail to St. Louis, where their first caller was Dr. Sneed—and there was no chair to offer him.

The family settled in, bought a refrigerator and gas stove and redecorated the house from top to bottom. Some money was put in Lincoln Trust, and the monthly note had to be paid on the property. Suddenly, the $3,000 insurance money no longer seemed like such an enormous sum.

Never before had the Heckmanns had to buy food. The wild game the men supplied, the chickens Mary raised, the milk from the cow and the huge vegetable garden all had been taken for granted. Except for the electric light bill, there had never been utilities to pay—the men kept the family in wood and the cistern supplied the water.

CHAPTER 17 ~ 'TIL DEATH DO US PART

Thank our kind Father was Mary's response when a telegram from Ed arrived in late October saying he would soon be home. Little did Ed know just what he was coming home to. By the time he arrived, Bob, Martha and Lottie all were out of work. *Boys all out looking for jobs, not successful up to date.* With commercial training and work experience, Lottie quickly found another job—her board money helped keep food on the table.

Ed had made good money in Alaska—$125 per month with all expenses paid. He had been saving his salary with the intention of coming home to marry his girl, Alice Bock. But now it seemed he would have to support his family instead. *Ed and I down town to Mr. Senn and to Real Estate Office, paid some off on the mortgage and fixed it up for another year.* Ed's desire to marry was thwarted by more than his family's situation—Alice didn't want to marry a steamboat man. His mother reported, *Ed is contemplating buying an interest in a market near here.*

Mary closed 1907 with these words:

So, good bye old year, I have written more in this book than to anyone, more than I have talked to anyone. It is a relief to tell all to my books, some day I may destroy them all. The old year passed away and the new came in while I knelt at the altar at church, I try to put my full trust in God.

Clothes still had to be washed the hard way, and the washings were still huge. The wash woman was almost a necessity, but it took money to pay her. Often Mary and the "girls" —Lizzie and Martha— did the wash. Daughter Mary, who was 16 and popular, was little help around the house and prone to bringing home great numbers of guests.

Mary often wrote in her diary of her complete exhaustion. She did manage to get to church, to prayer meetings and sometimes to WCTU meetings. Her interest in the latter had not waned, but her enthusiasm was tempered by lack of physical strength. As always the family took their mother for granted. They seemed oblivious to her failing health.

George was courting Helen Fallis in St. Louis, John was courting Annie Kuhn in Hermann, and Norman would later court and marry Irene Kuhn. The sad news of the death of a Kuhn sister, Martha, was followed in a few weeks by the death of another sister, Gretchen. Tuberculosis had killed their father and now claimed the two young women. Ed accompanied his brother, John, to Hermann for the funerals.

Cousin Victor Silber, the perpetual salesman, tried to sell a life insurance policy to Ed, but he failed the physical.

The M.D. told him he could not pass, owing to the condition of his leg and he also said, if he were to take a fever that ran up to 104 he could have blood poisoning inside of 24 hours and die, so Ed intends going to the hospital tomorrow and have an operation performed later.

Ed entered the Centenary hospital on February 17 and underwent surgery the next day. His brother John reported that Ed *was as well as could be expected.* On March 5 Mary wrote, *Ed surprised us by walking in this evening.*

The Heckmann estate was still in probate. On Feb. 25, Mary wrote that she *signed deeds of Mill and Islands to Leimhuehler and Langenburg today.* She received not a penny from the sale, but she was relieved from the burden of debt on the properties. Now her only remaining asset in the world was her small equity in the St. Louis house.

Whatever Ed's ideas about finding work close by may have been, he had to conclude that Alaska offered a far better solution to his money problems. *To be gone until November, gone to Alaska, may our Father keep him safely.* Before leaving on May 21, Ed bought paint and painted the porches and interior of the house. Lottie talked of trying to find work in Alaska, too, but in the end did not accompany her brother.

Warm weather meant jobs for the boys. George left on the steamer Bald Eagle, and Norman left on the steamer Silber. John and Bob were working, and daughter Mary was sent off on a five-week visit. The food bill diminished considerably, as did the quantity of laundry to be done.

On June 28 Mary wrote, *A beautiful day. I arose this morning feeling dizzy, before time to go to church, I had to lie down, was quite ill for a while, but was able to eat some dinner, and slept most of the afternoon.*

Before long, Mary was back to nursing her brood. George was quite ill for a month, from what his mother does not say. Just when he was starting to recover, Lottie fell ill, and Norman came home needing new clothes. *Norman and I went down town to get him some clothes, he is entirely out after six weeks in the country, got his first long pants.* Norman, who grew to be nearly 6-feet-3-inches tall, had a continual problem of outgrowing his clothes.

Girlfriends came to visit, and some were helpful. John's girl, Annie Kuhn, helped Mary with the ironing. This was a huge task, done with flatirons heated on the stove.

Ed returned from Alaska on December 6, and on Christmas Day Mary wrote: *Since writing last things have been going on about the same as ever. Monday morning Bob came home, Ed went to Tower Grove to get a basket of game, and Bob came home with it. John has been killing quite a lot of game and sent us some. The Christmas entertainment came off O.K. I and Ed were the only ones to remain at home, I was so tired remained at home to rest. Harriet was remembered by many, and is a happy child. John returned home 23rd. All are now in except George.*

On New Year's Eve Mary helped make coffee and sandwiches for "Watchnight" at the church. *Ed came up for me and remained to meeting, the New Year was ushered in while we all knelt in prayer.*

In January, Ed announced his engagement to Alice Bock. His mother was delighted with the news and made preparations to visit Hermann with a Valentine's Day gift for the bride-to-be. Aboard the train, Mary conversed with her seatmate about her large family, explaining how very proud she was of all her children. Suddenly, she gasped—and died in mid-sentence.

February 11, 1909—

Mrs. Mary Heckmann Dies on Train
While on Way to Hermann

Mrs. Mary Heckmann, widow of the late Capt. Wm. L. Heckmann, formerly of our town, but the last two years a resident of St. Louis, was a passenger on train No. 1, Mo. Pacific, last Thursday morning on her way to Hermann to visit some of her children who reside here; and as the train passed Labadie she suddenly fell ill, and before the people around her realized what was going on she was dead. Among the passengers was a physician who rendered what assistance he could, but death had already set his stamp upon her brow, and all the doctor could do was to announce that deceased came to her death from heart failure.

At Washington, Dr. Muench was called, but he too pronounced Mrs. Heckmann dead, and the corpse was permitted to complete the journey to Hermann, while Mr. Wm. Heckmann here was notified of what had taken place, and to prepare for the arrival of the remains.

Mrs. Heckmann was a daughter of the late Judge Sam Miller of Montgomery county, was married to Capt. Wm. L. Heckmann 38 years ago, and became the mother of fifteen children, fourteen of whom are yet alive and are as follows:

Mrs. Robt. Miller, Bluffton, Wm. L. and Sam M. Heckmann of Hermann; Mrs.
C. H. Miller, of Springfield; J. Fred Heckmann, of St. Joseph; Miss Elizabeth
Heckmann, Mrs. Martha Brennecke, Miss Charlotte V., Robert E., Edward,
George T., John H., Miss Mary I. and Norman J. C. Heckmann; all of St. Louis.
She was 62 years old at the time of death, an active church and W.C.T.U. worker,
and a woman of more than ordinary intelligence and force of character.

The ladies of the Home Mission Society of the Shaw Ave. Methodist Church
wrote of Mary Heckmann:

Very human she was, with an abundance of the saving sense of humor. Earnest,
sincere, true, willing. Not an angelic, unapproachable creature, just a wom-
anly woman, filled with God's Love! ... It is strange that with her steadfastness
in the right and her wonderful power for good, she was so lacking in self-
assertiveness. If we were to search for one single word in which to express her,
that one word would be "Faithfulness."

Mary Heckmann had been born in February, she had married in February,
and she died in February. Her funeral service was held at the Methodist Church
in Hermann. The congregation sang "Safe in the Arms of Jesus" in German, and
the church was filled with beautiful flowers.

EPILOGUE

The Legacy

$\mathcal{W}$hen Mary and William Heckmann died, about the only thing they left behind were their children. But that proved to be a very large legacy, indeed.

Justina Heckmann, Will's daughter from his first marriage, married Mary's brother, Robert Miller. Tina nearly equaled her stepmother in having babies, losing two and raising 11 children. The Millers lived on top of one of the highest hills at Bluffton, where it was said that they raised their children on asparagus and fresh air, a claim closer to the truth than one might imagine. Steamboat Bill added that the family got by with "not many doctor bills to pay, a few country midwives, a Bible and prayers." Yet, no one would have dared to call them impoverished. Steamboat Bill wrote:

> *Bob Miller was a character deluxe. He had a big band that offered love and music to the Hill Billies and their sweethearts around Bluffton for half a century. His style of singing and music was as amusing as the swimming monkeys in the Memphis Zoo. Uncle Bob's songs were mostly made up by himself. He would play and sing such melodies as "Said the Dominicker Hen to the Big Red Rooster, You Don't Come Around as Often as You Uster."*

Bob also worked a little on the boats and as a carnival worker during the summer. The children, all handsome and intelligent, did well. Son Roy Miller distinguished himself by becoming a famous steamboat pilot and serving in the Armed Forces during World War I. The French awarded him the Croix de Guerre for bravery after he saved a burning barge that was loaded with explosives on the Seine River near Paris. Another Miller son, William, also followed the river for a time.

William L. Heckmann Jr., the first-born son, was the crown prince who received the lion's share of his father's attention. Young Will grew up thinking that steamboats were the ultimate career possibility. His fame as Steamboat Bill came from two sources—his copious writing under that nom de plume and his long career as a Missouri River pilot.

His brothers could never equal his outpouring of words, but they could and did rival him on the river. Jealousy was not unheard of among the Heckmann boys. When a poem titled "Will Heckmann, Who Never Sunk a Boat" appeared in the "Waterways Journal," it was just too much for brother Ed, who countered with a verse of his own, "Captain Bill, Who Sunk One Boat," signed G. Haw Jr.

Will Jr. did not take kindly to being overlooked when something important was afoot on the Missouri River. When J. Patrick Hurley, U. S. Secretary of War, made an inspection trip up the river, Steamboat Bill was not invited. He solved the problem rather neatly, according to the Kansas City "Journal-Post." The story by Gilbert Smith, which was reprinted in the "Waterways Journal," captures the spirit of the man perfectly.

How Steamboat Bill Joined Hurley

Hermann, Mo., June 23 , 1932—*Nearly everyone has heard of Steamboat Bill, he who occupied a legendary niche in the hall of fame with Casey Jones and others made immortal by barbershop ditties. Today, Bill was the honored guest of Patrick J. Hurley, Secretary of War.*

Bill differs somewhat from Casey Jones in that he's still alive and more than a little active. His saga may have been outlasted by that of Casey, but that may be put down to the vagaries of a fickle public and the idiosyncrasies of radio announcers. Anyway, there are hundreds of trains where there is only one steamboat today, and that may account for the condition in which he finds himself. But Steamboat Bill has two claims to fame that Casey never possessed. He has been entertained by one of the nation's highest officials, and has the reputation of having tied a Congressional committee up in more knots than Houdini could unwrap.

Bill came alongside the Mark Twain, the steamer on which Secretary Hurley and his party are traveling, shortly after it docked below the toll bridge at Hermann. Bill was, and is, typically "Old Man River." He sculled alongside the shiny towboat in a skiff that has seen palmier days and rammed his craft into the bank alongside the Secretary, who was holding an official conference before going ashore.

Not in Company Clothes

Bill was hatless and certainly was not wearing his company clothes when he splashed alongside and looked up at the group two decks above. Secretary Hurley looked over the rail and clutched L. F. Phillips, Oklahoma oil magnate, by the arm.

"My gosh, take a look," exclaimed the Secretary, who is more than a little human. "Where did he get that whale?"

The "whale" was a 45-pound channel catfish that reposed amidship in the skiff Bill was holding against the current. It wore a half-inch line around its gills and gave every evidence of resentment at being forcibly brought to the celebration.

"Where did you get him?" Secretary Hurley shouted to the boatman.

"Out of the river," replied Bill. "It's a catfish."

"I can see it is," was the Secretary's comeback, "but I can't believe it."

Caught Him for You

"I caught him for you," replied Steamboat Bill. "We eat 'em."

The crew acted intuitively and soon Bill and his catfish were aboard. Cleveland A. Newton, general counsel for the Mississippi Valley Association and former member of Congress, was standing beside Secretary Hurley and taking in the riverman's repartee.

"I knew I'd seen him before, Mr. Secretary," he said. "That is the one and original Steamboat Bill. There's no one else like him on any river in the country—he knows more river than any other six men alive."

Bill arrived on deck before Mr. Newton completed his story and was presented to the Secretary of War, and immediately was seized by Mr. Newton and Maj. Gen. T. Q. Ashburn.

Steak for Breakfast

"Caught him out of the river just now, and thought you might like a steak for breakfast."

"I know I will," Mr. Hurley said, "but what about having dinner with me?"

"Well, I don't like to do that, Mr. Hurley, but I'd like to go to Jefferson City tomorrow on the Twain—sort of celebratin', if you get what I mean."

"The boat is yours, and we'll try that steak," the Secretary said.

When Bill went below to supervise the work of preparing his catch, Mr. Newton completed his story. Bill, it turned out was Capt. William L. Heckmann, who's father built and operated steamboats on the Missouri river when navigation was comparable to dime bets on a policy wheel. He also had piloted steamboats from St. Louis up the Big Muddy to Miles City, Mont., and had a cousin in town who had been a pilot for 32 years.

Called to Washington

"We had Bill back in Washington before a Congressional committee at one time," Mr. Newton related. "Someone got on the subject of what the barge lines might do to the railroads if the Government got the rivers open and asked Bill what he thought about it.

"'That's what we send you fellers back here to find out,' Bill told the inquisitor. 'We've got troubles of our own,' and that was all the satisfaction the committee got when it tried to question Steamboat Bill."

So Bill was the guest of the Secretary of War and catfish steaks were served for breakfast Thursday morning aboard the Mark Twain.

Topping Steamboat Bill or catching him in an unflattering situation was a game with all the river people. In July of 1921, a correspondent from the U. S. Government Boatyards gleefully reported one such incident in the "Waterways Journal."

Got it in the Neck

Gasconade, Mo., July 6, 1921—*If Steamboat Bill is missing from the columns of the "Waterways Journal" this week, there's a reason and an explanation. Let me tell it.*

Now, your regular Missouri River contributor isn't one of those land lubbering parlor navigators who makes out they can tell a capstan bar from a spud at a glance. Captain Bill is one of those who knows a steamboat from her keel up and from her boilers out; and while evenings he may burn the coal oil composing for the Journal, daytimes rivermen always find him standing in the pilot house of the Champ Clark, his right foot on a spoke, his swallow-tail coat flopping in the breeze, Fedora on eyebrows and both eyes peeled ahead for snags.

So it was that on a recent morning coming upstream from Hermann he pointed the nose of the Champ into the mouth of the Gasconade River—and the Gasconade was running out from the effects of prolonged rains back in the Ozark hills. Fifteen hundred feet above the mouth the Missouri Pacific Railroad crosses this river on a low bridge, all of whose spans are fixed. But the Champ is a boat designed for the streams she plies, and so on this occasion the combination of a low bridge and a flooded river didn't perturb "Steamboat Bill" a bit. He simply weighted his bucket planks, folded up the smokestack, dismantled the collapsible, take-down pilot house, and standing in the open, blew two whistles for full speed ahead. The little boat responded with a vim, and her steering wheel cleared nicely—several hair breadths, in fact. But "Captain Bill's" head and neck loomed above the wheel like an acorn on a spar, and a moment later his Adams Apple met the bottom girder, jarring the whole span. "Bill" did a back dive to the hurricane roof that was pretty to see, then bounced off and lit on a pile of sacked wheat on the boiler deck. When he came to the crew was bending over him.

"Boys," he whispered in a husky cracked voice, "Dempsey was the better man." Then, realizing where he was—"After this when we come to a low bridge I'm gonna crouch."

Steamboat Bill and "Will's Annie" were married for more than 60 years and raised four children—Monica, Hazel and Gladys, and one son, Rodney Massie, who was named for a well-known steamboat captain. After high school the girls all became teachers. Their father never forgave the State of Missouri for minuscule wages teachers were paid. It never ceased to rile him that his young deckhands earned more than his daughters did teaching.

After college, son Rodney attended Eden Seminary and became an ordained minister in the Evangelical Church. (Now U.C.C.) Bill was proud of his son, whom he dubbed "Sky Pilot," and wrote of him often. But he did not hide his disappointment that his son had not chosen a career on the river.

Samuel Miller Heckmann was a fat-faced child who bore a striking resemblance to Horace Greeley, thus the nickname Greeley. Capt. Sam Miller was an ardent hunter and fisherman and probably the most skilled pilot ever to turn a wheel on the convoluted little Gasconade River. He designed the steamers Julius F. Silber and the Cinderella.

Sam and his wife, Gusta Bensing, were the parents of four children, Harvey, Doris, Wanda and Sam. Wanda died young. Harvey followed his father on the river and was a partner in the building of the Cinderella and her barge, the Golden Slipper. Harvey for many years was the engineer on the railroad transfer boat near St. Louis. Sam Jr. worked for the U.S. Corps of Engineers his entire life, spending most of his time in the Jacksonville, Florida, office. Doris married and remained at Hermann.

Angelia Louisa Heckmann married Charley Miller, a distant cousin. They had two children, Ira and Elizabeth. True to the Miller tradition, after trying several other occupations, Charley ultimately became a nurseryman. Son Ira followed his father in the same business.

Julius Frederick Heckmann held both engineer's and pilot's licenses, but he never seemed to attract as much publicity as his brothers. Fred cubbed under his father and worked on a number of the Hermann Ferry and Packet Co. boats, as well as the Monitor and a few others. He bought and operated a little ferry-boat at Decator, Nebraska, until his untimely death at age 52.

The eagle eye of the family, Fred was known for his uncanny vision. It was a dangerous gift—Fred pulled stunts like shooting a corncob pipe out of the hand of a deckhand sitting on the prow of a moving steamboat.

Fred married Philopena Morlock, and they had one son, Fred Jr., who did his cubbing under his Uncle Ed Heckmann. Fred Jr. received his mate's license, but later enrolled at the University of Missouri-Columbia and became a stationary engineer.

Mary Elizabeth Heckmann never married. Lizzie spent most of her life as a housekeeper and companion for others.

Martha Eveline Heckmann was beautiful, talented and popular. She married William Brennecke, a young minister, and had a baby girl. Martha, who was widowed by the time little Harriet was 18 months old, eventually became a matron of a Foundling Home. She was always financially dependent on her family but somehow managed to find money for voice lessons for her daughter. Harriet went on to sing with the Metropolitan Opera in New York, where for a time she was understudy to Galli Curcci.

EPILOGUE

Charlotte Virginia Heckmann and her brother Ed were the ones who held the family together financially during the St. Louis years. When she was finally free of this burden, Lottie fell in love and married Hermann Hundhausen. They had four children, William, Gene, Robert and Virginia, none of whom developed any interest in the river.

Robert Evans Heckmann, the studious member of the family, was the one Heckmann son who did not fall in love with steamboating. After trying various occupations, Bob found his niche with the Santa Fe Railroad, working with refrigerated cars. He married Myrtle Lapham, and they had four children, Charles, Louis, Ruth and Mary.

Bob's son Charles developed an avid interest in steamboats in his later years and was a promoter of a large boat that was to run on the Sacramento River in California. The project received lots of publicity but never attracted enough money to get off the drawing board. Perhaps there is a gene that carries "Steamboat Fever."

Edward Heckmann, my father, was the only son with no middle name. In his declining years he took the maiden name of his paternal grandmother, thereafter signing himself Edward Rewald Heckmann. By the time Ed acquired his pilot's license, his father was worse than broke and no longer owned any boats. So Ed went to Alaska, where he steamboated for four seasons.

This resulted in what probably was the longest pilot's license ever issued to an inland river pilot. On January 10, 1939, Ed was licensed as Master of Steam and Motor Vessels, of all gross tons, upon all rivers. His first class pilot's license covered the Mississippi River from Chalmette Slip, Louisiana, to Rip Rap Landing, Illinois; the Ohio River from mouth to Cairo, Illinois; the Illinois River from mouth to Griggsville Landing, Illinois; the Missouri River from mouth to Fort Benton, Montana; the Gasconade River from mouth to Arlington, Missouri; the Osage River from mouth to Shipley Shoals, Missouri; and the Yukon River and its tributaries.

Mary was a faithful chronicler of family events, but occasionally she missed a big one. In 1908 Ed was on a ship that was lost at sea. The western newspapers all speculated about the disappearance of several ships. But if such reports reached the St. Louis newspapers, Mary either missed them or failed to realize their significance. Ed told the story of his harrowing experience in a letter to his "girl," Alice Bock.

June 26, 1908

Dearest Alice:

You surely haven't had any trouble to find time to answer all the letters you have rec'd from me lately. Well, I might have written to you every day, had lots of time and certainly thot of you more than once a day, but you see, there is no chance to mail a letter at sea. In case our ship had gone to the bottom, I had intended to write a note and mail it in a bottle. Perhaps years later it might have been found on some foreign shore and sent to you. I wonder what I should have written with death staring me in the face. I sent a card from Nome. A ship left there the day we got in. Don't know when you will get this. The mails are very irregular here.

I suppose you feel relieved since school has closed. I would. I haven't much to write so I'll give you a little history of a delightful ocean voyage, and then stop. The ship "Transit" left the civilized world on June 1st. After seven long days on the Pacific we entered the Bearing Sea on the 8th. Had the conditions been favorable we should have been in Nome on the 12th. But on the 10th we encountered ice. From that time on we were cruising around in the ice until the morning of the 24th. There was a solid field of heavy ice from King Island, north of Nome, to Mumiak Island south of the Yukon. A distance of 200 miles or more. The field was some 30 miles wide. At some places it was broken up; at others there were miles and miles without a break. Our captain, a Norwegian was lost. He had never seen such ice before. There were about 500 men on the ship and the poor man was worried to death. I don't mean that he died, but if worrying could have caused his death, he would have died. We ate up about all the provisions they had several days before we got to Nome. If the ice had carried the vessel north into the Arctic we might have been out several weeks longer and I really don't know what we would have eaten. I have often heard of men eating human flesh to save their lives. Of course, one can't tell what one would do under certain conditions but I have always thot that I would rather die than eat human flesh.

One day we saw five vessels drifting with the ice in the same condition that our ship was in. All the ships so far have gotten in excepting one of the Seattle passenger boats and a U.S. Revenue cutter. The Seattle ship, the "Ohio," left on the 1st and she hasn't arrived at Nome. We got real near to her about a week ago and got some provisions from them, but went off and left them. Up to that time they had no accident. It's too bad they didn't follow us but that Captain has an idea he's a navigator and doesn't want to be shown. He is the same man who took us to Seattle last fall. I have some friends on that ship. There must be six or seven hundred passengers aboard. I hope they will get in safely. The second boat to arrive at Nome came very near sinking. They must have gotten in to the ice with some speed. They punched a hole in their ship but didn't sink her. After that accident they were more careful. One day we saw a herd of walrusses on the ice. There must have been 200 of them. They are monstrous animals. Some of them must weigh a thousand pounds. I tried to get a picture of them, but there wasn't light enough. I did get some good views of the ice. Took 4 pictures of a beautiful sunrise at 2 A.M. We landed here yesterday at noon.

Ed survived his years on the Yukon. When he finally was relieved—almost—from the burden of supporting his younger brothers and sisters, he married Alice in September of 1911. I was their only child, born in Hermann, Missouri, on December 3, 1913. My first cry coincided with the 7 a.m. shoe factory whistle.

Ed probably had the most intense case of "Steamboat Fever" of any of the Heckmann sons. He claimed he fought the disease, and he promised my mother he would leave the river, even going so far as to go look at the farmland in Texas his cousin Victor Silber was selling. For a time Ed sold centrally installed vacuum cleaners in Des Moines, Iowa—and he and Alice nearly starved. He later said, "There just weren't enough people who would pay $300 for a broom."

So in the end, my mother capitulated, and the river won. Ed returned to steamboating, working on the Leavenworth, the little boat with the sweet whistle and a penchant for turning over. She turned over once for Ed when a windstorm caught her near Weldon Springs. Resurrected, she was a comical sight, indeed, returning up the river.

Next, Ed bought into the steamer Myrtle and began making good money—a welcome change. But apparently there was only one cure for his particular case of "Steamboat Fever." The following story, which appeared in 1977 as a three-part serial in the "Waterways Journal," tells the story. The only elements missing from the tale are the sacrifices Ed's family made to indulge his ailment.

The Leavenworth returns to home port after turning over at Weldon Springs.

Genealogy of a Steamboat

Complying with the persistent requests of my daughter I shall now write the story of the building of the steamboat John Heckmann, named for my dear brother Johnnie, and our trials and tribulations in the operation of this vessel on western rivers. As I contemplate how the fates conspired to lead me slowly but surely, relentlessly into this venture, I am convinced that the person who wrote, "There is a destiny that shapes our ends, rough hew them how we will" was on the trail of a profound truth.

From the time I first conceived the idea of building this vessel until she was completely dismantled, covering a period of ten years, I lived and breathed steamboat. She became a part of me, occupied my mind night and day and eventually turned out to be the albatross hung about my neck.

Before we start the actual building of the ship, I must attempt to show you how the fates (there must have been a gang of them) worked together in perfect accord to ensnare me.

This boat was unique in that she carried two separate sternwheels. We are now speaking of the era, before the advent of the diesel engine and the screw propeller vessels, when there were just two types of river boats; the sidewheeler and the sternwheeler. Both were designed to operate on shallow waters. the side-wheeler had one great advantage over the sternwheeler in that she could "round to," that is turn around in her own length by working one wheel ahead while backing the other. Whereas the sternwheeler required at least twice her own length in the same maneuver. The sternwheeler had the advantage in operating in narrow channels.

In the year 1904, after the devastating flood on the Missouri, there was a revival of interest in restoring what had been known as the "Golden Age" of steamboating on the wild Missouri. My brother, Capt. Sam, first conceived the idea of building a sternwheeler with two separate independent wheels. This type of construction would not only give the sternwheeler some of the maneuverability of the sidewheeler, but by employing two small, light wheels would cut down the terrific cost of repairs for replacing damaged parts and broken shafts on the larger wheel. Very few sternwheelers ever lived to a ripe old age without cracking or breaking the shaft.

The idea of building a two wheeler kept intruding and milling around in my mind until the fates stepped in years later.

My father engaged in steamboating some 10 years after he was mustered out of the Union Army. First as a pilot and master, then owner and manager. He continued active in this business until his death in 1907, leaving to mourn his passing Mother and 14 children, 6 girls and 8 boys. We, the boys, naturally took to the water like ducks and practically grew up on the steamboats operating out of this port, Hermann.

After serving as a deckhand, cook, fireman and all around roustabout for the time required by law, I took the examination under U.S. Steamboat Inspectors, Capt. Archibald Gordon and engineer William McDonald, later a major, (that was in the old St. Louis Customs House, 3rd and Olive, St. Louis, demolished years ago) and was granted license as first-class pilot and first mate at the age of 21. I engaged in steamboating with occasional ventures far afield until the year 1915 when I was financially able to acquire a three-fourths interest in a small steam towboat, the H. E. Myrtle.

The name was not the name of a man as one would suppose. This very fine little vessel was built at Hermann by the Hermann Ferry & Packet Company. My cousin, Capt. Gustave Wohlt, was the president and general manager of this company at the time. It was his privilege to select the name for the vessel. He had three *daughters and no doubt had in mind to honor one of them by naming the boat for her. Deciding he could not slight the other two, he named her for all three—Hilda, Edna, Myrtle. (On the pilothouse it became H. E. Myrtle.)*

This boat was a financial success from the start, always in demand for working on channel improvement projects. Being light draft we could operate it anyplace where it was wet. Any sane person would have continued to operate this boat while she was showing a profit; however, the desire to build the big "two-wheeler" had become an obsession, akin to insanity—that's just a polite way of saying I was nuts. So just remember, the fates are taking over from here.

High and Dry

The U. S. Engineers had lying high and dry at the Arsenal Depot at the foot of Arsenal Street in St. Louis, two small sternwheel towboats, out of commission and declared obsolete because they were too small to handle the heavier equipment they were building. The boats were old, but the engines were practically new. A marine engineer, Charlie Nash, who had been our chief engineer on the str. J. P. Light on the Yukon and was now working at the Arsenal, had told me these boats would be sold at auction and that he could notify me, suggesting we purchase one and build a towboat.

That was the last I heard from him but not the last I was to hear about the boats. In the spring of 1918 a friend, Capt. Hugh Blaske, notified me that these boats had been offered for sale but all bids had been too low and rejected. He learned, however, that the Engineers were anxious to dispose of them and would consider any reasonable offer. So we got together and made a deal, he to bid for one boat with option to purchase the other at the same price. The boats were identical twins, named Isle Du Bois and Aux Vasse.

Now here's where the double sternwheeler definitely enters into the picture. Capt. Blaske became the proud owner of a steamboat for the sum of $630. I purchased the other boat for the same price. We had a verbal agreement to form a stock company to build the big boat, turning over our machinery in exchange for stock certificates.

So now, we had solved the power, or propulsion problem; the next step was to find boilers. All this occurred at the time prices were going up and up. A battery of boilers suitable for our engines would cost about $3000.

Now, pay attention and you will see why I harp on the part played by fate in all these transactions.

In the summer of 1914 the large excursion steamer Majestic, a wooden hull boat, was proceeding to St Louis at night after completing a tour of the upper Mississippi. At that time the city of St. Louis was building a new water intake tower near the old tower of the Chain of Rocks. A cofferdam had been sunk, and the foundation for the tower had been poured. From all I could ever learn the pilot on watch had no knowledge of this obstruction which really was near the main channel. When he first saw the structure he was headed straight for it—

Str. John Heckmann

STEAMBOAT EXCURSIONS

2 Trips **SUNDAY, JUNE 10** 2 Trips

Boat leaves Hermann 1 p. m. sharp — Leaves northside, opposite courthouse at 1:30 p. m. — Arrives Gasconade 3 p. m.

See the ball game at Gasconade
Hermann vs. Gasconade.

See the big slide on Mo. Pacific — See the Gov. Boatyards.

Boat leaves Gasconade 5:30 p. m., arriving at Hermann at 6:30 p. m.

Fare Round Trip — Adults 75c Children 25c.

NIGHT TRIP

Boat leaves Hermann at 8:30 p. m. — Leaves northside at 9 p. m. — Arrive at Gasconade 10:30 p. m. — Leaves Gasconade 10:45 p. m. — Arrive Hermann 11:30 p. m. Fare Round Trip Adults 75c Children 50c.

Dancing Both Trips Free

EDW. HECKMANN, Master

too late to avoid a head-on collision—so he sheared off, and she struck the cofferdam amidship and just sort of draped the vessel over it. No lives were lost, but the boat was a most complete wreck.

There must have been a suit for damage against the city because the water department soon thereafter owned a battery of three marine boilers, no doubt the only thing in the old hulk worth salvaging. These were placed on shore above the high water mark at the Chain of Rocks, where they rested in plain view of every passing craft. Many a riverman no doubt cast covetous eyes at them. I, of, course, had them in mind when we purchased the small boats. I bought them from the city comptroller for $750.

So now we have the machinery, wheels and boilers. All we need is a hull and pilotwheel.

At the very time I purchased the boilers, the wharfmaster at St. Louis, Fred Hornbrook, purchased the hull and superstructure of a large towboat, the General Simpson, from the Army Engineers. He was disposing of the superstructure, as he wanted just the bare hull for a wharfboat. He sold me the cabin, decks, all kinds of hardware that we could use in the new boat, the pilothouse, the pilotwheel and whistle, all for $240.

253

The next step was to assemble and carry all this equipment up the Missouri River to our home port of Hermann, 125 miles from the Arsenal.

I soon learned that my friend, Capt. Hugh Blaske, was losing all interest in the big boat building project, knowing he could readily sell his boat at a nice profit, so I paid him $1,200 for his boat and $80 for an old, leaky barge lying at the arsenal. I then steamed up the Myrtle, proceeded to the arsenal and started dismantling the boats, loading all equipment on barge and steamer. We rolled the sternwheels out of the pillow blocks (main shaft bearings) and down the loading ramp on the barge. Everything worth salvaging that could be used in the new boat was taken aboard. (I sold the boilers from the two little boats as they were, and left the hulls where they lay.)

The barge was not what one would call seaworthy, or riverworthy either. But we managed to bring her, or it (it's all right to refer to a boat or ship as her, but a barge should be an "it"), safely into port and unloaded while still afloat. I then chartered a small barge from the Hermann Ferry and Packet Company and proceeded to the Chain of Rocks where we skidded the boilers from the Majestic down the bank and rolled them aboard the barge. This barge was only 40 feet long by 18 foot beam. The boilers weighed 12 tons, measured 12 feet in length and 8 feet high. I sighed with relief when this cargo was unloaded at the Hermann wharf. (We took two of the Majestic's boilers, the third went into the Robert Stewart.)

In the spring of 1919 we received two carloads of fir boat lumber and timbers from the west coast. This had to be loaded on a barge and moved downstream to the only available building site, a narrow strip of land claimed by the Missouri Pacific Railway Company. We were not financially able to hire a good lawyer, versed in riparian rights, to argue the case, so we actually paid $12 a year rental fee.

I suspect the owners of this company were terribly frightened, knowing that we were building this vessel to operate on the Missouri River to compete for freight with four giant railway companies: the Wabash, Rock Island, Katy and Missouri Pacific. Naturally, they would all be frantic with bankruptcy staring them in the face, so would make every effort to destroy us.

An now, my dear readers, if any, when your mirth has somewhat subsided, we will proceed.

EPILOGUE

Thus ended Captain Ed's tale, but it certainly was not the end of his steamboat. From an engineering standpoint, the vessel was a complete success. The concept of the twin sternwheels worked perfectly, and the John Heckmann could run on a heavy dew. Measuring 165 by 30-1/2 by 4-1/2 feet, she was thought to be the largest steamboat ever built on the Missouri River with private funds.

Financially, however, the John Heckmann was a disaster. Competition with the railroads was impossible in 1920. So after just one year as a packet, she was remodeled as an excursion boat, licensed to carry 1,200 passengers—a pipe dream on the Missouri River. Crew was carried for 600, a more realistic figure. She operated out of Kansas City and Omaha, tramping upriver from St. Charles in the spring, running excursions out of small towns along the way. The process was reversed the next fall. But she could never make a profit—not even by going south for the winter to haul apples, sorghum and cotton out of the Cumberland, Tennessee, Illinois and Ohio rivers.

The John Heckmann was completely dismantled after she was wrecked by ice at Hermann in 1929. Today her 9-1/2 foot pilotwheel is the focal point of the Hermann River Memorial at Hermann, dedicated to all of the rivermen of Hermann, past and present. The three-chime whistle found a resting place in the Maritime Wing of the Smithsonian in Washington, D.C.

After the demise of his boat, Captain Ed ran the steamer Ralph Hicks for the Kansas City Bridge Company and m.v. Sgt. Pryor for the U.S. Army Corps of Engineers. During World War II he served as a lieutenant commander in the Coast Guard. In retirement he returned to his hometown of Hermann, Missouri, where he became founder and curator of the River Room Museum. He died in 1974, just short of his 90th birthday.

George Talbot Heckmann was known for his mechanical skills and inventive genius. George believed in learning everything he could from a job, and he believed in education—a trait his brothers did not share. George enrolled in any engineering or mechanical course he thought would improve his skills.

The maverick of the family, George had a knack for getting into peculiar and dangerous situations. Always good for a story and a laugh, brother George could be a trial to the "big boys." The following incident occurred on the steamer W. H. Grapevine, the only boat the Heckmanns owned in the early days that had electric lights. After he had done his chores, George, the cabin boy, liked to spend time in the engine room.

The Grapevine's electric generator was belt driven from a steam engine. Her com-
mutator brushes were laminated copper. Soon brother Fred was pressing me into
service as his relief. (He could think of more excuses to leave the engine room.)
When he gave me my instructions about the Generator he told me to "watch for
sparks between the brushes and the commutator. When they show up take a piece of
sand paper and clean the brushes." It had to happen to me. In order to have light to
work with and at the same time have both hands free to work, I placed the extention
cord between my teeth. The moisture from my mouth soaked through the cord and
knocked me on my ass. Years later when I had a tooth pulled the dentist said,
"George, there is something strange about this tooth. I can't find any sign of a
nerve."

Having more than one Heckmann brother on a boat usually spelled disaster.
George wrote about several of his escapades.

Brother Greeley Heckmann was the captain and George Sneider chief engineer. Ed
was deckhand and cook and I was the other deckhand. When Sneider was called
away, they put me in the engine room.

We had one very swift crossing at which we had the habit of laying a line to
pull us over. While Sneider was away I suggested that with a little more steam we
would be able to push up over the shoal and save the trouble of laying the line. It
worked. We were working by the hour so not being in a hurry, we got rid of the
excess steam as soon as possible after getting over the swift spot. This was done by
'scaping her out on the roof.

Ed and I between us, decided that we were wasting a lot of steam for no reason.
So we took a two-inch piece of pipe about a foot long and set it at the proper angle to
form a shrill whistle and Boy, did it raise Hell. A wild herd of horses would be down
under the high bluff taking a drink of water and when we turned the whistle loose
the horses would leave for the hills, I think some of them are still running.

When the engineer came back, we did not tell him about the whistle arrange-
ments but did tell him about using the extra amount of steam to which he agreed.
He almost went nuts the first time he threw the 'scape pipe out on the roof. Ran up
on the deck, pulled our whistle loose from its foundation and threw the whole works
over board.

EPILOGUE

❧

At Mt. Sterling, Mo., on the Gasconade we had a load of telephone poles to be unloaded from an open hull barge. Ed, John and I were the deckhands. Rolling the poles out of the barge and up the bank one at a time with cant hooks was too much of a job. We placed a snatch block high up in a large cotton wood tree about fifty feet from the barge. With a set of ice tongs on the business end of the rope and the other end to the steam capstan on the head of the boat. The capstan had a high gear. It was a simple matter to drag the poles up the hill and drag the line back to the next pole to be unloaded.

When we had all the poles unloaded I decided rather than to climb the tree to retrieve the snatch block, I would tie a boline on the end of the line and have them hoist me up to the limb. My smart brothers decided to throw a scare into me and started to hoist me up at full speed. I don't think they wanted to kill me. The only thing that saved me was the knot in the line that stopped operation when it came to the snatch block. It threw me over the top of the limb but I was able to hang on.

❧

The steamer Kennedy was by far the fastest steam boat the Heckmann Clan ever owned, and going down that narrow river (the White) at full speed, she threw up quite a swell. During that time there were quite a lot of clam fishermen out in their row boats. When the swells hit them we could see the fishermen further down the river laughing their heads off about the sight, not thinking that it would hit them next. If the Heckmanns had been compelled to pay for all the row boats we turned upside down on that trip they would have been broke sooner.

❧

On one trip I was working under brother Bill and decided to change jobs. When the new engineer arrived he was quite a dutchman. Brother Greeley introduced him to my sister Lizzie. The engineer: "So this is Lizzie, you know I been a long time wanting to get familiar with you."

Not long after his mother's death, George married Helen Fallis. They had two children, James and Mary Helen. After Helen's death, George married Ora and they had a daughter, Gladys. A divorce ensued, and he married another Gladys and added two more children to the family, George Jr. and Elaine. Despite his daredevil ways, George lived to be 92 years old.

John Henry Heckmann was the darling of all—handsome, charming and gentle. A natural pilot, he took to the river, even without the guidance of his father. John spent the 1910 season on the Yukon River in Alaska with his brother Ed and later purchased the steamers Myrtle and Fairmont. He married Anna Kuhn, whom the family affectionately called "John's Annie." Their only child, Mary, was just 18 months old when her father succumbed to typhoid at age 31. John had contracted typhoid earlier in life, and his doctor thought he could not have the disease again, an erroneous assumption that cost a young man's life.

Mary Isabell Heckmann, the baby girl of the family, was a popular teen-ager who blossomed into a beautiful woman. She was 16 when her mother died, after which she was in the care of her sisters. Mary was the only daughter to receive music lessons, and she taught piano almost until the day of her death. She married Robert Doerges, and their union produced five children, Robert, Marianna, Norman, Jack and Virginia, none of whom was interested in the river. Robert did spend one summer decking on the steamer John Heckmann under his Uncle Ed.

Norman Heckmann, the baby of the family, was only 14 when his mother died. As a minor child and a son of a Civil War Veteran, he was eligible for a land drawing in Idaho during the reassignment of Indian Lands. Once during their travels north, brothers Ed and John looked at the land. They decided no one in the family would ever homestead there for the required five years and vetoed the project. Norman never forgave them—the land later was in the center of a gold field.

After his mother's death, Norman was making $5 a week working for a man named Briscoe, but his sisters were charging him $4.50 a week for room and board at the Russell Avenue house. Hearing of Norman's plight, his boss said, "Come live with us. We won't charge you that much." Norman did just that. Later in life, Norman returned to the river and obtained his engineer's license. Eventually he became a landlubbing stationary engineer. Norman married Irene Kuhn, sister of "John's Annie." They had no children.

A 6-foot-3-inch southpaw, Norman was recruited by Branch Rickey of the St. Louis Browns. But World War I interfered with his baseball career, and he wound up in France instead. While in France, Norman wrote home to the "Advertiser-Courier."

EPILOGUE

Plit Batting High

Norman (Plit) Heckmann, Hermann's well known pitcher, who is now twirling barges and tug boats around the streams of France, and is stationed at Rouen, France, writes the A-C the following very interesting letter, which as is characteristic of Plit, we are instructed to publish as written and with no metaphorical, grammatical or phraseological embellishments:

"Notice that many of the boys have written the home paper letters and have given interviews in regard to their experiences abroad. My department has not been heard from, so here's a letter for publication, but it must be printed as written. I've read several letters from men over here and in life I never heard them use such good grammar. I want the folks to recognize me before they read my name at the other end of this. For the benefit of the kids that don't know my name—this is from Plit.

"Being as Pete (Hugo) Bock is the only fellow from home in this outfit, I'll take it that you have heard nothing of this wonderful regiment of ours. I am in the 124th Co. I.W.T. and Pete is in the 125th. I have never seen him over here.

"Pete Detweiler, Bluford Jett and Roy Miller are also members of us. The majority of the men in this unit are enlisted men—I myself was drafted, but that don't seem to make much difference in the treatment you receive. Some of the drafted men know as much about boats as the enlisted once thought they knew.

"We are a part of the S.O.S. Service of Supply, and altho I never saw it, there sure must be an army or something was back of Paris, cause we used to handle a lot of things, ammunitions, tin, roofing, iron and everything, even tobacco and candy. We stevedored when we first came over and we all worked so hard that since then, we don't do a thing. I was due to go as engineer on a tug, in November, but for some reason or other they stopped sending so much stuff by water, especially ammunition. One thing I do know and that is that they quit sending shells from our base on November 1st, so some one must a been wise to something.

"Well—anyway, being as they run out of tugs before I got one, they gave me a barge and its the cutest little thing you ever saw. I am captain, top cutter, mess sergeant, cook, head deckhand and since they took my buddy away, I'm K.P. too. I have a guard house on board and, whenever I don't behave, I confine myself to quarters. I'd like to confine myself to francs, because quarters are nothing in this

259

ville de Rouen.

"*Some thoughtful friend has been sending me the A.C. and as no name appears on it, kindly let me express my thanks (merci). I've seen the letters Mickey Neumann and Jimmy the truck driver, wrote. Mickey says the army life is great stuff. I guess he'll get sore when he's discharged. I will too, but most of the soreness will be in my feet, trying to beat No.1 home.*

"*I've never been near the front. Was in Paris four months and have been here almost that long. Since the war's over, we all feel a lot safer, of course we never were in any danger here, but I was always worried for fear they'd send an order down for a couple of dozen soldiers. Altho we ain't soldiers, we wear the regular uniform and know how to salute and everything, some of us even know one or two of the General Orders.*

"*Now I'll tell you some river news. This is Rouen and must be about 20 miles from La Havre. The mouth of this river makes connections with some ocean down there. Ships—real ones, can come up this far—but here's where they stop, cause they figured it would be a lot cheaper to build bridges over this river, than it would be to walk around. Otherwise, I guess they could have sent the British Navy up this river and gone right through to Berlin. They unload the ships here, also at LaHavre, into barges—all sizes, from 100 tons up to 15,000 ton. Their tugs are nearly the same as ordinary tugs at home. No sternwheeler's on the river at all. They pull everything instead of push it—and the 1st barge is usually about 200 feet behind the tug and so on. Each barge has a rudder and the guy that shoves the rudder, is captain. Going up stream is tiresome but coming down there are so many bridges to miss that we have lots of fun betting on whether we'll hit or miss the next one. One of the barges had a pretty good record last trip—only missed two bridges on the whole trip. Some of the French barges are so long they have a man on the front end to signal the pilot which way to go. The one I'm on is not that long.*

"*We have real nice quarters and do our own cooking. We have plenty of coal and plenty to eat, but I've been stewed so often, I'm tired of stew. Usually there are three men to a barge, but just now I am alone. My buddy said he was getting tired of France and thought he'd try America. Guess I'll get tired of it too some of these days.*

"*There are soldiers and people from all the places on this earth here—and some from that place that's supposed to be the subway. I'll name them in the order of rank in my estimation: Red Cross nurses, Americans, English, Australians, New Zealanders, Indians, Jamaicans, Frenchmen, Scotch, Fins, Norwegians, Swedes, Jews, Waacs, Hindus, Coolies, Germans and all the other I forgot to mention.*

"This river has a 36 foot channel between here and LaHavre and 20 feet from here to Paris. It is clear water and usually tame, but they usually have high water in March and this year they had it in January. The only driftwood that you see is bottle corks; there's an acre of them ahead of this barge right now. This country is not dry and has no intention of ever being.

"Rouen is the place where Joan of Arc was caught, imprisoned and burned; its quite a place and very pretty the first few times you see it. They also have the oldest running clock in the world here.

"I notice that we have a bunch of young folks home that call themselves 'Sammy Girls.' Why, I dunno. If it's in honor of the U. S. soldiers, I would suggest they change it to Yankeyites or something, for no matter whether a guy's from Georgia or Montana, he's a Yank over here. If it don't cost too much, publish this. I only get mail about once a month, so if any of your or my friends care to write, please don't stop just because war's over. I'm going to be over myself soon.

"I was in one game of ball over here and the Captain saw me bat and so he made me a Sergeant."

Signed, Plit (Norman Heckmann)

Thus ends the saga of the Heckmann family, a true steamboat dynasty. One of the most astonishing periods in the annals of Hermann steamboating occurred just after World War I. The little German community still was reeling from World War I when the Volstead Act sounded the death knell for the town's wine industry and everything connected with it, from vineyards to cooperages.

In the midst of this total economic collapse came three Heckmann brothers, each promoting a new steamboat company. Steamboat Bill was running about town selling stock in his Big Muddy Steamboat Company. Brother Ed was beating the bushes for stockholders for his new Heckmann Packet Company. Brother Sam was touting his Gasconade River Farmer's Packet Company. In addition, the Ferry Company, which at least had an admirable track record for turning a profit, was selling stock for the building of another new boat.

This final burst of activity was the last gasp of the steamboat age at Hermann.

As usual, the Ferry Company did fine. But the other contenders did not fare so well. The Big Muddy died somewhere short of building a boat. (Will's Annie said "no.") The Heckmann Packet Company built the big steamer John Heckmann, later regrouped as the Missouri River Excursion Company, and still went broke with a boat that was too large and too late. The Gasconade River Farmer's Packet Company sold $10,000 in stock and built the steamer Cinderella and her barge, the Golden Slipper, but after a disastrous year sold out for just $3,000.

Founded in 1872 by Capt. Henry Wohlt, the Hermann Ferry and Packet Company had helped build a young country, carrying lumber, railroad ties and iron ore. By 1913 its boats were handling almost $500,000 worth of cargo a year. The company continued to run ferryboats until 1930 when the Missouri River bridge opened at Hermann. On December 31, 1935, the company sold its warehouses and last boat, the steamer Hermann, to the Schoellhorn-Albrecht Machine Company of St. Louis. Had the business continued until April 27, 1936, Fritz Lang, one of the original directors, would have celebrated his golden jubilee of active service in the river transportation business.

And so it was that the sound of the steamboat whistles was heard no more. Gone was the chug and huff of the engines, the splash of the enormous paddle wheels, the whoosh of 'scaping out, the snort in the stacks as the engineer pushed her, the sudden roar of the mud drums, the occasional screech of the "nigger" whistle, the insistent ring of the engine room bells. When the steamboats died, so did the joyful melodies of America's rivers, songs of romance, poetry and hope.

APPENDIX

Heckmann Family Geneaology

WILLIAM LEWIS HECKMANN
Feb. 27, 1845—April 24, 1907

MARY LOUISE MILLER
Feb. 7, 1848—Feb. 11, 1909

Married February, 1868

THEIR CHILDREN

Justina (Miller)
July 11, 1865—March 1952
(by William's first marriage)

William L. Heckmann Jr. March 7, 1869—Aug. 21, 1957	Samuel Miller Dec. 21, 1870—April 4, 1957
Angelia Louisa (Miller) Aug. 24-1872—Nov. 10, 1943	Julius Frederick Nov. 25, 1874—Jan. 5, 1924
Mary Elizabeth (Lizzie) Sept. 23, 1876—Feb. 29, 1963	Martha Eveline (Brennecke) Sept. 21, 1878—August 20, 1945
Charlotte Virginia (Hundhausen) Aug. 23, 1880—April 8, 1960	Robert Evans May 18, 1882—Sept. 13, 1956
Edward July 7, 1884—April 20, 1974	George Talbot April 21, 1886—January 1978
John Henry July 1, 1888—Jan. 16, 1918	Joseph Leising Nov. 18, 1890—April 18, 1891
Mary Isabell (Doerges) March 5, 1892—April 10, 1978	Norman J. Colman Dec. 19, 1894—Oct. 26, 1981

The Hermann Steamboats

1869	Steamer Washington	1898	Str. Columbia
1872	Str. Stem	1900	Str. Buck Elk
1873	Str. Light Western	1900	Str. Grapevine
1874	Str. R. W. Dugan	1900	Str. Henry Wohlt
1878	Str. Hope	1901	Str. Kennedy
1880	Str. Fawn	1904	Str. Wm. L. Heckmann
1881	Str. Vienna	1905	Str. Julius F. Silber
1882	Str. Dora	1905	Str. Lora
1885	Str. Royal	1909	Str. August Wohlt
1888	Str. Pin Oak	1910	Str. Mt. Sterling
1889	Str. Annie Dell	1911	Str. H. E. Myrtle
1890	Str. Gasconade	1912	Str. Hermann
1892	Str. Mill Boy	1920	Str. Cinderella
1894	Str. Peerless	1920	Str. Champ Clark
1895	Str. Kingfisher	1920	Str. John Heckmann
1897	Str. Jack Rabbit	1920	Gas boat Loutre Island

1869—The **Washington** was running on the Missouri River as early as 1867. She was built at Wellsville, Ohio, in 1867 and was of 53 gross and net tonnage. She had one boiler 40 inches in diameter by 20 feet long. There was one cylinder 12 inches in diameter with 3-1/2 feet stroke. She was owned by the Wohlt/Heckmann and other interests and burned at Hermann in 1878 while ferrying. Capt. Henry Heckmann in command.

1872—The **Stem** was a little experimental boat built on the Gasconade River by Capt. Henry Wohlt and William Lalk. The attempt was not very successful, and her life was short. No record exists as to what happened to her.

1872—The **Light Western** was built on the Gasconade River by Capt. Henry Wohlt, who received $650 toward construction from the town of Hermann. The Light Western, a center-wheel, boot-jack boat, became the ferryboat for Hermann. Capt. Wohlt later rebuilt her as a larger side-wheeler. Total original cost listed at $1,250. Crushed by ice in 1878 at foot of Hermann Island.

1874—The **R.W.Dugan** was financed by a company formed by William L. Heckmann and his brother, Edward Heckmann. Her value in 1875 was listed at $12,000. The brothers bought her from Capt. Joseph Kinney and later resold her to him for $8,000. She tried to run in opposition to the Star Line in the St. Louis and Portland trade, but could not compete.

1878—The **Hope** was built at New Albany, Indiana, in 1877 at a cost of $4,000. She was sold to the Hope Steamboat Company, comprised of Henry Wohlt, his sons August and Gustave, and William L. Heckmann, for $3,500. She towed ties for the Missouri Pacific Railroad and handled freight. Sold to southern interests in 1882. She was 107 x 29 x 3.5 feet, and her engines were 10-1/4 x 3-1/2 feet. One boiler, 42 inches by 22 feet. She ended her career by burning up.

1880—The **Fawn** was built by the Wohlt family at a cost of $3,000. This sternwheel ferry operated out of Hermann until the Wohlts sold her to Cliff Able of St. Charles. She sank at St. Charles near the wreck of the J. P. Gage. She was 91.9 x 19.1 x 3.4 feet.

APPENDIX

1881—The **Vienna** was purchased and rebuilt by Capt. Henry Wohlt and sons. First named City of Plattsmouth. The Wohlts petitioned to have the name changed in honor of the town of Vienna in Maries County, the head of navigation on the Gasconade River. Way's Directory says she was built at Plattsmouth, Nebraska, in 1879. This sternwheeler was listed at 73 tons, 89.6 x 24 x 2.3 feet. Engines, 8's-14". One boiler. The Vienna was used for tripping and ferrying at Hermann until purchased by New Haven ferry interests for $2,500 in March 1888. The Wohlts had sold the Fawn and the Vienna to Capt. Wm. L. Heckmann and Hale Talbot for $6,000 in 1886. The Vienna was snagged and lost one-half mile below New Haven on Dec. 10, 1889.

1882—The **Dora** was built by Heidbroeder and Boeger at Butcher Bluff (Boeger's Landing) on the Gasconade River. She was sold to William L. Heckmann and I. Hale Talbot the same year. This sternwheeler measured 90 x 20 x 3.6 feet and was rated 81.08 tons gross and net tons. One boiler, 18 by 42 inches, was allowed 120 pounds pressure. Engines of seven-inch cylinders with 34-inch stroke. Accident prone, she was sunk and raised twice. Her upper decks were torn off by tree limbs after she broke loose in ice. She finally burned at Madison Crossing, 17 miles above St. Louis. She had been sold to the Washington, Missouri, ferry interests before her final demise.

1885—The **Royal** was built at Hermann by Capts. August and Gustave Wohlt to run in opposition to the Ferry Company, owned at that time by Heckmann and Talbot. Heckmann and Talbot bought the Fawn and the Vienna from the Wohlts and then bought the Dora from Heidbroeder and Boeger. This sternwheel boat had the distinction of being the only steamboat ever to go up the Gasconade River as far as Arlington (Jerome). Her dimensions were 86.6 x 24 x 3. She was listed at $2,500.

1886—The rivalry between the Wohlt and Heckmann interests ended. Talbot sold his interest in the Fawn, Vienna and Dora to the Wohlt brothers. They, in turn, added their steamer Royal to the holdings. These boats formed the nucleus of the future Hermann Ferry and Packet Company.

1888—**Pin Oak** 95 x 17.5 x 2.2 feet. One boiler. It was said she could run on a heavy dew. She was listed at $3,000. The Wohlts sold her to Capt. Archie Bryan and E. W. Wild in 1896. She turned over and sank in Sandy Hook Bend, July 29, 1896.

1889—The **Annie Dell** was 70 x 16.6 x 2 feet and weighed 19.05 tons. Built at Hermann by Feagen and Iven of Osage County. Stockholders were the farmers along the Gasconade River. The boat first passed inspection on January 15, 1890. Later purchased by Capt. William L. Heckmann when he was living at the Heckmann Mill. Wrecked by flood waters there, she was stripped and rebuilt in 1897 as the Jack Rabbit. Cost $2,500.

1892—The **Gasconade** was built by the Hermann Ferry and Packet Co. in 1892 at the Loutre Island ferry landing. She was 107 x 23 x 3.5 feet. According to the "Waterways Journal," she had "white pine gunwales, her head, stern bottom, knuckles and grub streak were built out of three- and four-inch selected hill white oak without a knot or sign of sap to be found in same." The ships carpenters were Perrin Kay and Joe Shepperd. "Doc" Trail said, "Perrin Kay was perhaps the most versatile man ever connected with steamboats. He could build a boat complete, install all the machinery and then capably man every position." The Gasconade once came out of the Gasconade River loaded with 1,500 sacks of wheat and towing the steamer Pin Oak, which had 900 sacks of wheat on board. This was the largest trip on record down the Gasconade River. The Hermann Ferry and Packet Co. kept the Gasconade for 11 years and then sold her for more than she cost to build. During that time less than $700 was spent on upkeep and repairs, and the Gasconade never turned a wheel without "bringing in some bacon."

1892—The **Mill Boy** was built by the Hermann Ferry and Packet Co. She was 89.2 x 18.8 x 2.8 feet. Two engines, one boiler, 18 x 44 inches, 41 tons, 125 lbs. pressure. She was a light-draft, open-hull sternwheeler with geared machinery, drawing one foot light. Her first two years were spent in the Gasconade River packet trade, where she made good money. Then she was decked over and converted into a ferryboat. She lived out her life as a ferryboat at Hermann, New Haven and Washington. The Mill Boy was said to be the only loaded boat to come through Pryor's Bend after dark. She was lost in the ice while in winter quarters in 1910. Loss reported at $5,000.

1894—**Peerless** was built by Capt. Henry German, ship carpenter for Begeman and German. This boat was leased to the ferry company and finally bought by that company. She was a sternwheeler built for the Gasconade, but not as successful as the earlier boats. Cost $4,000. She was sold to Archie Bryan and E. W. Wild in 1896. She turned over and sank in Sandy Hook Bend on July 29, 1896, near Wyss Landing, Missouri.

1895—**The Kingfisher** was the lightest draft boat ever built for the Gasconade or any other river, according to Steamboat Bill Heckmann. She ran when they had to raft the ties flat to float them down over the shoals. With her open-hull barges she could come off the Gasconade on nine inches of water, with two large carloads of wheat. She was built at the Heckmann Mill near Mt. Sterling by Capt. Wm. L. Heckmann Sr. She measured 75.6 x 16 x 2.5 feet, Engines 6's -3 ft. She operated on the Gasconade for three years and was sold to a Mr. Terrel of Texas, who took her to Red River for the fish trade. Documented at Galveston, Tex., 1899. Apparently rebuilt at Fulton, Arkansas in 1901. Still registered in New Orleans in 1905.

1897—The **Jack Rabbit** was 73.6 x 16.2 x 3.3 feet. William L. Heckmann Sr. had bought the Annie Dell to use at his mill. While she was on the ways for repair, a flash flood tore off the superstructure. She was rebuilt as the steamer Jack Rabbit, but she was not well-named since she was anything but fast. Condemned at New Orleans in 1904. When the Heckmann Mill proved unsuccessful, Capt. Heckmann traded in the Jack Rabbit for stock back in the Hermann Ferry and Packet Co.

1898—The **Columbia**, according to Way's Packet Directory, was built at Osage City, Missouri, in 1898 for the St. Louis and Hermann Packet Co. and then sold to the Burress family of Miami, Missouri, on Aug. 5, 1903. She was sold again in 1907, at Memphis in 1913, back in St. Louis in 1914 and taken out of service on September 13, 1915. This boat is something of a mystery, as it is not mentioned in the Hermann newspaper or the diaries of Mary L. Heckmann. But Steamboat Bill said she was sold before the 1903 flood. No specifications have been found.

1900—The **Buck Elk**, a sternwheeler, was built at the Hermann wharf in 1900 by the St. Louis and Hermann Steamboat Company, with Capt. William L. Heckmann Sr. supervising and Dan Jackisch, William Heckmann Jr. and Tim Estes involved. She was a light-draft carrier, 100.7 x 18.3 x 3 feet. Later sold to the Buck Elk Steamboat Company and finally gravitated to the Yazoo River in 1908. Value, $5,000.

1900—**Wm. L. Grapevine** cost $10,000, the most paid for a Hermann steamboat up to that time. Also the largest Hermann boat, 142.5 x 30 x 3.5 feet, engines 10-inches diameter of cylinders by 4-feet stroke. Named for Capt. Wm. H. Grapevine, superintendent of the Missouri-Pacific's transfer boats. She had the machinery and part of the upper works of the J. A. Woodson. First owned by the Iron Mountain Railroad. Designed for the White River in Arkansas to connect with their trains. After brief service there she ran in the St. Louis-Rocheport trade for the St. Louis and Hermann Packet Co. Ran excursions at Kansas City in 1900 until purchased by Hermann interests. Sold to Capt. Doss Davis of Ironton, Ohio. On Christmas Day, 1903, she broke loose in ice at Cincinnati, hit the C. & O. Railroad bridge and sank. Her machinery went to a Big Sandy boat named Eclipse.

1900—The **Henry Wohlt** was named for the originator of steamboating in Hermann. She was 97.8 x 20 x 3 feet. Engines 7"-3 1/2 ft. Capt. Gustave Wohlt was in charge of this boat, which was built at Hermann by ship's carpenter, John Bohlken. A scow (square) bow boat, she was a good carrier, but never handled as well as the later August Wohlt. In the first year of operation, she earned twice what it cost to build her.

1900—The **Kennedy**, originally named the Mayflower, was built at Lyons Iowa. She was 121.5 x 24.4 x 3.9. Engines 19's-6 feet. Two boilers, each 36 inches by 18 feet. She was bought new by the St. Louis and Hermann Packet Co. (Capt. Way says "by the Heckmanns of Hermann") who ran her out of Batesville, Arkansas, on the White River, carrying railroad supplies to Buffalo Shoals. Returning to the Missouri River, she ran out of St. Louis during the 1904 World's Fair. The Kennedy played a big part in rescue work during the 1903 flood. She was sold to the Florida East Coast Railroad and went to the Florida Keys. She burned in the St. Johns River, Florida, on February 24, 1914.

1904—**William L. Heckmann** The Hermann Ferry and Packet Co. always built its own boats and named them for owners of the company. So even though both William L. Heckmann and his namesake son were with the rival St. Louis and Hermann Packet Company, the ferry company still named a boat for Capt. Will Sr. She was 95 x 20.3 x 3 feet and had the rating of passenger boat. Designed by a Mr. Pott and built by ship's carpenter John Bohlken, she was of very light draft—only 18 inches. She was the largest sternwheel ferry to operate at Hermann. She also operated as a Gasconade River packet. She ran for more than three years with the ferry company, during which time not a dime was spent for repairs of any kind. "Doc" Trail, river historian, said "Old Roughhead" Heckmann would not allow any steamboat to carry his name unless it was the very best. She was sold for more than she cost to build to parties at Canton, Missouri, on the upper Mississippi, where she shortly went up in smoke.

1905—The **Julius F. Silber** was built by the newly formed Buck Elk Steamboat Company at Osage City on the Osage River for $4,800. She was 101.8 x 21.3 x 3.7, and the ship's carpenters were John Bohlken and Albert Shubert. The Hermann Ferry and Packet Company absorbed the Buck Elk Steamboat Company in 1907 and put the steamer Julius Silber in commission on the Missouri River. In 1917 she was in the Omaha/Decatur trade. Sold to Woods Bros. in 1927, she was renamed the Clark Woods and used as a towboat.

1905—The **Lora** was purchased by William L. Heckmann Jr. after he had a falling out with his partners in the St. Louis and Hermann Steamboat Company and formed another company with two parties from St. Louis. The Lora, which was renamed the Omaha, was purchased from parties on the upper Mississippi. No listing in Way can be found, but Will Jr. said the Lora was bigger and faster than the Kennedy.

1909—The **August Wohlt**, named for the oldest son of Capt. Henry Wohlt, was built by John Bohlken of seasoned Missouri white oak at Hermann in 1909. She was 91.1 x 18.1 x 3.3 feet. The Wohlt once came out of the Gasconade River with a record 1,100 sacks of wheat, some of which were stacked in the engine room. Sold to the ferry interests at Rocheport, Missouri, and owned in 1926 by Capt. Edward C. Roehrig of Rocheport. The Glasgow Sand and Gravel Company took her over, and she was dismantled and abandoned in 1927. Steamboat Bill claimed, "This boat was the pride of them all, the best handling boat that ever ran on the Gasconade River."

1910—The **Mt. Sterling**, a low-water boat, was only 65 x 12 x 2.2 feet. Engines 6"-2 feet, 22 tons. One boiler. Built by the Hermann Ferry and Packet Company, which sold her after just one year to parties at St. Joseph, Missouri. There is only one legal recording, at St. Joseph, August 19, 1913, $1,700. While owned by the Buchanan Sand & Supply Co., a windstorm swamped her and laid her up at St. Joseph.

1911—The **H. E. Myrtle** was named for Gustave Wohlt's three daughters, Hilda, Edna and Myrtle, after he declined to have a boat named for himself. The name "Hilda-Edna-Myrtle" was too long to be painted on a pilothouse, so the name was shortened to H. E. Myrtle. She was sold in 1914 to Capt. John Heckmann, who sold her to his brother Ed in 1916. Parties from Chattanooga, Tennessee, later purchased the Myrtle for the Tennessee River trade.

1912—The **Hermann**, a steam ferry built by the Hermann Ferry and Packet Company, was the Port of Hermann's longest running boat. Built at the Hermann wharf in 1912, she was still running when sold in 1935. Her dimensions were 89 x 19.6 x 2.4 feet.

From 1912 until 1920 only one boat was built at Hermann— The Ferry Co. built the steamer Lexington for that city's ferry interests. She was delivered in July of 1918. But it certainly was not a period of inactivity for boats. By 1914 the river was dominated by Heckmann boys. William Jr. was on the Chester, Fred was on the Monitor, Sam (Greeley) was on the Silber, Ed was on the Leavenworth, John was on the Myrtle, and Norman was engineer on the August Wohlt. Two of their cousins, Oscar Heckmann and Roy Miller, also worked on the river. The Wohlts also were producing sons who took to the river. Gilbert, Allie and Wesley Wohlt had already joined Gustave on the boats—more cousins.

The years 1918-1919 saw a great rush of new steamboat companies, with three Heckmann brothers peddling stock—Steamboat Bill for his Big Muddy Steamboat Company, Ed for his Heckmann Packet Company, and Sam (Greeley) for his Gasconade River Farmer's Packet Company. In addition, the Ferry Co. was selling stock in its next steamer. The Big Muddy Company died a'borning, the Heckmann Packet Company built the steamer John Heckmann, the largest steamboat ever built with private funds on the Missouri River, the Gasconade River Farmer's Packet Co. built the little steamer Cinderella and her barge the Golden Slipper and the Ferry Co. rebuilt the Champ Clark. This was the last gasp of steamboating at the Port of Hermann.

1919—The **Cinderella and barge Golden Slipper** were built and promoted by Greeley Heckmann and his son, Harvey, just for the Gasconade River. This beautiful little steamer might have been a success if the elements had not interfered. The year she was hoping to make a big profit the wheat crop on the Gasconade was lost to flood waters. She was sold before ever really being tested.

1920—The **Champ Clark** was the last Hermann Ferry and Packet Company steamer. Built at Mudd's Landing, Illinois, in 1912, she was originally a towboat used by Rust and Swift, contractors. She was sold to the Rocheport Ferry & Transportation Co. The Hermann Ferry and Packet Co. bought her, lengthened her, and used her for a packet on the Missouri River. She was finally dismantled on the bank at Hermann.

1920—The **John Heckmann** was thought to be the largest steamboat ever built on the Missouri River with private funds. She was promoted and built by Ed Heckmann, the sixth Heckmann son. John Bohlken was the ship's carpenter. Ed Heckmann's Packet Co. financed this boat with an original stock issue of $15,000. She made her trial run in 1920 and after a year proved she was too much, too late for the packet business on the Missouri River. Another stock issue was presented for $45,000, and she was remodeled into an excursion boat by a new company, The Missouri River Excursion Company. She ran nine years, working as an excursion boat in the summer, tramping upstream in the spring and running out of Kansas City and Omaha, then tramping back downstream. She went south to the Cumberland and Tennessee rivers in the winter, hauling cotton, apples and whatever else was available for shipment. She was taken out of service in 1929 and tied up just below Hermann. She was lost to ice, hung on the bank for a while and finally collapsed in 1930, a total loss. Dimensions: 163.6 x 30.5 x 4.2 feet.

1920—The **Loutre Island**, a gas boat, was the last boat built by the Hermann Ferry and Packet Co. at Hermann. She served as a ferryboat until the Hermann bridge across the Missouri River was completed in 1930.

1935—**Hermann Ferry and Packet Company dissolves.** After being in business since 1872, the company sold its warehouses and last boat, the steamer Hermann, to Schellhorn-Albrecht Machine Co. of St. Louis on December 31, 1935. If the business had continued until April 27, 1936, Fritz Lang would have celebrated his golden jubilee of active service on river business.

Pleasure Boats—No account of the Hermann boats would be complete without mentioning the pleasure boats built by individuals. August Wohlt's steamer **Ideal**, John Bohlken's gas-powered **Peacherino** and other colorful little boats did their bit for the entertainment of the area. Also worthy of mention is the little **Exporter**, built by Kropp to haul ice-cold beer up the Gasconade and Osage rivers.

Glossary of Steamboat Terms

Beam: The width of a vessel. **Deep** refers to the draft of a vessel, the depth of the hull.

Bell Pulls: A bell cord with either a brass ring or a wooden handle that the pilot pulls to ring a bell or bells to signal the engineer in the engine room.

Bight of the Bend: The narrow turn of a bend, like the top of a horseshoe.

Bitts: Cast steel or wooden devices used to secure lines on a boat. Winding a line **too tight on the bitts** often caused it to part.

Bull Rails: Rails around the lower deck forming a fence. Boats usually had moveable sections of the same construction to confine livestock.

Capstan: A metal spool for winding up a rope. Placed upright on the deck, the capstan may be revolved manually or mechanically. A **capstan bar** is a wooden club, similar to a baseball bat, that can be inserted into a hole in the capstan to facilitate winding. Bitts at the bottom prevent the line from reversing itself. When steam operated, several gears were used to regulate the rate of revolution. A capstan could be used to pull a boat to shore, if necessary.

Cordelle: Rope or line from boat to shore used to pull a vessel over tight spots. Used to pull barge line boats, especially upstream.

Dead Low: Water in stream as low as possible.

Decked-Over: The opposite of open-hulled. Barges were often open-hulled. Boats more often were decked over, although old-time steamboats were sometimes open hulled.

Fantail: A continuation of the engine room guard or gunnel on a sternwheel boat, built with a steep upward curve to join the cylinder timber so the engineer could stand to lubricate various paddlewheel bearings and cams.

Flanking a Boat: A downstream maneuver for rounding a bend. The pilot would "drive her hard" toward the opposite bank, then "set her back hard" at the last minute and let the current swing the bow around.

French Landing: Steamboats typically land head upstream, stern downstream. Landing stern upstream is called a French Landing.

Gunnels: Sometimes spelled gunwale. The top edge of the first deck of a barge or boat.

Hail: Whistle blown to greet another boat or to signal approach to a town (or woodlot in olden times). Also a signal on shore for a boat to stop for cargo. This can be as simple as the waving of a handkerchief or newspaper in slow, deliberate arcs in daylight or at night by the wave of a lantern. Steamboats hailed one another to transact business in mid stream after the passing signals had been completed.

Leadman: A man who uses the lead line or sounding pole to judge depth of water, calling out the reading back to the pilothouse.

Loaded Flat, Laying Low: A boat so laden with merchandise or people as to be nearly flush with the water.

Mud Drum: A long tube built of boiler steel set under a battery of boilers and connected into each boiler by a mud drum leg. The sediment of raw river water settled in the mud drum and periodically was discharged overboard by opening a valve. The sound emitted was a peculiar, hoarse roar, quite disturbing to passengers not acquainted with steamboats. This procedure was called "blowing out the mud drums." When a riverman felt the daily urge, he excused himself by saying, "Well, I've got to go below and blow out my mud drums." (Courtesy, Capt. Fred Way)

Out on the Ways: When a boat was pulled out of the water for repairs, she was said to be "out on the ways."

Rounded to: Turn a boat around in mid stream.

Roustabouts: Men employed to work under the mate on the deck of a packet. The term usually referred to black laborers; white men thus employed were called deck hands.

Run into the River: When a chain on a chain-driven boat broke, it literally ran into the river, leaving the boat totally disabled.

Sack Pile: A pile of sacks of wheat or corn waiting for shipment on the bank of a river. Always a welcome sight for an approaching steamboat.

'Scape: Contraction of the word "escape." The rhythmic, periodic emission of exhaust steam from the engines. The term " 'scapes out on the roof" meant exhausted steam from the main cylinders was piped upward above the roof and released from 'scape pipes. These usually were located at the aft end of the roof, above the engines. Boats equipped with condensing engines did not sport 'scape pipes.

Spar: A stout pole used to fend a vessel off shore. Used in olden days to pry boats off sandbars.

Stacks: Smokestacks. On a vessel said to be **cramped in the stacks** the smokestacks are too close together, producing too little draft and making it more difficult to raise steam.

Stage: A built-up boardwalk, sometimes 40 to 60 feet long that was swung out and lowered at landings, with the heel on the forecastle and the other end on shore. Also called a stageplank. Invented about 1870, the stage was preceded by the gangplank.

Whistle Treadle: A steamboat whistle was blown by pressing down on a treadle, usually located to the right of the pilot wheel. On a triple-chime whistle, the first downward pressure on the treadle brought out the first note, and more pressure produced the second note. Flooring the treadle brought out the full-throated chord that shook the pilothouse and left the blower a bit deaf. It was a thrill to those on shore to hear the whistle of a steamboat, but the thrill was even greater when experienced in the pilothouse.

Wood Hawk: Man who handled the woodlots and the "wooding up" of the boats.

Gasconade River Miles

FROM MAPS AND SURVEYS MADE 1889-93

Locality	Bank	Miles	Locality	Bank	Miles
Mouth of River		0.0	Cox Ford Shoal		31.7
Missouri Pacific Bridge		1.0	Pryor's Island (head)	R	32.3
Gasconade	L	1.2	Pryor's Chute (head)	R	32.4
First Creek	R	2.6	Contrary Creek	L	33.4
Sunday Shoal		3.0	Clay Bank Shoal		34.0
Bock's Bar Shoal		3.6	Sand Shoal		35.4
The Basin		4.0	Mt. Sterling (bridge)		36.3
Stolpe Ferry		4.7	Mt. Sterling Shoal		36.6
Boecker's Shoal		5.9	Cooper Hill Landing	R	39.4
Long Shoal (head)		6.7	Cooper Hill Shoal		39.5
Round Island Shoal		7.3	Third Creek	R	39.7
Nigger Slide Off		7.8	Mistaken Creek	R	39.9
Stake Shoal		8.2	Massey Island (head)	R	40.6
Hardscrabble Shoal		6.4	Flat Brush Ford		41.4
Fredericksburg	L	9.1	Deer Slough (foot)	L	42.2
Upper Fred's Shoal		9.7	Deer Island (foot)		42.2
Woodpecker Shoal (head)		10.5	Deer Slough (head)		43.4
Beaver Shoal		11.2	Howerton Bluffs	L	44.4
Spohrs Shoal		11.9	Pointer Creek	L	45.2
Turnpike Shoal		12.5	Owens Creek	L	45.6
Turnpike Bluffs (head)	R	13.1	Lake Shoal		46.3
Gentle Shoal		13.3	Owen Mill Ford		47.9
Brandt Shoal		13.8	Stub Hollow Shoal		48.8
Browns Shanty	R	16.2	Seve Island Shoal		49.5
Catfish Shoal (head)		16.5	Buck Creek	R	50.3
Second Creek	R	16.9	Indian Creek	R	51.2
Second Creek Shoal		17.2	Rollins Whirlpool		52.7
Concrete Shoal		18.0	Swan Creek	L	52.9
Powell's Dam		18.6	Rollins Ferry Shoal		53.0
Fegler's Ferry		19.9	Rich Fountain Bridge		53.1
Fegler's Ford Shoal		20.1	Brush Creek	L	53.1
Lower Deppe Shoal		20.5	Wieger Shoal		53.9
Deppe Shoal		21.4	Ramsey Shoal		54.5
Lower Hensley Shoal		22.0	Ramsey Island (head)	L	55.4
Hensley Shoal		22.7	Scott's Island (foot)	R	55.6
Lottie Lewis Shoal		24.7	Scott's Island Shoal		56.5
Helming's Ferry		24.9	Little Hinchy Shoal		57.1
Helming's Ford Shoal		25.0	Big Hinchy Shoal		57.6
Campmeeting Shoal		25.5	Buck Elk Creek	R	58.2
Pinoak Creek	R	26.0	Buck Elk Shoal		58.4
Pinoak Shoal		26.4	Doggett Shoal		59.3
Perkins Shoal		27.3	Gascondy	R	61.4
Butcher's Shoal		28.4	Rock Island Bridge		61.4
Hope Landing	L	29.7	Paydown Ford		69.9
Cedar Creek	L	29.9	Vienna Landings		
Pryor's Chute (foot)	R	30.1	Indian Creek	L	77.3
Pryor's Island (foot)		30.1	Johnson's Ferry		
Pryor's Mill (in chute)			State Road		86.0
(Heckmann's Mill)	L	30.3	Gaines Ford		91.9
Lambeth Landing	L	31.0	Arlington Frisco Bridge (Jerome)		107.0
Cox Landing	L	31.4			

The Gasconade River

FROM GASCONADE TO VIENNA

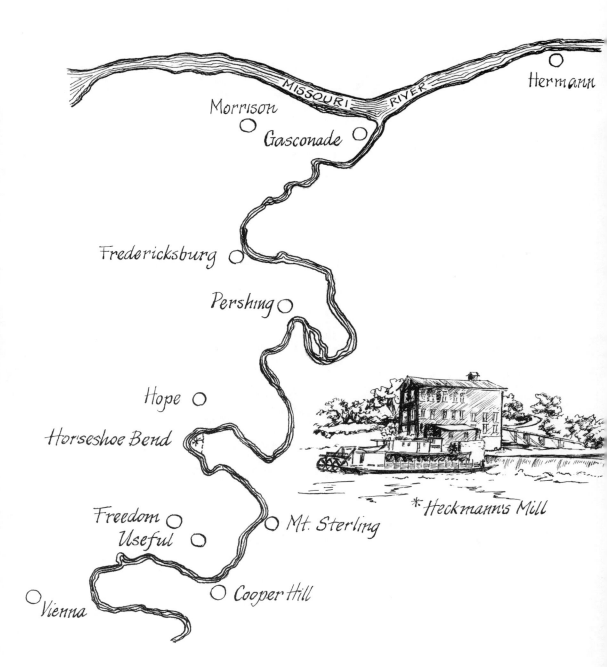

* *Heckmann's Mill*

ILLUSTRATION BY LINDA HECK

The Missouri River at Bluffton

DETAIL FROM 1884 MISSOURI RIVER COMMISSION SURVEY MAP

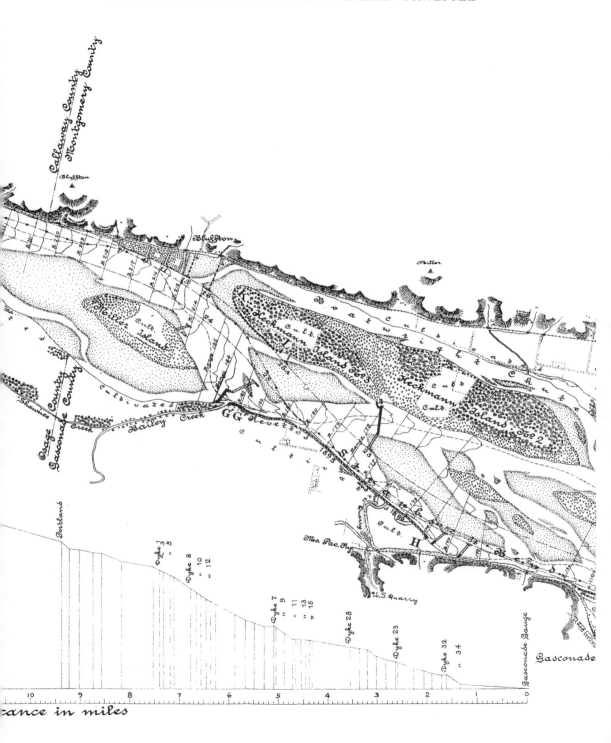

The Missouri River from Hermann to Bluffton

AS SURVEYED APRIL 25-30, 1879

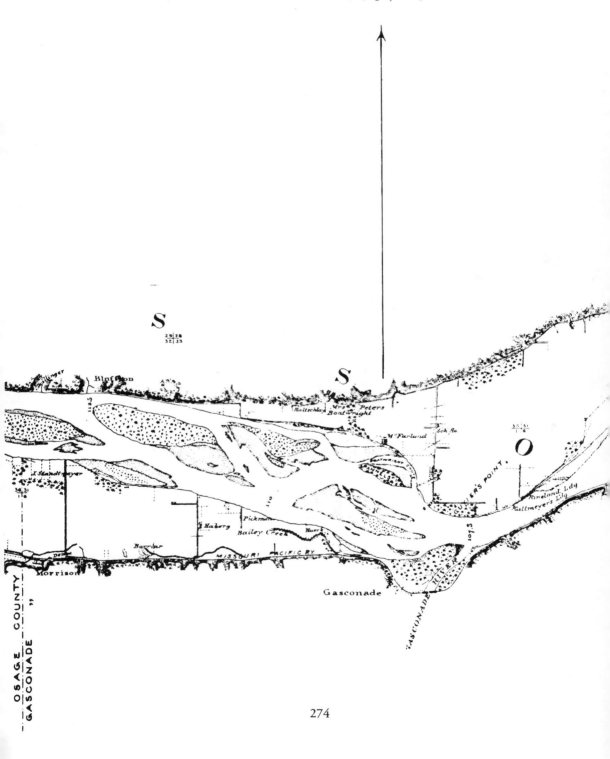

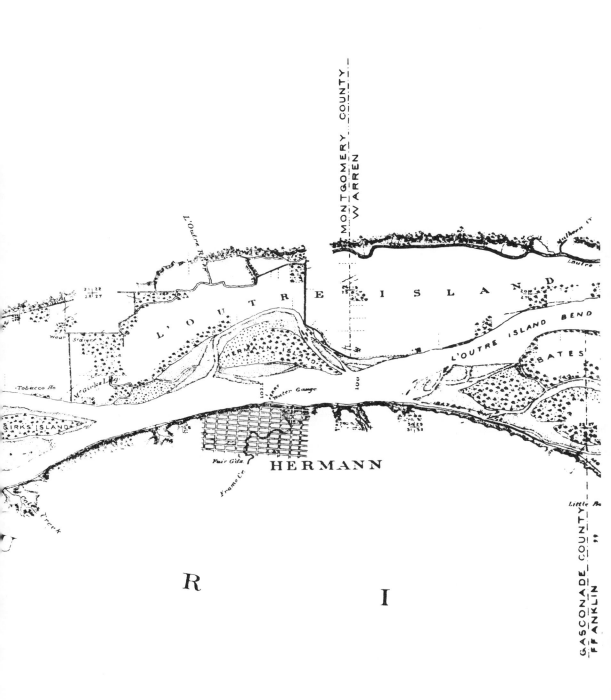

Alice and Edward Heckmann with their daughter,
Dorothy

About the Author

DOROTHY HECKMANN SHRADER was born December 3, 1913, in Hermann, Missouri, at the home of her maternal grandparents. She attended school in Hermann and spent her summers living and working with her parents aboard the Steamer John Heckmann.

Shrader received two degrees from the University of Missouri-Columbia—one in journalism in 1935 and one in education in 1947. Graduate study in Iowa led to work in special education. She was principal of Wilson School for the Educably Retarded and founder of the Beloit Campus School for the Emotionally Disturbed in Ames. At the same time, she ran her own small publishing business, editing and publishing "The Bulletin Board, a Guide to Ames" for 25 years and serving as the city's public relationist. In retirement, she has devoted her time to researching Missouri River history.

Dr. William D. Shrader, her husband of 58 years, is an Iowa State University emeritus professor of agronomy. The Shraders have three children, John Shrader, who is in engineering management at Aerospace Boeing in Seattle; Dr. David L. Shrader, dean of the School of Music at North Texas University in Denton; and Maggie Shrader Ford, program director and publicist for the School of Music, Virginia Commonwealth University in Richmond. They have six grandchildren and one great-grandson.